War on the Home Front
An Examination of Wife Abuse

PUBLIC ISSUES IN ANTHROPOLOGICAL PERSPECTIVES
General Editors: William O. Beeman and David Kertzer, Department of Anthropology, Brown University

Volume 1

> **Braving the Street: The Anthropology of Homelessness**
> Irene Glasser and Rae Bridgman

Volume 2

> **War on the Home Front: An Examination of Wife Abuse**
> Shawn D. Haley and Ellie Braun-Haley

Volume 3

> **A Sealed and Secret Kinship: Policies and Practices in American Adoption**
> Judith Modell

WAR ON THE HOME FRONT

An Examination of Wife Abuse

Shawn D. Haley and *Ellie Braun-Haley*

Berghahn Books
New York • Oxford

First published in 2000 by
Berghahn Books
www.berghahnbooks.com

© 2000 Shawn D. Haley and Ellie Braun-Haley

Library of Congress Cataloging-in-Publication Data
War on the home front : an examination of wife abuse / edited by Ellie Braun-Haley, Shawn D. Haley.
  p.   cm. — (Public issues in anthropological perspectives series)
Includes bibliographical references and index.
  ISBN 1-57181-117-6
1. Wife abuse—United States—Case studies. 2. Family violence—United States—Case studies. 3. Abusive men—United States—Case studies. I. Braun-Haley, Ellie, 1943–   II. Haley, Shawn D.   III. Series.
  HV6626.2 .W37 2000
  362.82'92'0973—dc21   00-058527

British Library Cataloguing in Publication Data
A catalogue record for this book is available from the British Library.

Printed in the United States on acid-free paper.

Contents

Preface   viii

Chapter 1 **Introduction**   1
It's War 2
Methodology 4
Types of Abuse 8
    Economic Control 9
    Psychological/Emotional Abuse 9
    Physical Violence 14
    Pattern of Abuse 17
    Acceleration of Abuse 19
Notes 21

Chapter 2 **Social Stigma and Silence**   22
Society and Spousal Abuse 23
    Individual Factors 24
    Family Factors 32
    Community Factors 40
    Cultural Factors and Mechanisms 43
The Official Position 68
The Personal Perspective 71
    The Helpers 71
    The Abused Women 75
Notes 77

Chapter 3 **The Impact of Abuse**   80
Domestic Violence 80

Personal Impact 82
   The Statistics on Abuse 83
   The Abused Women 84
   The Abuser 101
   The Families 103
   The Friends 111
Societal Impact 114
   Intervention 116
Lack of Support 138
Notes 138

Chapter 4   **Breaking Away**   140
Breaking Up Is Hard to Do 141
   Suffering Alone 141
   Holding the Family Together 146
   The Threads Unravel 152
Escape to Anywhere 153
   On Your Own 155
   Family and Friends 157
   Into the Arms of Strangers 160
   Legal Separation and Divorce 163
Long-Term Hiding 167
   Threats and Long-Distance Abuse 169
   Attacks on Friends and Family 172
   Stalking 174
   Police Intervention and Court Orders 176
Rebuilding a Life 177
   A Brand-New Life 178
   Living with the Memory 184
Notes 187

Chapter 5   **What Can We Do?**   188
Preventative Measures 188
   Potential Abusers 188
   Potential Victims 193
   Both Groups 197
Protective Measures 198
   Abusers 199

Victims 203
Both Parties 210
General Public 211
Discussion 213
The Couple 213
Family and Friends 214
The Professionals 216
General Trends 218
Notes 219

Chapter 6 **The Future of Wife Abuse**   220
A Backward Glance 220
Looking Forward 225
A Proposed Solution 225
Family and the Prenuptial Agreement 225
Redefining the Crime 227
A New Court 227
The New Procedure 228
A Step Back 233
A Final Statement 234
Notes 235

References Cited   236

Index   240

Preface

O ur first conversations with women who had been (or were still being) abused by their husbands took place almost a decade ago. From that moment on, "wife abuse" was not a distant, abstract social problem. It was personal. Women we knew, some of whom we knew well, had been physically and psychologically tortured by the one person who was supposed to love them. This we found appalling. Moreover, these women and society in general let the torture continue for years. This we found tragic. We also found it incomprehensible.

For several years after those initial conversations, we searched for understanding. We met with and became part of the lives of many abused women. We confronted abusive husbands. We discussed the problem with members of the helping professions. As we gained more information, we also acquired a new perspective. We realized that although the husband was and is guilty of wife abuse, society at large and every one of its members were and are guilty of aiding and abetting that abuse. We all must share the blame.

In this book, we present our findings in six distinct sections. We define wife abuse. We look at our society and the role it plays. We examine how wife abuse affects everyone. We discuss what is currently being done to halt abuse. We talk about proposed solutions offered by everyone involved, and finally, we offer short-term and long-term solutions that have arisen from our examination of the problem. We do not claim to have discovered the definitive solution to this barbaric and criminal behavior but we do believe that we know the direction society must go in to end the torture.

Although we, the authors, accept the ultimate responsibility for the content and the focus of the work, it is a product of many minds and many hands. William O. Beeman and David Kertzer, editors of the Public Issues in Anthropological Perspectives series, encouraged and supported us. The publisher and staff at Berghahn Books provided logistical support and assistance. The Rocky Mountain Institute of Anthropology helped financially. We are grateful to them all. We would like to dedicate this book to all the women who let us into their lives. We cannot name them, but they know who they are.

Chapter 1

Introduction

S ince international peacekeeping was first conceived, North American soldiers have served all over the world, insuring peace on Earth. Unfortunately, there is little peace at home. About half of the women in the United States and Canada have been physically or sexually assaulted after the age of sixteen (Statistics Canada 1993: 2). It would appear that North Americans are able to provide more caring and aid when dealing with complete strangers.

This concern for strangers was well demonstrated by the actions and compassion of two thousand peacekeeping soldiers in the former Yugoslavia. The soldiers were given guidelines, yet they ignored them to help the people of that war-torn country. They handed out food when they had been advised otherwise. They stopped to help the less fortunate civilians and put themselves at risk in doing so. In the town of Bakovici, a group of these peacekeepers worked under deplorable conditions to bring aid to a hospital of three hundred mentally handicapped children and adults. One reporter (Armstrong 1994: 22) observed, "We've served on every mission around the world since peacekeeping began and it is widely accepted that we are among the best in the world at the job, perhaps because we don't have enemies." Considering a 1993 Statistics Canada study on violence against women (the first national survey of its kind anywhere in the world), it would appear that some North Americans do indeed have enemies. However, these enemies are within their own borders.[1]

The victims are the abused and innocent women. Thousands of special shelters provide safe sanctuary for the women and their children. In 1992 in Canada alone, seventy-eight thousand women and children were admitted to protective shelters (C.A.W.E.S. 1993: 4). The number in the United States was roughly ten times the Canadian number. These women were seeking protection from their husbands, boyfriends, and lovers. Their need is apparent. "In each of the past two years [in Canada], more than one hundred women were killed by their male partners" (Franssen et al. 1994). In the United States, the number of women killed by a current or former spouse or lover was estimated at about 1,500 each year for the same time period (Silverman and Kennedy 1993).

That the violence is occurring at all is cause for concern. That 25 percent of all women have experienced physical or sexual violence at the hands of a marital partner is cause for alarm. Some 45 percent of all women surveyed have experienced violence at the hands of men known to them (Statistics Canada 1993: 2), but as yet no "peacekeeping" force has been deployed to bring protection and aid to these innocent victims. Violence against women is widespread. When these women leave their homes seeking sanctuary, when they try to start new lives free from pain, degradation, and violence, they discover that the abuse continues. For many of these women, the fear remains with them for years, often for the rest of their lives—a direct result of the abuse.

It's War

This is a chronicle of abusive relationships and how and why they fail. It describes not simply husband-wife relationships, but the broader network that includes all of the relationships an abused woman has with family, friends, and co-workers, as well as legal and social work professionals. The list goes on, and for some women, each and every one of these relationships fails them. Sometimes the results are deadly.

On a sunny day in 1995, Teresa left her place of work as usual. As she approached her car, she noticed that her tires were all flat. While trying to figure out what to do, she suddenly smiled as she saw her estranged husband coming towards her. She probably thought he would help her. He shot her at close range. She died on the way to the hospital; he went home and shot himself. Everyone expressed shock and surprise that he "… would do such a thing. He was always so nice." However, several of Teresa's closest friends confided that she had left him because he had beaten her on a number of occasions. Despite this, no one expected him to end the relationship by ending both of their lives.

On 28 June 1992, Kay Weekley heard her ex-husband, a brutal man with a lengthy record of physical violence including spousal abuse and assault, approaching the trailer where she'd been living since their separation. She was alone and terrified, and rather than face the inevitable beating or worse, she shot him with a shotgun. She later argued in court that she knew he was coming to kill her. "It's like going down the freeway, and you see these cars piling up, and you're going at a certain speed, and you know you'll hit the cars.… It's just something that a battered woman knows." He died, and she is currently serving a lengthy prison sentence (Gleick 1996).

No one is willing to accept that the only way for spousal abuse to end is with the death of one or both of the participants. Unfortunately, however, this extreme form of abuse is a reality. Abusers are killing their spouses or their spouses are killing them, while society at large wrings its collective hands and wonders how things ever got this bad. However, only a few know just how bad it really is. The general public receives only the end of the story, the extremely violent aspects of spousal abuse—the injuries, the severe beatings, the killings—primarily because they are graphic. A murder makes great headlines, but it is only part of a process. A murder takes only seconds to accomplish, but the abuse process goes on for years, even decades in some cases.

For many of the abused, death becomes a feasible and perhaps preferable escape because all their relationships with the rest of society have failed and all other escape routes have been blocked. There are, of course, two aspects of spousal abuse. Husbands abuse their wives and wives abuse their husbands. According to Lesley Gregorash (1994) of the Pastoral Institute, "The police still tend to believe that husband abuse doesn't happen." Statistics presented at the 1994 Conference on Men's Health Issues argue otherwise. The National Family Violence Surveys demonstrated that of the 28 percent of American couples surveyed in 1975 and 1985 who admitted to having some violence in their relationships, the violence was instigated by women at least 25 percent of the time. Despite this statistic, we have chosen to concentrate in this book exclusively on domestic violence directed against women. One reason for that decision was the willingness of the abused women to participate in the research. The men who suffered abuse at the hands of their wives were extremely reluctant to discuss it at all.

Methodology

We began exploring the problem of wife abuse in 1991.[2] The impetus for the study was a conversation one of the authors had with four close friends. Abuse came up in this casual conversation, and to everyone's surprise, all of the women had been abused at one time or another, two of them by the same man. These four women became the study's principal informants. Beginning with them, the authors conducted a series of interviews that tended to be informal and conversational. There was a series of questions that needed to be answered by each informant, but the authors decided to avoid using a structured interviewer-driven interview. Instead, an informant-driven approach was adopted. Usually, the questions were answered during the course of the interview. If they were not and the session was drawing to a close, the questions were inserted by the interviewer.

Initially, the interviewer and informant met for the introductory interview at a time and location chosen by the informant.

The reasons for the meeting were restated and the conversation begun. This initial meeting tended to be short (under 1.5 hours), but all subsequent discussions regularly lasted several hours. The information gathered at every interview included individual life histories, the informant's history of abuse, and the ways the woman had dealt or was dealing with its aftermath.

The authors encouraged the informants to speak to other women who had been abused. The informants were given written statements of intent (containing information on how to contact the authors) to give to the others in the hopes that they would also agree to become participants. Responses to this kind of request are usually few and far between, as most surveys rarely garner a return rate higher than 10 percent. In this case, though, almost all of the women contacted in this way responded positively and joined the group of informants. They contacted other women in turn, and by the end of the study, the authors had a list of several hundred contacts all across North America. Perhaps because of this kind of "snowball" sampling, the ethnic background of the women in the study was quite homogeneous. With the exception of a small group of Hispanic women from Central America and a few Native Americans, the group was white Euroamerican and middle to low class in economic status.

To deal with the women, the authors adopted a standardized approach that began with a telephone call initiated by the woman during which some basic information was gathered and an initial meeting was arranged. If a face-to-face meeting was impossible for logistical reasons, the interview was done over the phone at that time or over a period of several weeks. If an interview in person was possible, it was set up and one or both of the authors met with the woman.

After the initial interview, each woman was asked to participate in a series of interviews to monitor her progress. Usually, there were between two and eight subsequent interviews within two to three months of the initial interview. Contacts with the women who participated in these extended sessions continued with either telephone interviews or face-to-face meetings every six months or so. Some contacts continued for five years or more.

As the study progressed, the authors set up a series of group sessions where several abused women would meet to discuss common issues and problems. These sessions were held in one of the women's homes and became regular meetings, with the authors acting solely as facilitators. The women were aware at all times that the authors were taking notes and would be using the information gathered, but this did not seem to constrict their choice of topics for discussion. Some of the women admitted that they found it easier to participate in these sessions than in the earlier interviews, as they were not the focus of the conversation all of the time and so could relax, enjoy, and listen.

We also invited the women to involve their family and friends in the various discussions and interviews. Many were reluctant to do so but others readily agreed. Between 1991 and 1996, the authors interviewed about 100 women in the presence of their mothers, sisters, or female friends. On only a few occasions, fathers or brothers were also present during the conversations. These interviews were extremely valuable for two reasons. First, the authors gained valuable insights into the perceptions of the family and friends of the abused women. Second, the women themselves gained those insights. Several told the authors in subsequent interviews that the relationships they had with the people who had accompanied them to the discussions had strengthened considerably as a result of their participation in the joint discussions.

In order to expand the database, we kept records of the people who were somehow involved with the abused women and many of them were approached directly. Doctors, lawyers, psychologists, therapists, police officers, shelter workers, and others were contacted and invited to participate in the study. We did not identify the women who had provided their names, nor did we attempt to discuss specific cases. For these individuals, we utilized a more structured interview format and focused on each individual's experiences regarding wife abuse and their perceptions of the problem as a whole. Many declined to participate, citing as the reason the need for absolute confidentiality, a condition imposed by their employers. Others agreed to participate but almost all imposed conditions varying from guarantees of anonymity to having all questions submitted to them in advance. Several chose to respond in writing to those questions and then declined the request for an interview.

Contact was also made with a number of men who had been abusive toward their spouses, using a method similar to the indirect contact letter that had been used to alert abused women to the study. The letters were distributed by counselors who were conducting group sessions for abusive men, and by workers in various agencies that dealt with such men. The responses were minimal and the authors had the opportunity to interview fewer than twenty abusive husbands over the course of the study.

One of the biggest difficulties we had in conducting this study was the overwhelming amount of data. A statistical analysis was attempted, but it seemed too cold and did not properly convey the seriousness of the problem. Instead, the authors settled on a very personal approach. The women's stories would be told, thereby confronting the reader with real personalities, real pain, and real danger. However, as a concession to these women who all still fear for their lives, all names have been changed and all of the geographical and temporal information has been altered. In addition to following these women through their ordeals, the authors offer experiences and thoughts from abused women as well as from other individuals who have either helped or hindered the victims of abuse.

We decided to limit the analysis by dealing only peripherally with the root causes of wife abuse. These causes may be societal to some degree in that historical cultural precepts gave women the status of "husband's property." On the other hand, abusive behavior is personal and idiosyncratic. No one is able to explain why a man becomes abusive towards his wife when another man in exactly the same situation does not. It seems an abuser has a potential for violence that predates the abusive relationship. It has been argued that the abusive behavior was learned when (a) he observed abusive behavior in his role models (he watched his mother being abused by his father) or (b) he was abused himself or (c) both. However, when one examines the background of abusive individuals, one discovers that some abusive men have never had any of the above "learning experiences." More importantly, many individuals who have "learned" never become abusive themselves. Perhaps the propensity for violence exists within all individuals—a pre-existing condition, if you like—but some men will become abusive while others will not.

There are two ways to view this. People could simply deplore the situation and recognize that spousal abuse is inevitable and there is nothing they can do about it. This is a convenient way to abdicate responsibility and has been used on occasion by caregivers and others in authority. On the other hand, they could suggest that all humans have the capacity for violence but societies have developed cultural and individual mechanisms to hold that violence in abeyance. It is our opinion that the spousal abuse that is occurring here and now is partly the result of changes in the cultural and individual mechanisms that should be controlling the violent behavior. The mechanisms seem to be ineffective as far as spousal abuse is concerned, and more men are becoming abusers because they can get away with it. One of the goals of the research was to look at those cultural and individual factors and the reasons for their failure.

Although the study initially focused on the problem of spousal abuse in Canada, the number of informants in all categories from within the United States increased until nearly half of the total informants were American. At that point, we were confident enough with the data to expand the parameters of the study. With that in mind, the following discussions should be considered to apply to North American society in general, rather than to Canada or the United States specifically.

Types of Abuse

As noted earlier, the general public usually is exposed to the criminal aspects of the abuse—the assaults and the murders.[3] There are many other kinds of abuse that vary in intensity and severity, although they cannot really be ranked since a single type may be inconsequential to one woman but have a severe impact on another. Therefore, the impacts on either the abused or the abuser are highly idiosyncratic and situational, but all of them center on the imbalance of power between the abuser and the abused. It has been argued that the "... purpose of the assault is to control her behavior" (Edmonton Women's Shelter Ltd. 1995: 1). If so, all forms of spousal abuse can be interpreted as the actions of a man to gain, maintain, or exert control over a woman (usually his wife).[4] The various types of abuse can be grouped under three major headings: economic control, psychological/emotional abuse, and physical violence (also referred to as criminal abuse).

Economic Control

By controlling finances, the abuser gains control over his spouse, often preventing the victim from working outside the home. For example, a former neighbor once confided that her husband would not let her work. His reasoning was that he did want to have to admit that they needed her income to get by. He was embarrassed by that possibility. She felt that he wanted to keep her totally dependent on him.

If the victim is employed outside the house, the abusive spouse can interfere with that work by embarrassing his wife in her employer's or co-workers' presence or by making her late for work. Also, if the victim attempts to increase her efforts to improve economically, for example by taking a training course or the like, the spouse may sabotage those efforts by raising roadblocks.

It is likely that an abusive spouse will deny the victim access to many things. For example, the abusive spouse may withhold any money from the victim, including the money she earns from her employment. Without money, the victim becomes isolated. In addition, she may be denied use of the car, the telephone, or other services.

Psychological/Emotional Abuse

VERBAL ABUSE

There are a variety of ways that a man can verbally abuse his spouse, either in private or in public. He can call her names or mock her with words, humiliating remarks or gestures. He may criticize her in a destructive way. He might blame her for something or accuse her of doing something. Any of these can be done quietly, providing the right amount of sarcasm is used, or he might raise his voice and yell at her. Alternatively, he may remain silent, letting his total lack of communication speak volumes about his displeasure.

APPLYING PRESSURE

A clear form of abuse is the application of pressure or intimidation by the user to get the woman to do what he wants her to regardless of her wishes or needs. For example, he could sulk or use guilt to get what he wants. He could apply pressure by threatening to withhold money or use the children (a form of withholding) to force the woman to make a decision against her will, or he may use deprivation. For example, a man who wants his wife to do something (like have sex with him or change her mind about something) may simply prevent her from sleeping until she complies.

If children are involved, the abusive spouse will threaten to report the victim to any of the various watchdog agencies that oversee child welfare. The possibility, however remote, that the mother would lose her children is an effective control mechanism.

AUTHORITARIANISM

There is a fine line between the exercising of authority and the over-exercising of that authority. In a functioning (non-abusive) relationship, generally the couple makes all decisions, especially important ones, after appropriate discussions. In an abusive relationship, a man may exercise control by making major decisions unilaterally. For example, one abusive husband told his wife that he had taken a new job and they were moving at the end of the month to a new town several hundred miles away. His announcement was the first she had heard about it.

In addition, an abusive husband will always claim to be right. His decisions are the right ones (regardless of outcome—indeed, often when the outcome is negative, the husband will shift the blame onto his spouse), and he will frequently tell his spouse what to do and how to do it. In the latter case, the instructions can be extremely petty and involve something of very little consequence. For example, one abused woman described how her husband insisted that all of the canned goods be stored in the kitchen cupboards in alphabetical order (ostensibly because that was the way his mother did it). He would yell at her and/or beat her if the smooth peanut butter was on the wrong side of the crunchy peanut butter.

Another informant said that her husband controlled the foods that she ate and what foods came into their home.

> If I did bring mayonnaise into the home, it had to be kept at the back of the fridge—out of sight, out of mind. If I made sandwiches for lunch, as soon as he came into the kitchen and saw my sandwich, he'd want to know where was the knife that was used to make his sandwich? Was his sandwich put anywhere near my sandwich? If we went somewhere for a barbecue and Caesar salad was offered and if I actually had the audacity to eat it, he was angry as hell. He would spend that whole night and maybe a good part of the next day not talking to me because I actually had eaten that garlic.

DISRESPECT

Showing disrespect is very closely related to verbal abuse, although the disrespectful behavior almost always involves others. A man may, in the presence of others, interrupt or change the topic of conversation without regard for what his spouse has been saying or doing. He could simply ignore his spouse and not respond to any questions or statements that she makes. This demonstrates indirectly to the wife, and to the others present, that she has no value. He may directly demonstrate her lack of value by putting her down (or her family or friends) in front of other people. Yvonne mentioned that at Christmas time, her husband would make a very big deal out of giving presents to his children and friends (including his secretary) while making sure that everyone was aware that he had no gift for his wife.

ABUSING TRUST

A fundamental aspect of a functioning relationship is trust, and one form of abuse involves the repeated violation of that trust in a variety of ways. For example, a man may withhold information from his wife, lie to her, or be unfaithful to her. On the other hand, instead of taking advantage of a trusting wife, he may exhibit lack of trust in her. One informant described how her husband would randomly phone her at home from work and if, for any reason, she was not there to answer his call within four rings, he would fly into a rage. When he returned home that evening, he would accuse her of sneaking out to see other men and then proceed to beat her. If the phone were busy when he called, he would get angry and accuse her of phoning her "boyfriends." That too would result in an evening beating. She learned to remain home close to the phone whenever he was at work so that she would not miss any of his calls. She rarely made phone calls out or stayed on the phone long whenever anyone called her. In that way, she hoped to reduce or limit the number of beatings she received at his hands.

Another participant gave a similar example of an everyday occurrence and the disproportionate and unreasonable jealousy generated by it. She said:

> I knew that when we were driving down the streets not to stare out the window although I was the passenger, because if he, as the driver, spotted, say at a bus stop, two guys, then as we drove by the bus stop if I'm still looking out the window once we got past the bus stop he'd have a freak out. To him, I must have been staring at those guys at the bus stop.

She said that even if she was just daydreaming, she always had to remember not to have her head turned in the direction of the window, or else she might be accused of looking at other men.

WITHHOLDING EMOTIONAL CONTACT

Most individuals require some kind of emotional support. An abusive husband can take advantage of this need by withholding any kind of emotional contact. When one informant asked her husband why he never said anything about the food she prepared for him, he responded: "I'm eating it, aren't I? If I don't like it, I'll let you know." Invariably, any comments that he made concerning his wife, her appearance, or her accomplishments were negative. Few abused women ever receive positive reinforcement from their abusive spouses.

MINIMIZING

In a way, minimizing—that is, making light of abusive behavior—
is abusive. By downplaying the abuse or even denying that it ever
happened, the abuser reduces the worth of the victim. Phrases
like "I didn't hit you that hard," or "You are overreacting" are
common forms of minimizing, reducing the importance of the
abuse. Often, when the abuser cannot minimize it in these ways,
he will turn it around and blame the wife. "You made me do it,"
"You made me angry," and "You stupid bitch, if you did it right, I
wouldn't have to punish you" are all blaming/minimizing tactics.

ISOLATION

In an attempt to control his spouse, the abuser may resort to isolation tactics. He may generate roadblocks that prevent the wife
from seeing friends and relatives. One informant mentioned
that immediately after their marriage, the husband accepted a
job two thousand miles away from the wife's nearest relatives.
He told her that they would move back when they could, but at
the same time, he told several friends that he would never move
back to be near her family.

The abuser may also control where his wife goes and whom
she sees. "I don't want you going to see her anymore. She's a
bitch" was what one husband told his wife about her best
friend, a woman she'd known all her life. He gave no reasons
but implied that there would be severe repercussions if she dis-
obeyed him.

In addition, this abusive husband (and many others) tended
to monitor phone calls made by or received by his wife. He would
remain within earshot or listen on an extension phone. This
monitoring would prevent the wife from saying anything to anyone about the abuse, or about anything personal at all.

HARASSMENT

We have already noted that an abuser may make the occasional
telephone call to check up on the abused spouse, but the harassment can go much further. He may show up unannounced at his
wife's place of work, or any place she happens to be visiting, just
to make sure she is "not doing anything she shouldn't be."
Michelle summed it up this way:

I had a job where I did a lot of ordering and I had to meet with salesmen, and 90 percent of sales people are men. Well, it was common. You take all these big catalogues. You go sit down somewhere. You have a coffee and you spend five hours writing up an order. And I was always very nervous, because if that happened to be the day that my spouse decided to come and have a coffee with me, and walked into my office and I was sitting there placing an order with a man or sitting in a food court placing an order with a man, it was hell to pay. So you think it would be okay if it was a saleswoman? No, if it was a saleswoman then he used that as his example to prove to me that he worked harder than me. His job was more demanding of him physically and mentally. All I do is visit and drink coffee. So he deserved more catering than I did when we got home because I didn't do anything all day. He had seen. He had caught me having coffee with the saleswoman and didn't recognize it was a business meeting. It was just sitting and having coffee with some woman.

Physical Violence

This category of spousal abuse includes most forms that are interpreted by people in general as being abuse. It is criminal in nature, and this type of criminal abuse rarely occurs in isolation. Rather, it begins after a pattern of other abusive behaviors has become well established. In fact, it augments the abuser's already extensive repertoire of abusive techniques.

SEXUAL VIOLENCE

Only in recent years has the idea become acceptable that a woman's body is her own, and therefore does not automatically become her husband's property after the marriage ceremony. Today, any form of sexual intercourse between husband and wife must be mutually agreed upon. Otherwise, if one partner does not consent to having sex, the intercourse becomes rape—sexual violence. An abusive spouse may treat the abused spouse in a degrading manner based on sex or sexual orientation. He may use force, threats, or coercion to obtain sex or perform sexual acts. He may engage in sexual touching or fondling that is nonconsensual, or he may show no respect for the victim's personal privacy. Any and all of these activities, assuming that the wife has, by word or action, signaled her non-interest, belong in the realm of spousal abuse.

INTIMIDATION AND THREATS

In North American society, violence is not condoned. The threat of violence is equally condemned, although threats in an abusive situation are rarely public affairs. Threats are forms of intimidation and can be either physical or verbal. In the former, the husband may make angry or threatening gestures, use his physical size to intimidate, stand in the doorway during arguments (to prevent the wife from escaping), or drive recklessly with his wife in the car. In the latter, he may threaten to hurt his spouse or another person who is important to the wife.

DESTRUCTION

An abusive husband will often use dramatic gestures to underscore his threats. He will throw and/or break things primarily for emphasis—although occasionally, these things are used as weapons against the wife—or he will demonstrate his superior physical strength by, for example, punching holes in walls. It could be argued that these items are used and destroyed during the heat of an argument, but when one examines what items are destroyed, there appears to be some form of premeditation involved. For example, in almost all of the cases of wanton destruction in abusive situations, the destroyed items belonged to the abused wife rather than to the husband or to the couple. Indeed, they were usually of some sentimental value to the wife, and as such represented her life rather than his. In one case, the abusive husband tortured and then killed the wife's cat while the wife was forced to watch.

Elizabeth's body is covered with scars from cigarette burns, knife cuts, and blows with blunt instruments, including fists, but she readily notes that she cannot remember getting half of them. However, she does remember the time her pets were killed in front of her. She described it this way:

> He came home one night and said to me, he said, "You know you aren't even worth a f__ing licking." And the things I loved the most in my life were my cats. I had two half grown cats. He made me sit on the couch and he shot them ... through the arm pit area. I had to sit on the couch and watch my cats flip around and die. It took about an hour for them to die. And that was more effective than any beating he ever gave me because basically what

he said to me was "You could be that cat" plus every day I had to look at the bloodstains in the rug that I couldn't get out. I'll always remember that.

The action, in the eyes of the abuser, accomplishes two goals: first, it lets the wife know that the husband is capable of this kind of violence and therefore increases his control over her; second, it hurts the wife seriously without leaving a visible mark on her.

ASSAULT

The physical destruction of symbols representative of the wife rather than the wife herself is relatively common in abusive situations. As noted above, objects of sentimental or real value to the wife are destroyed, but when that violence is directed at the woman, the abusive behavior becomes assaultive.

The kinds of violence used by an abusive spouse are limited only by the perpetrator's imagination. He can slap, punch, grab, kick, choke, push, bite or burn her. He can hurt her just once or twice, or continue until he runs out of energy or rage. According to the women, the assault can be over in a few seconds, or it can last for several hours, with rest breaks alternating with severe beatings.

Some abusive husbands will involve others in the physical violence. Sylvia told of the time when, after her departure from an abusive relationship and the subsequent incarceration of her estranged husband for stalking and assaulting her, she heard a knock at the door. For some reason, she did not respond. Instead, she waited and watched from an upstairs window until two "bikers," as she described them, left. Within minutes, the phone rang. It was her estranged husband phoning from prison to ask if she had "received his message." He had sent two friends to beat her since he was unable to do it himself.

ASSAULT WITH A WEAPON

The use of weapons occurs with regularity as well. The abuser may begin by using these weapons, showing them to the spouse, or simply letting her know he has one. This is an attempt to intimidate by directly or indirectly threatening the woman into submission. Phrases like "I have a gun and I'll use it on you if you get out of line" or "Don't make me shoot you" were heard regularly during the interviews.

These threats to use weapons such as guns or knives are frequently followed up. A husband may shoot or stab his wife (or use some other form of weapon such as a hockey stick or baseball bat). Of course, these types of incidents generally have legal ramifications and tend to occur quite late in the abusive relationship.

MURDER

The final abuse is simply a matter of degree. Sometimes, the abuse is severe enough to result in the death of the victim. That makes it murder. It is estimated that about one hundred women in Canada and more than ten times that in the United States are murdered by their male partners annually. Some make the headlines, if the events surrounding the crime are spectacular enough. A case in Alberta dominated the North American news for several weeks in 1997 and 1998. An estranged husband abducted his ex-wife from her family's home in the middle of the day and drove off in a camper van. The couple disappeared and, despite a massive manhunt that lasted about a week, there was no sign of them until he appeared at a convenience store alone. It took several more days for the searchers to find the van and her body. He had beaten her to death with a club-like weapon.

In another case, the estranged husband walked into his former wife's home, doused her with gasoline, and set her afire. Her house was destroyed and two of her children died in the fire, but it took her a year to die from the burns she suffered. In both cases, the lack of remorse shown by the husband[5] and the nastiness of the murder kept the public interested, and so kept the crimes in the news. However, most of the deaths attributed to the ultimate form of spousal abuse receive little or no mention in the media.

Pattern of Abuse

Some would argue that certain items classified above as abusive behavior are simply parts of everyday life. They contend that actions such as yelling, interrupting, not paying attention, and infidelity, all mentioned above as abusive behavior, may occur between a husband and a wife during the normal course of a marriage and so should not be classed as abusive. Indeed, when they occur infrequently and in isolation from other abusive behaviors, they are not necessarily abusive. For example, if an otherwise caring husband hits his wife in anger once, it is not considered to be wife abuse, although that behavior is unacceptable. He is not labeled a wife-beater. However, in an abusive situation violence is not an isolated incident, nor does it occur only once. Usually these kinds of controlling behaviors occur in clusters as part of ongoing abusive behavior referred to as the Pattern or Cycle of Abuse.

The Cycle of Abuse can be divided into four stages (Edmonton Women's Shelter Ltd. 1995):

1. The Build-up. Stressors such as employment or money troubles trigger this stage in which negative thought processes (blaming and anger) become dominant. During this stage, the anger and blaming become directed at a specific target—usually the spouse. Abusive behaviors increase.

2. The Acting Out. At a certain point, the abuser lashes out, usually with physical abuse. The behavior can range from a single slap to inflicting serious injury with a weapon. It can also occur as a single incident or a series of repeated assaults over an extended length of time.

3. The Rationalization/Justification. Both individuals use defense mechanisms to justify or rationalize the assaultive behavior. The abuser may deflect the blame away from himself and divert any consequences of his actions; his spouse may become an enabler and allow the abuser to deflect the blame. Indeed, she may accept the blame herself, suggesting that she deserves to be beaten.

4. "Pretending Normal." With the justification firmly in place, the couple portrays the relationship as "normal." Both husband and wife deny that anything is wrong and, without adjustments or attempts to break the cycle, the Build-up phase begins again. This stage and the preceding one are often combined and referred to as the "Honeymoon Stage."

We suggest that although this model is useful in evaluating specific relationships, it ignores many causative factors and other elements that affect spousal abuse.

The dynamics of a relationship between an abusive husband and his abused wife are worth noting. Typically, an abuser, through successive beatings or abusive episodes, demonstrates his control or power over his wife. As he does so, he tends to gain an inflated sense of his own power. As he dominates, he develops a "need" to dominate. Conversely, the abused spouse suffers from extremely low self-esteem, tending to blame herself for the abuse: "He beats me, therefore I am a really terrible person." As the abusive relationship continues, the wife, seeing herself as incapable of fending for herself because of low self-esteem, develops a strong need to be dominated. Dominance begets dominance and powerlessness begets powerlessness. Both partners need each other to maintain their own self-images, and this need is strong and emotionally long-lasting.

Acceleration of Abuse

It is obvious that a man who abuses his spouse has an enormous choice of methods ranging from psychological to physical abuse. It is impossible to predict which abusive method (or aggregate of methods) an individual will choose, although it could be suggested that there are two factors that affect the choice: (1) the husband wants control over his spouse and will use whatever form of abuse that is necessary to obtain that control. If verbal abuse is sufficient to obtain and maintain control, the abuser may not use any of the more violent methods. (2) the abusive husband has a psychological need to demonstrate the control he has over his spouse. Whatever method satisfies that need will be used. Often, the abuse will be excessive (beyond the level perceived as necessary by the abuser), simply to reassure him of his own power over his spouse.

If the abuse is sufficient to maintain and demonstrate the control and the power, it will remain stable. We repeatedly listened to the stories of women who endured years and even decades of verbal abuse, for example, that did not change from the first demonstration of power to the last. One widow told of over thirty years of degradation and isolation: "My husband was a bastard. He'd scream at me and call me all kinds of names. After a while, I learned to do what I was told. He still screamed and yelled but I tuned it all out. I stopped listening and he didn't care as long as he got what he wanted."[6] Incidentally, this woman did not realize she was being abused until she started attending a self-help group several years after her husband's death.

It is our impression that once an abuser establishes control to his satisfaction, he is content with the status quo and will not alter his pattern of abuse. It is only when the situation changes that he begins to accelerate the abusive behavior. Participants in the study identified three scenarios that tended to have an impact on the abusive behavior.

OUTSIDE INFLUENCES
It appears that when other areas of the husband's life begin to change for the worse and he sees his control slipping away—for example, when his job is threatened—he will begin to focus more on those areas where he still maintains some degree of control. He will take out his frustrations on his wife even if her behavior has not changed.

PREGNANCY AND CHILDREN
In general, as long as the couple remains childless, the husband has the wife all to himself. He maintains control. However, when the wife becomes pregnant, his control apparently weakens in his estimation. She is often tired and unable to fulfill his every desire. He will not react with understanding but will become more abusive. In addition, babies are demanding and the husband finds himself playing second fiddle to a helpless infant whose cries cannot be ignored no matter what the husband requires. This is a loss of control that will have a strong negative impact on the husband's behavior. The marked increase in abusive behavior against pregnant wives has been documented repeatedly.

THE WIFE'S ATTITUDE
As long as the wife is acquiescent and docile and all other conditions remain unchanged, the abuse will continue but will not

accelerate. However, as soon as the spouse becomes resistive, the husband will fight harder to regain control over her. We have listened to many women tell us that the most dangerous time during the relationship was the time when the wife was attempting to end the relationship. Beatings, physical confinement, and murder are all possible, indeed likely, responses to the wife's seeking a divorce. Sandra described how her estranged husband sent his sister to a shelter pretending to be on the run from her husband but really seeking to discover if the wife was in residence there. His intent was to kidnap her. Another woman discussed the time when she went to her sister's house for a few days to get away from the abuse. She knew that when she returned home, "… he was going to beat the crap out of me."

The wide variety of forms that abuse takes is quite disturbing, and to someone who has not experienced it, it might seem unreal. However, listening to the abused women describe the emotional and physical abuse perpetrated against them in their own homes makes it very real. There is no exaggeration, no embellishment. They simply describe their experiences.

Notes

1. No comparable survey exists for the United States, but it is felt that the American statistics would be comparable to the Canadian figures.
2. For the purposes of this analysis, the terms "wife abuse" and "spousal abuse" are used interchangeably to refer to violence perpetrated by the husband against the wife.
3. Many forms of abuse are not considered illegal, which prevents the criminal justice system from becoming involved. The abuser cannot be compelled to change his behavior.
4. The term wife is used in the sense of a woman who, whether legally married or not, carries out the role of wife.
5. The man who bludgeoned his wife to death was described as "smirking" throughout his trial.
6. In a relationship involving an abusive wife, she is most likely to use this form of abuse. The husband is then usually referred to as "hen-pecked."

Chapter 2

Social Stigma and Silence

It is perhaps significant that the abused women who participated in the research (including a few who were still in the
abusive relationship) spoke easily about their problems and
experiences. The frank and open discussions brought to light
events and experiences that ranged from amusing to horrifying,
but there were no moments in these women's lives that were
forbidden. The women opened their wounds and talked about
everything, without hesitation and certainly without any attempt to sugarcoat or minimize.

On the other hand, those in the helping professions—the
shelter workers, police officers, and lawyers in particular—were
quite reluctant to talk to us. When one of the authors sought an
interview with the manager of a shelter, she was given the third
degree, and at one point there was a veiled suggestion that perhaps she was misrepresenting herself. Perhaps the manager
seriously considered her a government investigator sent to "spy"
on the shelter's operation, or a cohort of an abusive husband
seeking information. It took some convincing and eventually the
manager cooperated, but the cooperation was far from unconditional. Suspicion is a natural state of affairs at emergency shelters and we were not offended by it. Like security at airports, it
can be annoying but it serves a greater good. Shelters routinely

refuse to divulge any information about their clients, and with good reason. Sandra was not the only woman to describe attempts by an abusive husband to locate and "reclaim" his spouse. Because of the potential danger to clients, the shelter operators are naturally suspicious of any requests for information, regardless of the source of the request.

The police, whose activities are essentially open to public scrutiny, should have no foundation for suspicion; however, they too openly questioned the motivation for the study. Eventually, official and unofficial channels began to open up though it took the intervention of a police sergeant, a close friend of the authors.

As an aside, an Internet surfing session revealed another societal reluctance. Using a standard search procedure, all references to "spousal abuse," "wife abuse," or "wife beating" were requested. Despite expectations of a huge list of occurrences, the computer registered fewer than a dozen hits. The information being sought was found under the collective heading "domestic violence," a label that effectively distances the topic. Domestic violence is impersonal, neutral, and as devoid of emotion as "wife beating" is personal and intensely emotional.

Society and Spousal Abuse

It is generally recognized that the problem of spousal abuse has been around for a very long time, perhaps since the first families came into being. Most animals (humans included) will attempt to gain dominance over others of their own kind. The stronger members of a species will dominate the weaker ones, and in a sexually dimorphic species—one with distinctive physical differences between males and females—the dominant-subservient division usually falls along gender lines. The observation that for centuries women were referred to as the "weaker sex" attests to this. In addition, some individuals, usually males but not always, will exhibit violent behavior towards members of their own families regardless of the safeguards that are in place.

Having said this, we would like to examine some of the factors that affect and permit spousal abuse despite the stated ideal that "people are equal to one another and no one has the right to abuse another."

Individual Factors

That each human being is genetically unique, with the exception of identical twins, is an accepted fact. That every human being is *behaviorally* unique is an idea that is rapidly gaining acceptance. It is argued that a human, as he or she grows, acquires an aggregate of temperament (a general demeanor, perhaps a result of the unique genetic makeup of the individual), learned behaviors (acquired largely by observing others—parents, siblings, peers, and so on—at a young age), knowledge (acquired through experience and education), and attitude (more properly described as perspective or "worldview"). This aggregate or collective acts together to generate a set of adult behaviors. People who share much of their genetic makeup and the same life experiences will, to slightly varying degrees, exhibit similar behaviors. For example, siblings of approximately the same age who grow up together, share the same friends, and attend the same schools will tend to behave similarly (making allowances for difference in temperament). Conversely, people who share none of these things will act quite differently from one another.

Temperament

Temperament can be described as the characteristic physiological state of an individual that tends to condition his responses to life's situations. Individual temperament varies greatly, so that one person will stoically accept a loss of a job while another in the same situation may become wildly angry. A person can be moody or optimistic or resistive. These variations in temperament tend to explain how, when confronted with the situational factors that often accompany spousal abuse, one person will not become an abuser whereas another, confronted by no factors linked to abuse, will be abusive. Psychologists have been struggling with this diversity of temperament since the beginning and are no closer now than they were at the turn of the century. This recognition that, all things being equal, some men will abuse their spouses while others will not, seems to have resulted in a generally fatalistic attitude towards spousal abuse: many believe that no matter what is done there will always be abusers.

LEARNED BEHAVIOR

> Early childhood experiences are the most critical in forming an individual's personality and in socializing the individual to the ways of the society. These early experiences are, for the most part, unstructured and unplanned. Much of early childhood socialization is not the result of acts explicitly aimed at shaping the child's view of the world, although some acts will be. Rather, most of what goes on in the socialization process during this period is informal, as people feed, care for, and play with the child (Howard 1996: 148–9).

In earlier generations, the people largely responsible for teaching the child proper behavior were the parents (usually the mother), siblings, and other family members. Although these people are still involved in the process, others such as day care workers and television personalities are now having an impact as well. The circle of socializers has increased, and as a result the parents, the primary caregivers, though they remain the most influential role models for the very young child, have less control over the socialization process then they once did.

The adult personality is shaped by early childhood experiences and relationships. What one internalizes and organizes unconsciously as a child will affect what he or she does throughout life. Some parents in our society recognize and act on this, and make a conscious effort as parents to rear their children according to guiding principles set out by professionals in child psychology. Others will try to emulate their own parents and raise their children as they themselves were raised. However, all parents are amateurs at raising children since socialization is a cultural process and is largely unconscious. There are no curriculum guides available, despite what one would think looking at the self-help and family sections of the local bookstore. Adults automatically react to what their own children do without conscious thought. For example, a mother with a fear of spiders acquired sometime in her unremembered past may, when she sees her child with or near a spider, react by screaming and wrenching the child away from the spider. The displayed fear, if repeated a number of times, will become part of the child's own fears to emerge as a hysterical fear of spiders acquired sometime in his or her unremembered past. Interestingly, a toddler left alone with a spider will not show any fear whatsoever.

In addition, adults do not need to be interacting with the child to be "socializing" her or him. If the adjective "normal" is defined as meaning "what we are used to," a normal family life is what the members of the family are used to. If children are raised in a nurturing, loving relationship, that will become the norm for them when they grow up. If, however, there is an abusive relationship, the children interpret and internalize that behavior as normal. As Sandra, whose mother was abused and who married an abusive man, told us: "I used to go to friends' houses for dinner and wonder why their fathers didn't smack their mothers around. I watched their mothers do and say things that'd get my mother a black eye or worse but nothing would happen. I remember spending hours and hours trying to figure out why my friends' families were so weird."

Children "… suffer the consequences of their parents' battles simply because they exist … people who as children had observed their parents engaging in physical violence were more likely to engage in the same sort of activity with their own spouses than those who never saw their parents fight" (Martin 1983: 23–24). In other words, children in abusive homes learn that violence in the form of wife beating is normal and will, as adults, behave normally. Research indicates that a high percentage of men who abuse their partners had as children witnessed their fathers abuse their mothers.

KNOWLEDGE

As people grow and mature, they acquire knowledge that enables them to be aware of, understand, and interpret the events around them. It can be suggested that the greater a person's understanding of the world, the better equipped he or she is to thrive in it and presumably, the less likely he or she would be to become an abuser or an abused spouse. This observation is true, but it often prompts the offering of educative solutions to the

spousal abuse problem. "Obviously, if certain knowledge promotes understanding and understanding promotes reduced violence, everyone can be provided with that knowledge and the
problem will cease to exist." It is not that easy. Knowledge *per se*
is often confused with education in a formal sense, but there are
really two aspects to the acquisition of knowledge and they exist
independently of one another.

Formal Education. At school children learn prescribed cur-
ricula, skills, and sets of data. The more formal schooling one has,
the better educated one is and the more knowledge one has. For
example, a person with a Ph.D. is considered to be more knowl-
edgeable than someone with only a high school diploma. If formal
education were all that is necessary, one would expect that incidents of spousal abuse would be significantly fewer in families of
well educated people. Consulting the statistics, it does seem that
lower-class families (if limited education can be correlated with
low socio-economic status) have a higher rate of reported incidents of spousal abuse than do middle- and upper-class families.
However, most authorities suggest that this difference is more
apparent than real, since middle- and upper-class incidents of
spousal abuse are underreported.

> Lower-class families have fewer resources and less privacy, and
> are more apt to contact public social-control agencies ... which
> compile domestic-disturbance statistics. Middle-class families
> have greater access to private support services ... who do not as a
> rule compile statistics.... These differences make lower-class vio-
> lence more visible (Martin 1983: 55).

As reporting techniques improve, more and more middle-class
spousal abuse cases appear in the statistics. The authors have
interviewed abused spouses whose husbands were dentists, doctors, accountants, lawyers, and psychologists. Formal education,
then, is no guarantee of a reduction in the violent behaviors.

Socialization. As stated earlier, this process of learning is
informal and occurs as children watch the world around them
and the people in it. If they are in the proper environment
with suitable role models, they will absorb and assimilate the
awareness and understanding they need to function as "good

citizens." This informal process is life-long but most critical in the formative years. For example, it is as toddlers that everyone learns the basic rules for appropriate interactions with others. Unlike formal education, socialized learning is extremely difficult to unlearn.

Sometimes socialized learning is linked to maturity in the public's mind. A "model citizen" who deals with people in the appropriate ways is mature and "worldly." Someone who uses inappropriate methods is socially "immature." Abused women often referred to their abusive husbands as immature and childlike, saying they displayed childish behaviors such as temper tantrums and the like at inappropriate times.[1] Thus, the degree to which one has learned the appropriate lessons is what affects the occurrence of spousal abuse.

ATTITUDES

> Worldview concerns the fundamental assumptions of a people about the nature of the world, as expressed more or less systematically in their philosophy, ethics, ritual, and scientific beliefs (Howard 1996: 142; also see Wallace 1970: 142–3).

People who live in a society share similar views of their world, and bound up in that worldview are sets of values which are emotionally charged beliefs "... about what is desirable or offensive, right or wrong, appropriate or inappropriate" (Howard 1996: 145). "Attitude" is the combination of worldview and values.

Within a society, there is a set of core values that provides a basis for social behavior and for the goals pursued by most of the members of the society. There is, of course, considerable variability in worldview, values, and attitudes among the various sectors of society (for example, "middleclass values" or "smalltown values" and so on). Moreover, not all members of a society or a segment of society share the same worldview or the same commitment to the values of that society. In general, spousal abuse (or any form of gratuitous violence) is considered offensive, wrong, and inappropriate. However, not everyone in our society shares this opinion. To some, wife beating is desirable or right or appropriate. These people are the abusive husbands.

As with all cultural beliefs, the belief that violent behavior is acceptable cannot be counteracted with logical arguments—any more than a faith in god can be crushed by scientific evidence to the contrary—because it is propped up and supported by many other cultural attitudes and perspectives. One interview was an incredibly frustrating discussion with a wife-beater/rapist, frustrating because his core values were completely different from the societal norm. He was guilty of violating society's sense of rightness, since wife-beating and rape are clearly "wrong." His worldview prevented him from seeing that interpretation as correct. He defined "right and wrong" as "right-for-me and wrong-for-me," without any regard for the well-being of others. That being the case, beating his wife was "right" because it got him what he wanted. Conversely, being arrested and jailed for beating his wife was "wrong," since it denied him his freedom to get what he wanted. He resented the authorities for doing that.

Needless to say, there exist a huge number of possible attitudes that individuals can have, even within a single society. For example, the person mentioned above saw the world as a resource to be exploited at will for his own gratification. Another abuser described his world as a vicious, nasty place where everyone was out to get him. "No matter what I do, I get screwed. I behave. I go by the rules and I get hassled. Hey, I'm going to get hassled no matter what I do so I might as well enjoy myself." Obviously, these attitudes, and many others reflective of certain worldviews and values, allow for the perpetuation of violence against spouses and others.

THE AGGREGATE OF INDIVIDUAL FACTORS

Certain combinations of personal or individual factors predispose a man towards spousal abuse. Given the right conditions in his environment, he will abuse his wife and, quite likely, his children as well. Unfortunately, there is no way to quantify or predict which precise individual factors in exactly which combination will combine to form the personality of the abuser. For example, a man who is moody and temperamental, grew up in an abusive home, has experienced successive failures in his life, and sees the world as actively hostile towards him will probably, given the chance, abuse his wife. However, he may not become abusive at all. Alternatively, a cheerful man who grew up in a loving home, is eminently successful in his chosen career, and sees the world as "his oyster" will probably not abuse his wife, regardless of environmental conditions—but, on the other hand, he might become an abuser. Nothing is absolute.

It is virtually "… impossible to give an exact description of an abusive man" (Focus 1987: 2), although this does not prevent researchers from trying to do just that. Some of the characteristics of the abusive man found in the literature are:

- low self-esteem
- emotional dependency
- strong denial mechanisms
- internalization of the traditional male role
- feelings of isolation
- extreme insecurity
- fear of intimacy
- strong need to control
- extreme possessiveness
- inability to express emotions other than anger
- inability to trust others
- inability to nurture others or express need
- "Jekyll & Hyde" type of personality
- history of childhood violence (Focus 1987: 2)

Abusive men may exhibit some or none of these characteristics. Other men who exhibit them will not be abusive. Therefore, we recommend extreme caution when applying this kind of personality trait list.

From time to time, it has been suggested that there are two other factors that affect the aggregate personality and so alter the individual's behavior. They are alcohol or substance abuse and mental illness.

Alcohol Use. Many abusers engage in violent behavior only when drunk. "When the husband is sober he is 'pleasant' and "charming'; when drunk he is 'a monster' or 'a bully.' Many wives say that they were beaten only when their husbands were drunk" (Martin 1983: 56). Crystal was one of those wives. She said that almost every Friday, her husband would call to say that he was going to have a few "quick ones" with the boys from work.

> That meant he'd be home about midnight, drunk and nasty. Those nights I'd get beat up. It got to the point that as soon as I got the call, I'd start drinking too so that it wouldn't hurt so much when he hit me. That worked well for a while.

This cycle of sober pleasantness and drunken abuse has led to the postulation of a "Dr. Jekyll and Mr. Hyde" syndrome. However, researchers in New York have determined that alcohol consumption plays a relatively minor role in cases of family violence. In only about a quarter of the incidents were the assaultive spouses drinking, and in many cases the investigating officers did not think the abuser was intoxicated (Bard and Zacker 1974).

The use of alcohol is not a primary cause of spousal abuse; rather, it is an excuse. Alcohol is a chemical depressant that suppresses logical mental functions and other control mechanisms. It reduces the individual's ability to keep violent tendencies in check, but those tendencies must be present already for the alcohol to have that effect. Alcohol does not make a person violent. It simply allows the violence to emerge.

Also, alcohol is often used as a justification for the violence. Consider the phrase "under the influence." This implies that when a person is drunk, he is not responsible for his own actions. Jake, described by his wife as a Jekyll and Hyde abuser, readily admitted using alcohol as an excuse.

> Everyone thought I was stone drunk when I beat Julie, and I was sometimes. But not always. Lots of times, I'd had a few beers—so I'd blow over the legal limit [on a police breathalyzer] just in case someone called the cops.
> If you beat someone when you're sober, they charge you with assault, which carries jail time. But if you're blotto, or they think you are, the charge is drunk and disorderly. They toss you in the tank overnight and that's it.

He also recognized the value of alcohol consumption as an excuse within the family.

When you're sober the next day, people are forgiving. Everyone, my wife included, would be really nice and understanding. Rather than harp on the beating she'd gotten the night before, Julie would get after me about the drinking. I'd promise to stop and everyone would be happy.

Not all abusers who consume alcohol before beating their wives are as cognizant of its benefits as Jake was, but some are. Others accept it and use it subconsciously.

… a person who is potentially violent can drink with the sole purpose of providing himself with a "time out" in which he can lay the blame for his violent actions on the alcohol. "Thus, individuals who wish to carry out a violent act become intoxicated *in order to carry out the violent act*. Having become drunk and then violent the individual either may deny what occurred ('I don't remember, I was drunk') or plead for forgiveness ('I didn't know what I was doing'). In both cases he can shift the blame for violence from himself to the effects of alcohol" (Martin 1983: 57–58; also see Gelles 1972).

Mental Illness. In the quest for the root cause of spousal abuse, people often resort to simplistic adages such as "any man who beats his wife must be crazy." If that were true, the problem could be easily solved by treating all abusers for mental illness or, better yet, developing a vaccine or serum to give to all boys to prevent abuse. Unfortunately, the problem is not that simple. Some abusers may be mentally ill and therefore not responsible for their violent actions. However, such cases are rare, although many abusers claim temporary or situational insanity ("I just snapped. I don't know what happened"). A plea of temporary insanity might be acceptable if and only if the abusive behavior was an isolated incident rather than part of a repeated pattern.[2]

Family Factors

In a traditional marital relationship of two generations ago, the expectations of both partners were different than they are today. Men expected the woman to stay at home, raising children and keeping the home fires burning. Women wanted a husband to provide financial and personal security. A quarter century ago, Bernard (1972: 41) observed that:

Girls are reared to accept themselves as naturally dependent, entitled to lean on the greater strength of men; and they enter marriage fully confident that these expectations will be fulfilled. They are therefore shaken when they come to realize that their husbands are not really so strong, so protective, so superior.

In the 1990s, women were not seeking strength, protection, or superiority in a mate. They are looking for someone to share their life with. They want someone to work with them to build a life together. The characteristics most often mentioned are sensitivity, compassion, and understanding. They don't want someone to look after them. They want someone to talk to and to be with. Almost invariably, they define a marriage as a partnership of equals. Men, on the other hand, still tend to cling to the ideals expressed by their parents' and grandparents' generations. They want a wife who will look after them and the home.[3]

In any case, each individual brings to the marriage his or her own temperament, learned behaviors, knowledge, and attitudes. These individual factors in their unique combinations will affect the way the marriage is perceived by each spouse. The result is a dynamic relationship subject to the influences and expectations of each spouse as well as external forces. Over time, the relationship becomes patterned and, to some degree, predictable. For example, spouses who have been together for a long time are able to finish each other's sentences.

SPOUSAL RIGHTS

As we suggested above, each spouse enters the marriage with a certain set of expectations pertaining to the other spouse and to the marriage itself. Some of those expectations relate directly to the rights of the individual partners within the marriage. There are two aspects of this that need to be explored.

Divergence. One does not necessarily expect that both partners will view the marriage in the same way and grant their spouse the same rights and responsibilities that that spouse feels she or he should have.

Margaret ran into difficulties early in her married life when she wanted to go out and get a job. She wanted to be "gainfully employed." Her motivation was simple. She wanted to contribute to the family income and to achieve some status in the community other than as someone's wife. Her husband, however, envisioned his wife staying home, looking after the house, making meals at set times, and caring for the children. Clearly, there was a divergence of expectation. Having first tried to prevent his wife from working (and failing to do so), he constantly denigrated any job she got. He refused to acknowledge her financial contribution to the family (he simply stopped giving her any money from his income) and criticized her every time dinner was late, the laundry wasn't done, or the house wasn't clean. Margaret accommodated him by simply accepting his criticism as the price she had to pay for having a job outside the home. She also stopped talking to him about the job and began looking after the household and child rearing expenses without consulting him or asking for a contribution. He felt he had the right to prevent his wife from working; she felt that she had the right to work outside the home and he did not have the right to prevent it.

Most commonly in abusive situations, according to the research, one of the major difficulties was in the husband's attitude towards the rights of the wife. Typically, the husband viewed the wife as his property to do with as he pleased.[4] She was expected to obey him and be ready to do his bidding at any time. He felt that he was able to do whatever he pleased, but she was not. If the wife held different views, tension resulted and the cycle of abuse would begin. The abuser would demonstrate his views as to her rights and "beat them into her."

Dominance/Submission. Even if the partners share the same views of their rights within the marriage, abuse may still occur. For example, both husband and wife might see the wife's position in the marriage as subordinate to that of her husband and agree that he may beat her if he thinks she needs it. Some, in such a case, have argued that if both parties agree that wife beating is right, then there is no abuse. However, the legal system declares that assaultive behavior is illegal whether it is consensual or not.

In both situations, the rights of a spouse tend to be related directly to the culturally accepted gender roles discussed later in this chapter.

ABILITY TO COPE WITH STRESS

One could argue here that the ability to cope with stress is an individual characteristic, and it is. Still, the occurrence of spousal abuse can be affected by the family's ability to cope with stress as a unit. In a functional relationship, partners tend to act as stress releasers for each other. They provide opportunities for a person to vent—to complain about situations or individuals that are causing distress in his or her life. One partner listens to the other and offers empathy and understanding and occasionally advice, if called for. The partner could also provide opportunities for positive activities that require the expenditure of physical or mental energy. Thus the couple does things in general that take the stressed individual's mind off the problems. When problems occur that affect the couple as a unit, they have mechanisms in place to deal with them and help to reduce the stress those problems may cause.

Few abusive relationships are functional in the way described above. Abused spouses complain that "he never talks to me" or "we never do anything together." Abusive husbands commonly state that their wives do not understand them. There is little or no positive interaction between husband and wife. There is no couple. There are two people who share the same household but interact only minimally. One informant said her husband refused to speak to her or even to acknowledge her existence for several weeks. One night, "he started yelling and hitting me. I don't know why but when I went to bed that night, I recall, I was happy because he was talking to me again." Another said that her husband regularly gave her the silent treatment but she was glad when he did, because then she didn't have to listen to his putdowns and snide remarks.

AVAILABLE RESOURCES

The family unit has both financial and emotional resources on which it can draw, and there seems to be a direct link between access to these resources and spousal abuse, although the emotional resources are more important in the long run. Certainly short-term financial strains or chronic cash flow problems increase stress and can lead to or increase the incidents of spousal abuse, but these are situational problems. The denial of access to emotional resources is far more critical.

A couple needs emotional resources to make a marriage work. Ideally, there is a relative or set of relatives willing to listen, help, or just encourage the couple in times of difficulty. Without those resources, the couple may not have mechanisms in place in order to cope. At the same time, each partner needs access to his or her own set of emotional resources to draw on when needed.

Mary had access to her sister by telephone and used to call her almost every day. Her sister was always supportive and willing to listen. When Mary's husband assaulted her one night, she called her sister, who immediately offered her a place to stay and made the two-hour drive the next day to pick her up. She helped her find a job and was the "voice of reason" when Mary's husband tried to convince Mary he would change and she could come back to him. Mary did go back to her husband after a few weeks, but her sister continued to stand by her. When her husband hit her again, Mary once again called her sister and the whole thing was repeated. However, this time Mary refused to return to her husband. She filed for divorce and is doing well. "We [Mary and her sister] are closer than ever. I can't thank her enough for being there for me, even when I was an idiot and went back to that jerk."

Joan's story is quite different. She had no emotional resources to draw on. She had been abused repeatedly over a number of years before she decided to seek help. She talked to her mother, who responded with "That's between you and your husband. Leave me out of it." The rest of her family said more or less the same thing, and her friends offered advice that was clearly meant to put Joan off. "Have you tried counseling?" and "talk to the minister" were typical remarks. "No one I knew offered to get personally involved. They either told me to shut up or suggested I go see someone else. All I needed was someone to listen and say I was doing the right thing." She ended up staying with her husband for another four or five years before finally abandoning her home and entering an emergency shelter.

Sometimes an abusive husband will recognize the value of emotional resources, usually members of the wife's family, and will attempt to cut off those resources so that the abused wife is isolated and totally dependent on her husband for emotional support. For example, Sandra's husband Alan arranged a job transfer in order to move his wife two thousand miles away from her family. He then had the telephone company restrict the number of long-distance calls that could be made from their home phone (to restrict the frequency and duration of direct contact between his wife and her family) and had the phone company provide a detailed billing each month so he could personally keep track of the calls she made, including local calls. The absence of familial emotional resources in Sandra's case prolonged her marriage to Alan by at least three years in her estimation. It should be noted that even when the resources are in place, the woman does not easily talk about or refer to some forms of abuse (usually physical abuse) while she remains in the marriage.

PATTERNS OF RELATING

As noted earlier, spousal relationships become patterned and predictable. As two people get to know one another, they find ways to communicate and to interact with each other. If they work, these interactive techniques quickly become habitual.

If the personal interactive history of a married couple is examined, it can be seen that each of the individuals progresses through a series of roles, or social identities, relative to the other person.[5] Each of these roles carries with it a set of rights and obligations that are defined by the society at large but interpreted in specific cases by the individuals involved. To begin with, a typical couple would be "strangers" to one another and as such have no social rights or responsibilities relative to each other. If they meet and become "acquaintances," they are then compelled to acknowledge each other's existence and to greet one another when they meet. Nothing else is required of "acquaintances." If, however, they become "friends," there is an expected sharing of thoughts, feelings, plans, etc., which becomes more intense should the pair become "good friends" or "best friends." When a romantic or sexual aspect is added to the relationship, there is a subtle shift in roles and attendant rights and obligations. The two become more than friends; they are defined as "boyfriend" and "girlfriend." As the relationship becomes more involved, the roles once again change and each becomes each other's "steady." That indicates they have agreed to restrict all romantic and sexual activity to within their relationship. Two more role changes—from "steady" to "fiancé" and "fiancé" to "spouse" (husband or wife)—complete the creation of a legally binding and socially sanctioned economic and sexual union. They have formed the core of a family.

It is not necessary to detail the specific rights and obligations of each of the above roles. It is sufficient to recognize that each new label, each new social identity, has its own distinct set. Now, with the couple married and having assumed the husband and wife roles in the relationship, they must adjust to those roles. Further, they must adapt to the probably divergent interpretations that each has concerning those roles.

Margaret's husband interpreted the role of "wife" as carrying the obligation of being a homemaker who looked after his needs and those of the children and who, in return for fulfilling those obligations, was looked after financially and emotionally. His response to Margaret's refusal to accept the role as he saw it was predictable. He first objected to her desire to work outside the home. He then denigrated and minimized her outside employment while criticizing her "homemaking" as inferior. He abdicated his responsibility for her, both financially by no longer providing money for household expenses, and emotionally by being less than supportive and pleasant in his interactions with her. He abused her for failing to live up to her obligations as a wife.

He saw his role as Margaret's husband as being responsible for getting her to conform. He had to criticize her homemaking, minimize her employment, withhold financial support, and beat her for not conforming. Anything less and he would, in his mind, be failing to fulfill his own obligations. He had become locked into a pattern of negative feedback. It was a habit that proved impossible for him to break.

Margaret's story is typical of many in which the wife would try to eliminate the motivation for the abuse but the abusive behavior did not change. Once the interactive pattern was established, as in Margaret's husband's case, the actual motivation becomes unnecessary and recedes into the background. The interactive behavior becomes automatic. An abuser does not consciously decide to offer negative rather than positive feedback. He does not decide to hit his wife. He simply does it. Margaret's interaction with her husband was just as predictable. In addition to maintaining a job (except for the time she tried being a homemaker for him), she worked furiously at the housework, making sure that the house was spotless by the time he got home. She made the meals so they were precisely on time. She stopped asking for money for household expenses and made do on what she earned. In this way, she attempted, to minimize the contact they had with each other and thus cut down on the criticism and the abuse. Again, it was automatic and patterned. It was something she developed into a habit.

In general, there are a number of interactive techniques that many abused women adopt. They stop listening to their husbands' complaints or begin to complain back. In some cases, they may take the criticisms to heart and make an attempt to improve. The possibilities are endless, but once a pattern is set, it is set. A common pattern among abused women seems to be an acceptance of both verbal and physical abuse as right, coupled with an assumption that somehow she deserves the treatment she is receiving.

Whatever patterns are established, a routine of married life is created. Both partners know what the other will do or how the other will react in a given situation. Interestingly, or perhaps ironically, many couples in an abusive relationship define that relationship as comfortable. It may not be altogether pleasant, but it is secure and predictable with no surprises. Several women noted that while they were married to "him," they felt their lives were pleasant enough. Some did not realize that the relationship was abusive until much later—usually after the relationship had been terminated. It seems that it is only when one partner seeks to change the interactive pattern that problems arise, usually in the form of an escalation of the abuse.

THE FAMILY AGGREGATE

The family factors just discussed combine to initiate and per-petuate spousal abuse. Each factor contributes something that augments the impact of the individual factors discussed earlier. Disagreements regarding spousal rights and obligations provide a source of tension and friction. A lack of family resources, such as supportive family members, and limited stress releasing re-sources increase the tension that is relieved by an abusive act. Repeated abusive acts form a pattern that begins to perpetuate itself. Obviously, if a couple agrees on spousal rights, has positive family resources to draw upon, and has ways to relieve stress healthfully, its interactive patterns will tend to be non-abusive and healthy. Also, if the abused woman has supportive family or friends, the abuse may be mitigated.

Community Factors

A community is two things. It is a geographical region, an inter-active sphere, within which an individual conducts his or her daily existence. It can thus be a city, a town, a village, a neigh-borhood, or even a building. In addition, and more importantly, a community is a set of people with whom the individual inter-acts or who are available to the individual for interaction. Some researchers like to suggest that all of the people available to the individual live in the geographical interactive sphere and so see no need to divide community into two components. That proba-bly was true in the past, when most people spent their entire lives within a short distance of their birth place, and communi-cation and travel outside that distance were difficult, dangerous, and slow.

However, the trend towards urbanization (the clustering of large numbers of people into cities with rapid reliable trans-portation and instant communication) has, in our opinion, neces-sitated the division of community into its two distinct aspects. For example, a friend in New York lives in an apartment building that houses over twenty thousand people. It is a small city unto itself, and yet most of the people he interacts with on a regular basis do not live in that building or even in his neighborhood. In his case, the two aspects of community overlap only slightly.

The community as a whole, including both the social network and the geographic interaction sphere, contributes to the existence of spousal abuse in at least two ways.

AVAILABLE SUPPORT

It goes without saying that large population centers have more physical support facilities and support services, such as governmental agencies and private foundations, than do small towns and villages. However, the abused and the abuser alike tend to avail themselves of this type of "stranger" support only as a last resort. They prefer to utilize the people they know, that is, the people within their social network, if at all possible.

Abuse tends to occur less frequently when the couple's social network is extensive or intensive. In other words, if there are some "good friends" around on a frequent or regular basis, abuse is usually less common. Conversely, a weak social system lacking in "good friends" leaves the couple isolated and alone for much of the time and tends to generate a situation wherein abuse is far more likely to occur.

Over the years, we have spoken to many "army wives," whose community seems especially conducive to abuse.[6] Generally, a military man is posted to a base for no more than two or three years, after which he and his family are transferred to another location. The wives, and indeed the husbands too, do not have an opportunity to integrate into the community. They are provided with housing on the base, which physically separates and isolates them from the non-military "local" community, just as the knowledge that their time in the geographic community is limited emotionally isolates them from locals. The wives do not bother "putting down roots," and the locals do not welcome them into their network since they will be leaving soon.[7] The friends a wife may make are usually other military wives who come and go on the regular military rotation. The end result is a social network that consists of constantly changing "new faces" who are completely replaced every time the husband is transferred. Military wives complain that they have no one of significance to talk to other than their husbands. They feel isolated and vulnerable.

Potential abusers surface rather quickly in this kind of unstable social network.

People living in urban settings in the United States (over three-quarters of the population) can face a similar kind of isolation, the lack of social network resources. Modern couples are highly mobile and relocate frequently. As they relocate, they lose established social networks and must develop new ones. At least three abusive husbands admitted that they changed jobs and cities for the express purpose of destroying their wives' social networks and thereby making the abuse easier to maintain.

> Man, her friends were starting to get down on me. A couple of them were saying to me [about his wife's bruises] that she seemed to be running into a lot of doors lately. They were suspicious and they were telling me so. I thought, "Hey, I'm going to have to be more careful when I hit her. Otherwise, one of the bitch's friends is going to call the cops."
>
> That was a real drag and she wouldn't stop seeing her friends. One of them lived next door. What'd I do? I got myself a new job and off we went. No more nosy neighbors.

In a different case, a couple showed up for their regular weekly Bible study class. She had an obvious black eye, which naturally prompted questions. One woman asked her if she'd fallen down or run into a door. She replied, "No. He hit me," as she pointed out her husband. He was immediately confronted by the whole group. Subsequently, the beatings became quite infrequent as the abuser did not want to risk his standing in the community. His wife effectively used their social network to control his abusive behavior.

ATTITUDES ABOUT FAMILY

Members of a community tend to share a set of common interests, goals, and values that is to some extent what draws them together and binds them into a social network. As was already mentioned, a community can be a valuable resource for either increasing or decreasing the occurrences of spousal abuse, but just how valuable a resource it is depends on the values and attitudes the community holds in common concerning marriages and the respective roles of husband and wife. Obviously, if the

social network shares the view that (a) whatever happens between a husband and a wife is private and no one should interfere; or (b) the husband is the boss and the wife should always
"obey" him or suffer the consequences; or (c) a wife has no more
rights than a child, the social network as a resource for reducing
spousal abuse is ineffective. If there are certain subjects that
the community feels do not belong in polite conversation and the
topic of spousal abuse is one of them, the community is a poor
resource. Naturally, there is another side of the coin. A social
network that believes in gender equality and forthright and
open discussion of social issues is a strong advocate for nonviolence and, therefore, a positive resource.

THE COMMUNITY AGGREGATE

In order for the community to have an impact on spousal abuse,
the abused spouse needs two things. First, she needs a social network, a group of people with whom she can relate or interact on
a personal emotional level. Second, that network must have the
attitudes and values that advocate nonviolence against women
and gender equality in a marriage. If neither condition exists,
the community will be ineffective against spousal abuse.

Cultural Factors and Mechanisms

Just as an individual has a way of seeing the world and a set of
values and attitudes that stem from that worldview, societies
and cultures share a worldview and a set of values. For example, the modern North American culture tends to share what
could be described as a metropolitan or urban worldview. This
perspective tends to identify social relationships as being somewhat impersonal. This is clearly visible in the interactions of
people with the government, in that people seek some form of
assistance or information from strangers rather than friends
or relatives. Indeed, when dealing with the justice system, the
people charged with dispensing justice *must* be strangers. A
judge, prosecutor, or prospective juror who knows the accused
in a criminal case is expected to bow out of the process to avoid
a potential conflict of interest. Also, in an urban setting, most
of the people a person comes into contact with every day are

effective strangers, people passing by on the street, riding in the same elevator or eating nearby in a restaurant.

Emerging from the North American worldview is a set of values, emotionally charged beliefs about right and wrong, desirable and offensive. In a society, there can usually be found a set of what are called "core values"—systematically related central values which provide the basis for the social behavior and goals pursued by the members of a society. Of course, core values do not apply equally to all members of a society,[8] and what constitutes the core values of a society may be subject to controversy. Often, a person's definition of core values will reflect his or her own political and economic status in that society.

Core values tend to be resistant to radical change, while subsidiary values change quite rapidly. However, under certain conditions even core values can undergo rapid and drastic alteration.

The cultural mechanisms that existed for centuries, granting a man complete control over his wife and children but also limiting the form that control could take, have eroded significantly. It is possible these changes have acted to increase the incidence of spousal abuse; or, rather, perhaps it is a combination of the weakening of these cultural controls and the failure to replace them with other protective mechanisms that have created the problem. Thus there are new mechanisms that make spousal abuse possible, while there are also a number of cultural elements that have remained unchanged and have the same effect.

CULTURE CHANGE

First and foremost, it must be recognized that the twentieth century has been the time of greatest change in the history of humankind. Most of what is thought and done now would have been impossible a hundred years ago. The conveniences modern families enjoy did not exist and, in most cases, were unimagined a century ago. For example, the airplane was invented and first flown during our grandfathers' time. Their children knew about it, but few ever took a trip in an airplane until quite late in life, if at all. Their grandchildren, the "Baby Boomer" generation, began to travel by air as young adults, and their children (the great-grandchildren of the people who introduced air travel) accompanied them for the first time as infants. A hundred years ago, the majority of people were born, lived, and died within a hundred miles of their natal home. The average family of the 1990s frequently relocates a considerable distance from its members' natal homes.

The commonplace today was exotic a few generations ago, and the pace of change shows no evidence of slowing down. Less than a hundred and fifty years ago, communication was, by modern standards, extremely slow. A letter sent from the United States to Great Britain took up to six months to arrive at its destination in the 1870s. Today, communication is instantaneous. The telephone, television, radio, and computer connect the entire world in a matter of seconds. Analysts predict that videophones (already being used on the Internet) will be the norm in a few short years. The adage for the twentieth century is "There is nothing so constant as change."

This rapid change has lead to a confused state of affairs. What is considered the norm changes with each new generation. What was right for Dad and Mom is not right for the children. No one knows what the ideals should be, and any attempt by a generation to impose its moral values on another is met with fierce resistance. This confusion regarding roles, rights, and responsibilities contributes significantly to the occurrence of spousal abuse.

THE ENGLISH LANGUAGE

There can be little doubt that the English language itself, the dominant language of North America, is male-oriented. "Consider any number of paired sets of words—*master/mistress, bachelor/spinster*, governor */governess, courtier/courtesan*—and you can see in an instant that male words generally denote power and eminence, and that their female counterparts just as generally convey a sense of submissiveness or inconsequence" (Bryson 1994: 354) [italics in original]. Recently, there have been a number of attempts to eliminate the gender bias in the language. Some have been quietly successful, such as the 1987 American Roman Catholic Church's "Revised New Testament of the New American Bible." As Bryson (1994: 355) points out, this

Bible version is entirely non-sexist, and few, if any, readers noticed the changes. Unfortunately, a number of aspects of the bias-free speech movement have been overzealous and patronizing (itself a gender-based word derived from the Latin *patronus,* meaning "one who protects the interests of another, as a father does" [Ayto 1990: 386]). Some have introduced totally new biases. For example, one of the movement's proponents demanded that expressions such as "A man's home is his castle" be outlawed but defended statements such as "A woman's work is never done," arguing that the latter is true while the former is false (Maggio 1991). Also, "[w]hen the University of Hawaii proposed a speech code for students and staff,... a professor of law endorsed the ideal but added the totally arresting belief 'Hateful verbal attacks upon dominant group members by victims is permissible'" (Bryson 1994: 357). These extremist views have led to an anti-political correctness backlash that has belittled legitimate attempts to rid the language of words that promote or support male dominance.

THE FAMILY UNIT

A family, according to Murdock (1949), performs four vital functions better than any other social unit. They are

    a. sex: sexual needs are satisfied with a minimum of competition;

    b. reproduction: a woman is protected during her pregnancy and mother and child are protected during the extended lactation period;

    c. education or socialization: the co-resident man and woman provide all of the necessary knowledge to maintain the cultural values;

    d. subsistence: a gender-based division of labor makes the production of food and other goods essential to survival more efficient.

The dominant, but by no means sole, family structure in North American society is the "nuclear family," which consists of an adult male, an adult female, and their non-adult children, who share a common residence and cooperate in all things. Linton

(1959: 52) held the view that this structure was the "bedrock underlying all other family structures," and Murdock (1949), who conducted an extensive cross-cultural study, concluded that the nuclear family was a human universal found in every society. Howard (1996: 225) argues from a different direction.

> The nuclear family group is fairly rare ... [and] ... is most often found in segments of societies like the United States where housing is not in short supply and where social mobility, the hunt for jobs and improved social status, and the existence of specialized support systems (such as schools and nursing homes) reduce the central caring role of the family.

In previous generations, the nuclear family unit was sacrosanct. Divorce in North America was difficult and resulted in social stigma. A woman who divorced her husband for whatever reason was socially disgraced and her children came from a "broken home." The marriage vow in many churches contains the phrase "... till death do you part," and anyone who divorced was therefore in clear violation of his or her religious vows. Both husband and wife were expected to sacrifice their individual wants and needs for the sake of the family. Several of the informants recounted their attempts to speak to professionals regarding their abuse. In 1957, one woman went to her priest to seek some way out of an abusive marriage. The priest listened intently and offered the following advice:

> You were married under the eyes of God and the state of holy matrimony cannot be broken. You must go home and make the best of it. Do what your husband commands of you. In Heaven will you reap your just reward for your sacrifice.

This brief statement clarifies several things about that time period. First, the use of ritual language suggests that the priest was uncomfortable dealing with the situation. He did not know what to do and so resorted to citing Church policy. Second, male dominance is exhibited in that he tells the wife to do what her husband tells her (and implies that this will resolve the problem, as if it were somehow her fault for being beaten). Third, the value the Church placed on the sanctity of marriage was very high, since even physical danger was not a sufficient reason for termination of the union.[9]

If the woman sought advice in her home, she found herself under a tremendous amount of pressure from her own family to return to her husband and accept her lot in life.

Just one or two generations ago, there were few options for an abused woman, but there also seems to have been less spousal abuse. Of course, it can be assumed that many cases went unreported because reporting mechanisms were weaker. However, there is another reason that could be offered for fewer incidents. Before 1970, when divorce laws began changing, the concept of marriage was different from what it is today. A woman entering a marriage was expected to "obey" her husband, and there were a number of cultural mechanisms in place to insure that she did. A woman could not take on debts or engage in certain financial transactions without the written authorization of her father or husband. Generally, all assets were held solely in the husband's name.

A divorced woman was looked upon as a threat by all still-married women, and she would find herself ostracized by her circle of friends if she "abandoned" her husband. The legal system also reflected this negative image of the divorced woman. For example, in Alberta before 1970, a law stated that if a husband got a job in a new city and the wife refused to move to the new location with him, she could be divorced on the grounds of abandonment. Alternatively, if the wife got a new job in a different city and her husband refused to move with her, she could still be divorced on the grounds of abandonment. Either way, it was her fault that the marriage failed. Other jurisdictions shared the same kind of male-oriented laws.

Despite a strong anti-woman bias in the laws of a few decades ago, one thing that was quite clear was the definition of a marriage and what the husband's and wife's roles within it were. Both partners knew what was expected and what to expect.

Incidents of spousal abuse increase somewhat as the definition of marriage changes and more women feel sufficiently confident to report the abuse. As divorce laws become more lenient, as women gain more stature and power outside the home, as the husband's and wife's roles become more equal, the power of the husband erodes significantly. In previous generations, for example, a husband had merely to announce that the family was moving, and the family moved. Today, when a husband is offered a new job, society expects him to discuss it with his wife. The couple should then evaluate as a team the impact the new position and new location would have on the wife's career and the couple's plans in general. If the husband insists on taking the new posting and the wife chooses not to accompany him but selects divorce instead, he not only loses control of the family, he is also likely to lose the children and at least half of the assets he considered his.

The structure of the family is changing radically (see Haley 2000). For example, among couples under 30 years old, the divorce rate is approaching one out of every two marriages. The rate in1990 is thus four times higher than it was in 1960. Also, fewer people are getting married, and those who do are waiting longer before getting married (Otten 1991). However, more people are remarrying. About 20 percent of all marriages are remarriages with at least one previously divorced partner. "So marriage itself as an institution is not in decline. What is in decline is monogamous marriages that last until one of the partners dies" (Harris 1993: 461). People are practicing "serial monogamy"—one partner at a time—rather than the traditional monogamy—one partner for life—although the latter is still an expressed cultural ideal.

NEOLOCAL RESIDENCE
"[O]ur households are based upon a marital relationship relatively isolated from kin" (Johnson 1993: 164; also see Bohannan 1971). The structure of the modern family, a phenomenon that is a product of the Industrial Revolution, which required a large and mobile workforce, requires that a new family (usually just the new bride and groom) establish a new place of residence based on employment factors rather than family considerations. The new couple will go where the work is, and that usually means moving away from the parental home. The result is isolation from relatives who once served as a day-to-day support group for

the individual. A woman who had previously spoken to her parents on a daily basis finds that contact limited immediately after marriage because of the cost of long-distance communication.

PSYCHOLOGICAL DISTANCE FROM KIN

As well as being physically distanced from relatives, many newlyweds must also confront a psychological distance sanctioned by North American society.

> Psychological distance also is likely due to the strongly endorsed norms of independence, the mandate of privacy for the nuclear unit, and the belief that marriage should entail a sharp break between parents and adult children. Nevertheless, our kinship system has a matrilineal emphasis, so subsequent kinship relationships are usually linked and orchestrated by women (Johnson 1993: 165; also see Newman 1986; Troll 1971; Yanigasako 1977).

This psychological distance has two major effects in terms of spousal abuse. First, the abused wife does not have immediate access to her natal family. She is reluctant to involve her parents in the marital arena because she would be admitting failure. "Running home to mommy" has severe negative connotations. Second, the parental discipline structure that helped control the husband's violence is removed. The new husband is a man now and his parents are, from a societal perspective, out of the picture. Should either set of parents attempt to intervene, they will be seen as interfering.

INDIVIDUALISM AND INDEPENDENCE

> Most Americans believe that individuals are stable, autonomous entities who exist more or less independently of whatever situations or statuses they occupy. As Americans move from status to status or place to place—from student to husband or wife, to employee, to father or mother—they believe themselves to be the same persons nevertheless.... In this regard Americans are highly individualistic (Robbins 1997: 135–6).

This view that members of a society are individuals separate from the whole gives each person significant value. From this "egocentric" perspective, "each person is defined as a replica of all humanity, the locus of motivations and drives, capable of acting independently from others" (Robbins 1997: 136). Social relations are contracts between free-acting agents, and this, by extension, generates the idea that everyone is responsible for who they are and what they do.

By being an individual, one becomes isolated from his or her past, family, and other helpers because the only way to be deserving of achievements is to succeed through one's own efforts. Young people in American society strive to make it "on their own," to demonstrate that they are able to "stand on their own two feet." They must be independent, self-reliant, and self-supporting in order to conform to the society's view of an ideal person and so earn the respect of their peers (Bellah et al. 1984).

To see how a society views its ideal members, the society's mythology must be examined. Campbell (1949: 388) despaired that we live in an age without myths; or with myths existing only "in the individual." Perhaps there is simply a different type of myth. Using Hiatt's (1975: 5) idea that myths "constitute a conservative, socializing force whose function is to sanctify existing institutions and foster the values of sociality," one can turn to the movies, one aspect of popular culture that is a source of mythological scenarios.

First, movie heroes have certain characteristics in common. They are indeed independent, strong, confident, and capable. They are powerful and tend to be non-conformist and think for themselves. They achieve accomplishments largely on their own, with only minimal help (or acknowledgment of that help) from others. This is clearly the personification of the ideal individual. The audience members seek to emulate their hero.

Second, movies contain a consistent scenario that goes something like this: a hero, somehow isolated from his family, home, and society, goes on a journey in search of something (either external or internal, or both). Somewhere along the way he may acquire a mentor who conveys some kind of power or information to him. A powerful force (for example, monsters, aliens, gangs, ruthless governments) intervenes in the quest and makes it difficult for the hero to complete his task, but he perseveres. By facing death, conquering his fears, and overcoming overwhelming odds, he ultimately reaches his goal. The hero triumphs. This scenario is essentially a plot summary, with some minor variations, for many North American movies, including *Star Wars* (all three), *Raiders of the Lost Arc, The Wizard of Oz, The Net, U.S. Marshals,* and *The X-Files.*

By watching these films and identifying with the heroes, people learn about the American values of finding oneself and becoming successful. In order to succeed in American society, the message dictates, you must be just like the hero and do it your own way. You must be strong and independent.

This emphasis on individualism and independence has profound implications for spousal abuse. The "dangers of violence are greater when they are veiled in privacy and secrecy. When women live as isolated individuals, they are far more vulnerable" (Ward 1996: 253), yet society promotes just that. Individualism promotes isolation. As Julie told us,

> I wanted to go home. I wanted to leave my husband but I couldn't. If I did that, it would be like admitting I was wrong. Mom and Dad didn't want me to marry him but I did anyway. I made my choice. Now I have to live with it.

Stephanie's friend Mary knew she was being abused and needed help but didn't know how to offer that help.

> All through high school, Stephanie was fiercely proud of her accomplishments. She always said she was an honor student despite her parents. She never needed or wanted help from anyone. I felt that if I even hinted I thought Steph was in trouble, she'd jump all over me, accuse me of thinking her weak. I couldn't do it so I just started visiting her less and less. I couldn't stand to see her in pain. Eventually, we lost touch altogether.

Ironically, at the same time Stephanie was searching for just the kind of help her friend wanted to offer.

> How I wished someone would rescue me from him. I used to lay awake at night praying for that. I'd always pictured myself as tough, able to look after myself. It was a real blow to my self-esteem to realize I couldn't handle the situation on my own. Sometimes that was worse than the beatings themselves.

When asked why she didn't ask for help, she replied that her self-esteem couldn't have withstood the embarrassment. "I just couldn't admit I was a total failure."

The cultural ideal of an independent individual prevents people from seeking or offering help. At a more general level, it also seems to place the blame for abuse on the victim herself.

> Police, who are notoriously loath to intervene in domestic disputes,[10] too often take the attitude "well, if her husband beat her, she probably deserved it." They often assume that women who accuse their husbands of beating them are vindictive, and will only prosecute if they are convinced that the wife is a "worthy victim." And in courtroom after courtroom, it is the battered woman's responsibility to persuade the judge that she is really a victim—a judge who may ask her what she did to provoke her husband's attack (Margolis 1982: 25).

She is, as an individual, liable for the consequences of her own actions, and the legal system is reluctant to accept that she, as an individual, is not in control of her own life.[11]

CAPITALISM AND THE PATRIARCHY

Despite major strides toward gender equality, North American society is still in spirit a patriarchy, defined as a male-oriented culture wherein men hold most of the power. For example, a nuclear family, as mentioned before, is a social unit consisting of an adult male, an adult female, and their unmarried children. However, this social unit looks different in the context of its Judeo-Christian basis. The nuclear family, in the original European sense, was a social unit consisting of a man, his wife, and his children, since the man, being of the superior gender, was the master of the house and his wife, being of the inferior gender, was in his charge. This is the form that was brought to the Americas by European colonists. A marriage was a strictly monogamous lifetime commitment, with procreation as an essential component and labor divided strictly along gender lines (Weitzman 1974: 1,169). The structure of the family was strongly patriarchal. In early English common law, when two people got married, they became one. "By marriage, the husband and wife are one person in law.... The very being or legal existence of the woman is suspended during the marriage" (Blackstone 1765: 442). Under this law, the husband was entitled to beat his wife to keep her under control.

A patriarchal system is based on the idea that there are natural roles for men and women based on biology. "Many people believed that women's bodies defined both their social position and their function, which was to reproduce, as men's bodies dictated that they manage, control, and defend" (Robbins 1997: 175). With that justification, men could continue to subjugate women for their own good since they were incapable biologically of surviving on their own. Although this so-called biological justification is nonsense, it continues to have an impact on modern life.

During the modern-day marriage ceremony, for example, the father of the bride gives his daughter away to her new husband, thereby symbolically passing control of his daughter to her new master. The more conservative brides, still the majority, assume their husband's name and any children born to them automatically receive their father's family name.[12] Indeed, the family structure is the primary socialization unit that perpetuates the patriarchy, the male dominance, in North American society.

As times change and the ideal shifts towards equality of husband and wife, there is an increase in the incidence and the reporting of spousal abuse. The male, who has been raised to expect to dominate, is losing control. He must now negotiate rather than command; he must ask rather than demand. He is poorly equipped to do either. The modern male grew up in a conservative, traditional family that taught him to dominate, command, and control. Brian was one of those modern males.

Brian knew men looked after their spouses as their fathers-in-law had done before the wedding. He also knew that wives were supposed to cook and clean and obey their husbands. When, at age twenty, he married his childhood sweetheart, he found himself in a quandary. His wife would not obey. He would tell her to do something, and she would tell him to do it himself. His response was to decide that he obviously hadn't been manly enough. He reasoned that if he behaved in a more manly fashion, his wife would respond by acting more womanly. In other words, he had to be more assertive in order for her to be more submissive. He hit her.

To his surprise, she hit him back. This was not at all going the way he expected. He hit her again. Harder.

When one of the authors first spoke to Brian, he was in the second year of a seven-year jail term for manslaughter. His wife had been killed by that second blow. He was still very confused about what had happened, still wondering why she hadn't done what he'd told her to do.

In addition to being a patriarchy, North American society is capitalist. Capitalism is

> a political economy in which money can buy anything. This being so, everyone tries to acquire as much money as possible, and the object of production itself is not merely to provide valuable goods and services but to increase one's possession of money; that is, to make a profit and accumulate capital. The rate of capitalist production depends on the rate at which profits can be made, and this in turn depends on the rate at which people purchase, use, wear out, and destroy goods and services (Harris 1993: 249).

Inevitably, wealth-based inequalities develop in a capitalist system. Some people become capitalists, the owners of the means of production. They are wealthy and politically powerful. The vast majority of the population, though, become the workers and consumers. The capitalists get rich by paying their workers as little as possible and by encouraging those same workers to consume more of their goods.

In order to maintain the economic inequality that favors them, the capitalists (company owners) support, probably inadvertently, the patriarchal system. For example, a boss knows that if a worker is married and has a family to support, he is going to be more reliable than an unmarried, and thus unencumbered, worker. The married worker is also more pliable in that he is more willing to absorb pay cuts or increased hours of work in order to keep the steady job and meet the financial needs of his family. An unmarried worker, on the other hand, is more likely to quit and seek employment elsewhere when faced with the same negative changes.

One organization in Ontario, as recently as 1975, developed the perfect way to acquire the ideal family. It offered home mortgages to its married employees only, at interest rates well below those given by banks. This financially obligated the worker to the company. One condition contained in the mortgage loan agreement was that the couple could not earn more than a certain amount of money in a year. As the income cap was only slightly higher than the yearly salary of the worker, this effectively prevented the wife from seeking employment outside the home.

GENDER RELATIONS

Many aspects of the relations between men and women have already been discussed, both generally and specifically, but there is a little more that must be said. In recent decades, women have attained many new opportunities, particularly in the realms of education and career, opportunities that were not available to their own mothers and grandmothers. However, these have been obtained at the expense of long-held cultural values that placed men in the superior or dominant position. Many men have seen this erosion of traditional values as threatening and dangerous, and have resisted it as much as possible.

Women in the Workforce. In traditional preindustrial societies, there was generally a clear division of labor along gender lines that was, broadly speaking, based on biological differences between men and women. Men tended to do the dangerous jobs and the tasks requiring strength or endurance, while women tended to do those tasks that were compatible with child rearing, which was seen as the primary function of a woman. This meant that when the economic systems of Europe and North America shifted from a subsistence base (where the primary producer was also the primary consumer) to an industrial base (focusing on money and wage labor), women were already culturally conditioned to remain in the home while the man went off to work.

A major change occurred during World War II when, in America, there was an acute shortage of male workers, many of whom were in the military. In order to keep the industrial economy working, thousands of women moved into traditional male jobs. Naturally, when the war was over and the men began to return, they expected the women to hand the jobs back to them and return to being full-time homemakers. This met with resistance.

Shortly thereafter, the focus of the economy shifted to the information and service sectors, which together with the automation of many industrial plants, combined to eliminate the presumed biological differences between the genders. Since a woman could sit at a computer or run a factory machine as well as a man, men's superior strength, a long-time justification for preventing women from working, was negated. The result was the feminization of the workforce and the destruction of the male breadwinner family (Harris 1981). Women's rights rose as the strategic value of masculine muscle power fell. "In 1960, only 32 percent of married women worked outside the home; in 1989, 58 percent were wage earners" (Robbins 1997: 162).

Men, still retaining much of their economic and political power, fought against what they saw as an erosion of traditional values. They could not prevent women from working so they used another tactic—the paycheck. They paid women less than men received for the same work.[13] The result is what has been described as the "feminization of poverty": "Two out of every three poor adults were women [in 1990], including more than a quarter of all women over 65 who were not living in families" (Robbins 1997: 162). Every woman considering leaving her abusive husband has to face economic reality: should she do so, she will face an immediate and dramatic change in economic status.

This is still the case, although most governments have recognized the problem and introduced "equal pay for equal work" legislation and "affirmative action" programs designed to make the numbers of men and women in certain jobs reflect the population proportions. In other words, since roughly half the working population is female, 50 percent of the jobs in all categories should be filled by women.

In 1994, in the Royal Canadian Mounted Police, Canada's national police force, fewer than 10 percent of its members were female. In order to correct this, it stopped hiring male recruits and, for two years, hired only females. The Canadian Correctional Service, responsible for all Canadian federal prison facilities, gave preferential treatment to women applicants. For example, during training, women had to meet easier physical endurance and strength requirements, despite the fact that both men and women would be required to do the same tasks once on the job.[14]

In the 1990s, the number of women in almost all job areas rose significantly. However, men did not accept this change readily. For example, "officers [in the L.A.P.D.] distinguish "traditional" police—those hired before affirmative action programs were implemented—from "new police" those who were hired under affirmative action guidelines" (Barker 1993: 350).

> Male officers suffer an assault on their self-esteem through their perception that standards of physical fitness and job training have been eroded as a result of affirmative action. They also see "easy promotions" for women as devaluing the work of people [that is, men] who, in their view, had to wait much longer and work harder for the same recognition (Barker 1993: 350–1).

This kind of resentment is common in many sectors of the economy. Men fear that women are taking their jobs away or they do not trust in the ability of the women to do the jobs. In trying to right a wrong and accelerate the balance of men and women in the workplace, governments have inadvertently created a source of tension between the two genders.

People born after 1960 are generally more accepting of the equality of women and men on the job. Many men under thirty do seem to be more ready to work with women and have a wife who will be working outside the home. All of the men we talked to who held this view had grown up in a family with a working mother. Some who were raised in a "traditional male breadwinner/female homemaker" family have the perspective that women belong at home and resist women in the workforce—except in the traditional female roles of teacher, nurse, or secretary. Women under thirty follow the same pattern. Daughters of working mothers are pursuing career goals, while daughters of stay-at-home mothers are concentrating on starting or raising a family. Of course there are exceptions to the rule and there are transgenerational conflicts.

One woman told the story of how her conservative and traditional parents, a mill worker and a housewife, wanted to find a good husband for their daughter. They decided that they should send her to university because the best and the brightest bachelors would be there. She agreed to go, but not because she wanted a husband. She wanted an education. She got what she wanted, a degree, but her parents were disappointed. She then suggested that her parents should send her to a prestigious university to do graduate work. She assured her parents that she would find an even better husband there—perhaps a doctor or a lawyer. They agreed, glad she was taking the search for a husband seriously. She obtained an M.Sc. and a Ph.D., but she remained single. With her education, she now has an excellent job and extremely bright career prospects. She is happy, although she feels a little guilty about using her parents the way she did. Her parents, on the other hand, have never acknowledged or recognized her academic or career achievements. They are distressed over their lack of a son-in-law and, more importantly, their lack of grandchildren.

The Education of Women. It has always been to a man's advantage to be better educated than his spouse. Even when "universal" education was put in place early in the twentieth century, parents were reluctant to send their daughters any longer than absolutely necessary. Only those who were destined for teaching, or secretarial or nursing jobs, went beyond high school, and usually they took that additional schooling in segregated and specialized facilities such as a "secretarial school" or "teachers' college."

As the economy changed and more education became a priority, women stayed in school longer but found their options still restricted. Everyone knew that women were intellectually inferior to men and could not learn or understand mathematics or science.[15] Women were effectively barred from careers in physics, chemistry, pharmacy, dentistry, and medicine, except as nurses.

When the notion of gender equality began to gain real strength in the 1960s and 1970s, all barriers started to fall. Women were admitted to faculties that had been denied them. Current university students in all disciplines generally accept the coed nature of post-secondary education, but in previous generations, the presence of a woman in an astrophysics or medical anatomy course was cause for concern. The male students often went to great lengths to force the "interloper" out. Although that battle has been lost and women routinely take these career paths, there are still a few areas of education that actively resist the participation of women. The most notable example of late is the U.S. Marine Corps training facility. The media have reported extensively on the trials and tribulations of women trying to become Marines who are being rejected, not only by the instructors but by the students as well.

It should be noted here that there is some anecdotal evidence for a link between the education of women and spousal abuse. However, it is not so much tied to a concern for overall education of women as to the relative education of a husband and wife. Our findings reinforce those of Martin (1983: 56) who writes, "I found in discussion with wife/victims, husbands suffer less from a lack in their own education than they do when their wives are better educated than they are."

In many cases of spousal abuse that we investigated, the abused wife was either better-educated than her abusive husband or had a better job than he had.

The Feminist Movement. By the mid-1970s, American women had banded together to fight for equality with men. There were two reasons for this. The first, and most obvious, was that their society was male-dominated and women, for reasons already discussed, were second- or third-class citizens. Changes needed to be made if women wanted to improve their situation. In order to get their fair share, they needed to create a united front. The second reason was that for the first time in recorded history, women could stand up against the men. Their increased levels of education and experience in the workforce demonstrated to themselves and to men that they could survive in the world as independent individuals rather than mere appendages to their husbands. This gave them the power to stand up.

Because of this feminist (or women's rights) movement and other social trends, women and men are more equal to one another than they have ever been in North American history.

However, there is a downside to this otherwise positive trend. It has created additional conflicts between women and men in the home. Many men want to maintain the traditional male-oriented structure of the society and family. Women want the new liberal structure. The result is an increase in the amount of violence, of spousal abuse, in the home. In addition, stresses are created within an abusive situation in that an abused woman is bombarded by commercials, public service announcements and other media devices stating that the only way to stop abuse is to end the relationship. If she does not, for a variety of reasons, she is not a "modern woman," and her self-esteem (one of the only primary defensive weapons she has) suffers badly. Yet if she does accept the feminist dogma and end the relationship, she quickly discovers that the infrastructure, the support system that is supposed to enable her to make it on her own, simply does not exist.

ATTITUDES TOWARD SEX

Helen's husband abused her and then took her to bed. As the abuse became more frequent, she noticed that he stopped having sex with her at any other time. For him, abuse became foreplay. In addition, according to Helen, the sexual intercourse itself became more violent. "Some nights, I felt I was being raped."

The way North American society perceives sex has a great deal to do with the often-quoted phrase "battle of the sexes." In North American society, manhood is defined by sexual prowess. As Sanday (1990 as quoted in Robbins 1997: 145) notes, "the deployment of the penis is a concrete symbol of masculine social power and dominance." Single males brag to one another about their "conquests" or how they "scored." It establishes their masculinity and improves their status within their own social circle. Some men, then, perceive the conquest as vital to self-esteem, and therefore rejection may have negative effects: they may become angry and violent.[16]

It has been argued that aggression is a normal part of sexuality. For example, Storr (1970: 39) feels that "only when intense aggressiveness exists between two individuals ... [can] love arise. Even sex itself does not seem to overcome aggression." He argues that some men do not see sexual intercourse as a physical expression of affection but as a battle wherein they can act out their aggressor/vanquisher fantasies. Several other researchers (for examples, see Rheingold 1964 and Lederer 1968) have supported an innate or biological link between aggression and sex, but their arguments tend to be simple justifications for blaming women for the consequences (violence) of rejecting a man's sexual advances.

At fault for the link between sex and male aggression, and for the "sex as conquest" ideology, in our opinion, are the traditional values held by previous generations, which are still taught to some extent today. Historically, men were supposed to be masterful in the bedroom, and husbands were expected to take the initiative. Conversely, women were not supposed to enjoy sex. They existed for their husband's pleasure, not their own. That women should enjoy sexual intercourse is a relatively recent phenomenon.

For men who learn that sex is a battle, that women are to be conquered and made to surrender—many are still learning that—the distance between aggressive sexual intercourse and physical assault is not great. If sex is a dominance issue for men, and for some it is, then sex and abuse can become confused. In either case, that learned behavior stems from cultural perceptions of sex.

ATTITUDES TOWARD VIOLENCE AND THE USE OF FORCE

Modern industrial states have a "monopoly on the legitimate force in the society, for it alone has the right to coerce subjects into agreement with regulations, customs, political edicts, and procedures" (Ember and Ember 1996: 269). When force is used by someone other than an agent of the state, that use of force is called a "crime." In North America this is the ideal, but it is far from the actual. Non-legitimate force in the form of interpersonal violence is unfortunately commonplace.

Many anthropological studies on violence have suggested that in societies where war is frequent, and the United States and Canada certainly fit in that category,[17] boys are encouraged to be aggressive in order to grow up to be warriors. However, as the studies show, this socialization affects other aspects of society.

Criminal violence, including spousal abuse, is an unintended consequence (Ember and Ember 1994). In other words, if children learn to be aggressive, the likelihood of spousal abuse and other forms of interpersonal violence is greater than in societies that lack training in aggression.

Children in North America learn that aggression and violence are acceptable modes of behavior. This is particularly true for boys as much of the socialization is directed at them specifically, but as gender equality permeates the social system, there is an increasing frequency of violent behavior among girls and young women. They are starting to receive as much aggressiveness training as the boys do.

As noted earlier, children learn what is acceptable and what is not, what is appropriate and what is not, through the process of socialization. They unconsciously absorb and assimilate what they see others doing. Young children do not process information the same way adults do, as they lack the experience to evaluate what they see. "For example, children between the ages of 6 and 10 may believe that most of what they see on TV is true to life" (Health Canada 1994a). They tend to take all they see at face value, and much of what they see advocates violence as an acceptable behavior choice.

The Media. Let us start with the media, which include radio, books and other printed material as well as television, which is the principal medium as far as children are concerned. Television is certainly the most influential of all the media forms. "The average time children spend watching television rises from about 2 1/2 hours per day at the age of five to about four hours a day at age twelve" (Health Canada 1994a). That represents between 15 and 25 percent of their waking day, and although some made-for-children television shows such as *Sesame Street* are carefully non-violent, others take up the slack. Some of the shows most popular with young children are cartoons that often are little more than violent incidents separated by very brief bits of dialogue.

In general, television is violent, and that includes the news. During the 1992 Rodney King case, for example, the videotape of police officers beating Mr. King was shown repeatedly on virtually every channel at all times of the day. It became impossible to avoid seeing it. Of course, television is also an invaluable source of educational learning for children, but evidence suggests that children who prefer violent television shows will probably be more aggressive later in life, and also be more accepting of violent behavior in others. This speaks to the issue of temperament that was discussed earlier.

Toys. Not all of the blame for violence can be laid on television watching. As noted in the Health Canada (1994a) study, "pre-schoolers who were given guns and other violent toys to play with were found to commit more aggressive acts than preschoolers who had merely watched a television program with violent content." By playing actively with violent toys instead of passively watching violent television programs, young children are socialized to violence very quickly, and there is no shortage of violent toys, which range from military vehicles such as tanks and airplanes to water pistols, slingshots, and "action figures."

It is interesting that even when parents make a conscious effort to avoid providing their children with violent toys, there always seem to be well-intentioned relatives or friends who supply them, or neighboring children from whom the youngsters borrow them. One ingenious boy of six, lacking the armament for participation in a block war game, created his own. He took harmless balloons, filled them with water, and bombed the opposition. He was, as it turned out, the hero of the day among his peers.

Recent generations have been introduced to an entirely new kind of violent toy, the video game. As computers improve, video games take on an eerie realism so keen that it is as if the player is really in the environment depicted on the screen. Most of them are war games with the player representing a hero with some type of martial arts skill or amazing weaponry. Usually the sole goal of the game is to go from one point to another (either to rescue someone or to gain a prize), killing, maiming, or destroying large numbers of people or human-like creatures in the process. To fail in some of these games is to "die." Some of the newer games even show blood spattering on the wall and body parts sailing through the air when the enemy is destroyed. For some children, the video game has almost replaced television, and it is possible that it may have an even greater impact on adult violent behavior than the violence on television (Anderson 1997; Anderson and Dill 2000; Dill and Dill 1998).

Warlike Sports. Societies that are involved in wars tend to have sports and games that are male-oriented and warlike in structure. Two very popular sports of this type are football and hockey. The object of both games is to move the playing piece (the football or puck) into the other team's goal, as in many other sports such as basketball and soccer. However, in contrast to these other games, hockey and football players must dress in heavy padding because interpersonal violence is a large part of the game. Players are checked, blocked, tackled, and otherwise beaten and abused.

These two sports enjoy considerable popularity as both spectator and participatory activities. In Canada, the majority of boys play hockey. In autumn and winter, pick-up games seem to be everywhere. There are organized leagues for all ages ranging from old-timer (50+) to young lads barely old enough to skate. In Red Deer, Alberta, there is a league just for boys between five and seven years of age. According to one of the hockey organizers for that city, there are between two and three thousand boys under the age of fifteen involved in organized hockey. The total number of girls playing hockey, on the other hand, is under two hundred, less than one-tenth of the number of boys.

There is no doubt that coaches (and fathers) encourage their boys to be aggressive in hockey. The children learn to "check" their opponents. They are ordered to push themselves into the play and "blast" the puck at the net and the goalie. Anyone who attends a game or a practice will hear coaches and parents praising aggressive acts and berating the child for being timid or avoiding aggressive behavior. Incidentally, the city tried to involve boys in a "no-contact" league, but it did not last due to lack of interest.

Schools. Children spend a great deal of time away from their parents. At the age of four or five, they go to preschool or kindergarten for three to three and a half hours a day, five days a week. As they enter the regular education system, many children find themselves in school seven or more hours a day. (This is almost the same amount of time over a year that he or she will watch television.) Whatever happens in school will obviously have some impact on the socialization of the child. In most schools, teachers tend to be positive influences and the planned curriculum does not intentionally promote or advocate the use of violence, but children tend to be exposed to much more than the teachers and the lessons. They are in contact with their peers and with older children as well, who become a primary source for socialization that differs from formal learning in that it is only rarely intentional. It is a byproduct of everyday inter-action and social contact.

The increasing violence in American and Canadian schools is having an effect. For example, metal detectors and police offi-cers permanently assigned to schools send the message that the world is a violent place and violent behavior is expected in the school. Fights between individuals or groups on school grounds tell young children that they are an acceptable way to resolve conflict. Although no quantitative studies have been done on the effect schools have on violence and aggression, there is little doubt that violence occurs at school and young children witness or participate in it.

Role Models. Despite all that has been said so far, the par-ents, and all others with whom the child shares a residence, are still the primary role models for young children and are respon-sible for most of their socialization. If a child witnesses a parent exhibiting violent or abusive behavior, violence will become part of that child's adult persona, so powerful is the parental influ-ence. North American children, who see that violence is accept-able on television, in sports, at school, and at play may infer that it is acceptable in other aspects of social interaction as well, espe-cially if they see their role models acting abusively in the home.

THE CULTURAL AGGREGATE

What binds a society together is its culture—a set of learned and shared beliefs, values and behaviors. Not all members of a society learn or share exactly the same beliefs and values due to individ-ual variation, but each society accommodates some variation by creating a set of norms—standards and rules concerning what is acceptable behavior—and then allowing some flexibility around those norms. For example, there are standards of appropriate clothing for certain social situations. The clothes that are acceptable for an evening of dining and dancing are different from those acceptable on a beach or in a classroom. If someone wore casual clothes to a wedding or other formal affair, there would be a certain amount of negative reaction in the form of derision or social isolation, but if one chose to go to that same affair naked, the reaction would be swift and decisive: he or she would be arrested for "indecent exposure."[18]

The importance of the norm can be judged by how the members of the society respond when it is violated. To voice the idea that "God is dead" today would invoke little or no reaction. To have made that same statement five hundred years ago would have branded the speaker a heretic and probably resulted in his or her death. Durkheim (1938) argued that culture was something that existed outside the individuals and exerted a strong coercive effect. Because of the process of socialization, people conform to the kinds of thought and conduct that their culture requires but only really notice the constraints when the norms are violated.

These norms, these learned and shared beliefs, values, and behaviors, are not just a random assortment of customs cobbled together over the centuries. Generally, they are, more or less, consistent with one another. Culture tends to be integrated, and cultural characteristics tend to appear together as "bundles" from which it is impossible to extract a single trait without significantly affecting all other traits in that bundle. Our society is attempting to change the belief that "men are superior to women" to "men and women are equal." This change, although apparently simple, has so far had far-reaching consequences in the areas of language, the family, sex, education, economics, and more.

Attempting to change societal norms regarding the appropriateness or inappropriateness of spousal abuse will have similar broad consequences. Indeed, it will have impact in areas where none would normally be expected.[19] Many aspects of society support or encourage spousal abuse directly, while others support the characteristics that encourage spousal abuse. All will have to be amended.

Of course, cultural norms are always changing, but "core" values are resistant to change and will tend to remain in place long after they have become maladaptive or even directly harmful. For example, North Americans use automobiles as a primary mode of transportation even though there are many more efficient, cleaner, and less expensive alternatives readily available. There are better ways to get around, but since the use of the car is equated with independence and freedom, its use will continue.

The Official Position

In the United States, "[d]uring 1992 approximately 28 percent of female homicide victims (1,414 women) were known to have been killed by their husbands, former husbands or boyfriends. In contrast, just over 3 percent of male homicide victims (637) were known to have been killed by their wives, former wives or girlfriends" (Bureau of Justice Statistics 1995:1; also see Bachman and Saltzman 1995). To put it another way, more than twice as many women than men were killed by their spouses in that year. To be fair, there is no way of knowing if a history of spousal abuse preceded the murders but one can suspect there was since a violent crime committed against a spouse is rarely an isolated event.

It is difficult to describe the "official position" on spousal abuse because there are a huge number of jurisdictions (national, state or provincial, county, municipal), each with its own official position. There is no unifying mandate or principal to allow any kind of consistency.

Many jurisdictions take an apparently straightforward response to wife abuse but also tend to avoid confronting the problem to some extent. They declare that "Family violence is a crime" (for example, see Alberta Solicitor General n.d.: 6). However, the definition of family violence conforms to the criminal code description of assault (physical and sexual abuse) but excludes emotional, psychological, and financial abuse and isolation, which are unacceptable but not punishable by the Criminal Code.[20]

Once a violent incident is reported, the authorities are compelled to react, although they often do so reluctantly. The police officers view "domestic disturbance" calls as the worst possible type of call. They are never sure what to expect and, according to one Montana officer, more police are injured on domestic disturbance calls than on all other calls combined. However, they do react and will, in most cases, arrest and charge the abuser. Often, because of chronic overcrowding of jails, the abuser is not incarcerated but is released immediately after processing.

In some jurisdictions, only the prosecutor can withdraw a charge once it has been laid. In the case of spousal abuse, he or she is, in accordance with departmental policy, usually unwilling to do so even if the abused woman desires or requests it. In many other jurisdictions, a spouse can withdraw a complaint and have the charge dropped: a woman cannot be compelled to testify against her husband, and if she is unwilling to testify, the court will dismiss the case for lack of evidence. The prosecutors usually withdraw the charge rather than waste the Court's time, or the police may be reluctant to even lay a charge.[21] This creates a situation that may be quite dangerous, since "... [t]he police do not have the authority to remove an abuser from a home if he is entitled to be there, so it is often the women and children who leave" (Alberta Solicitor General n.d.: 9)

Even after the charge has been laid against an abuser, the abuse may continue since the courts can deal only with the incident that led to the charge.[22] It is left to the abused spouse to resolve the ongoing situation. In Alberta, there are two legal options. One is a peace bond, a court order requiring an abuser to keep the peace that can include a condition forbidding the abuser from having any contact with his spouse. In order to obtain a peace bond, the woman must indicate to the police that she is worried about her safety and then must present her concerns in court. The other option is a restraining order, which requires an abusive partner to "stop molesting, annoying or harassing" his wife (Alberta Solicitor General n.d.: 16). This option requires a lawyer's involvement and stipulates that the abused spouse must either file for divorce if married or start a civil assault action if in a common-law relationship (that is, the common-law spouse must initiate a civil suit claiming damages for personal injuries against her common-law spouse). Once a restraining order is obtained, it allows the abused spouse to call the police as soon as her estranged husband appears, rather than wait until he becomes abusive.

Both of these options presume that the couple is residing at different locations. They are obviously final steps. They offer no protection for a spouse who remains with her abuser. For her, they are not available options.

It seems that in all jurisdictions, there are legal avenues for arresting the abuser and keeping him away from his spouse (assuming that he is otherwise a law-abiding citizen). One Montana police officer described the situation quite well:

> We have a family that is a constant headache for us. Two or three times a month we get a call from their neighbor that the Hammonds [a pseudonym] are at it again. We go out and the place is generally all busted up. Mrs. Hammond is all beat up too. Usually by the time we get there, Mr. Hammond is passed out cold. We offer to take her anywhere she wants to go. She doesn't want to go anywhere and, no, she won't charge her husband with assault. There is nothing we can do so we leave.
>
> My biggest fear is that one of these days, we're going to get the call and we're going to take our time because it's going to be just another waste of time but when we get there, she'll be dead. Then the media'll be all over us. They'll say we knew he was beating her and they'll want to know why we didn't put him in jail before and why we didn't get her out of there before. Why didn't we, the police, save her. They won't listen when we say that we can't make him leave. We can't get her away unless she wants to go. We can't file charges against him if she won't testify. We can't do a damn thing but the media will crucify us.

In other words, the police can only obey the law and work within it. Assault is a criminal offense, but a charge will only go to trial if there is sufficient evidence. Often the police can only stand by and wait until the abused spouse is determined to do something about her situation. In fact, it appears that most jurisdictions have left the onus on the abused spouse, the assumption being that the only solution is to dissolve the relationship. The

Alberta Social Services Department, in a pamphlet called "Wife Abuse: What is it? What to do about it," suggests that there are some things a woman can do about the abuse while still in the relationship but prefaces the list with the observation that "It is often difficult for abusive men to change their behavior without outside help. Instead, the abuse almost always gets worse" (Alberta Social Services n.d.: 3). In fact, most of the pamphlet deals with how to leave the relationship and offers information about legal and financial aid. The government of Alberta, like all other jurisdictions, tacitly acknowledges that in order to stop spousal abuse, the relationship must be sacrificed, and should an abused spouse not wish to make that sacrifice, she is on her own until her abuser commits some act that is criminal and does not require her as a witness.

It is safe to assume that the various jurisdictions are at a loss as to how to deal with spousal abuse. They do the best they can within parameters set out in the various criminal codes, but it is insufficient. They are losing the war on the home front and do not know how to alter that fact.

The Personal Perspective

Many people in the helping professions working with abused women were reluctant to discuss wife abuse. However, those most directly affected, the abused women themselves, were open and frank in their discussions. None of them showed the slightest hesitation, and indeed many of them sought the authors out with the express purpose of talking about it. In trying to make sense of this dichotomy, we detected some interesting and surprising perspectives shared by all abused spouses, as well as other positions shared by all those charged with helping stop the abuse.

The Helpers

There are two broad categories of helping professionals.[23] There are those who are directly involved on a day-to-day basis with the victims of abuse who, for them, have names and faces. This category includes such front line workers as Victims' Services personnel, shelter workers, and police officers. The other category includes people who are involved only peripherally, or who see spousal abuse as an abstract problem rather than a personal one. This group includes politicians, judges, and others. As conversations with the various professionals were evaluated, an acute difference in tone and content discernable between the two categories.

The professionals who approach the problem from an abstract point of view[24] tended to downplay the importance of the problem. One local politician, when asked to rank the problems facing his administration, placed spousal abuse, which he called domestic violence, fifteenth on the list behind garbage removal and animal control. He did not think it was a big deal.

> What happens in the privacy of your own home is up to you. The government cannot legislate your every action. Besides, we have laws already in place. If your husband beats you up, call the police. They'll arrest him. You'll be safe. That's the end of it.

This Councilman, incidentally, was responsible for overseeing the operation of city-run shelters for abused women. Despite having had that responsibility for about four years, he had yet to set foot in one of those shelters. Another politician, a state legislator from a western state, denied there was a problem.

> I think the issue has been blown out of proportion. A few women may be getting knocked around by their husbands, but they have to work out their differences. I get calls from women saying I have to do something. As soon as I realize what the call is about, I have my secretary refer them to Community Services.

In general, there exists a state of denial with regard to spousal abuse among those who operate at arm's length from the problem. When several politicians, police chiefs, lawyers, and judges were presented with a copy of the Statistics Canada (1993) study indicating that about 30 percent of all married women suffer from some form of abuse, the immediate responses were: "Not another damn survey!" and "Nothing we can do until someone breaks the law" and "My office is already swamped. Don't ask me to take on anything else" and "You should be talking to Social Services, not me."[25] They clearly do not want to get involved.

By contrast, the front-line workers perceive the problem as enormous and chronic. "It never ends," stated one shelter worker. "No sooner do we get one woman out of here and settled in her own apartment, we have another knocking on the door wanting the bed we just emptied." A number of workers stated that at times, the shelters have been overcrowded and women have not been able to get in at all.

Although the "public" face of the front-line worker is positive and friendly, in private it is anything but that. The workers tend to speak about their work using negatively charged words, phrases such as "we are overwhelmed" or "we are struggling to keep our heads above water." One Victims' Services employee who spoke encouragingly and optimistically to a woman who had just been beaten admitted to one of the authors moments later that "nothing I do makes a bit of difference." She went on to say:

> I took this job because I wanted to help, but after four years, I am burnt out. Before, I knew I could make a difference. Now I know better. It is hopeless. We talk. We provide information on what to do and where to go. Sometimes they take it. Sometimes they don't. But it doesn't matter because as soon as I'm done with one woman, I've got two other calls stacked up and waiting for me. All I want to do is get through the day and go home.

A former shelter worker explained why she quit:

> I just gave up when I realized that often we were doing more harm than good. We had to advise the clients to leave their husbands, to file for divorce. That was shelter policy. But what we weren't telling them was that things were going to get a lot worse once they did. That was shelter policy too. I couldn't take it any more. Knowing that they'd be back in an hour, in a day, in a week, with a hell of a lot more bruises than they left here with.

Many front-line workers are frustrated, angry, and bitter because they really care about their clients but are nowhere near a solution to the problem. They feel helpless and hopeless.

Many, like the Victims' Services worker, simply go through the motions. Others become hardened and resort to bureaucratic procedures to get them through.

> It's always the same. A woman comes in here complaining that her husband beats her. I give them all the same lecture and then hand them a bunch of forms to fill out. I can handle 20 or 30 in a day like that. One day, I processed 42 women. That's my personal record.

Still others are profoundly affected emotionally and suffer from depression, nervous disorders, insomnia, or other maladies. In the extreme case, they can become part of the problem they are trying to eradicate. For example, Paul, who currently teaches psychology at a university, was employed by a social service agency for several years.

> I used to run group therapy sessions for abused women. Some of the stories they told were really horrific. I started doing one-on-one sessions as well as the groups because they really needed my help. I'd get so angry with the abusers. It got to me. One night, after a particularly harrowing day, I went home and struck out at my wife in anger and frustration. I didn't hit her but I came awfully close. I wanted to. I sat down and asked myself, "What am I doing?" That scared me so much, I quit my job right then and there. I called the boss at home and quit. I never went back.

The pessimism of the front-line worker and the denial of the workers in the other category combine to generate the feeling that there is no solution to the problem. Both attitudes speak to a recognition that society and the system are failing to address the problem appropriately, failing to solve the problem. (Some workers suggest that they are making it worse.) The professionals are failing the abused women they are trying to help. As one shelter worker put it:

> They come to us for help. We do everything we can for them but it is never enough. And you know what's the worst? When they come in here, they are so grateful for what we do. You can see it in their eyes. They think they've been rescued. They think they are safe but we know different and yet we smile and say "you're welcome." That is really hard.

Everyone involved with spousal abuse seems to have feelings of guilt and frustration that manifest themselves as denial or in a pessimistic outlook. Either they can't do anything about it so they might as well ignore it, or they can't do anything about it but they'll pretend they can until someone comes up with a better idea. It appears they are embarrassed by their failure (or their perception of failure) and so use defense mechanisms to protect themselves from it. Perhaps this explains the general reluctance to talk about the problem at all, to anyone.

The Abused Women

Some of the women in the study had already extracted themselves from the abusive relationship or were in the process of doing so. In general, in marked contrast to the helpers, their perspective tended to be positive and optimistic.

> I put up with eight years of crap from that bastard but now I am free to get on with my life. It is wonderful. Oh, sure, I don't have half the things I had when I was married, but who cares. I have one thing I didn't have then—self-respect.

They look forward to new experiences. Many are just now discovering how much they were missing. Interestingly, many of those things are seemingly insignificant. Consider this:

> Sometimes after work, I'll stop off at the coffee shop. I'd sit and read the paper and sip my coffee. When I was married, if I was two minutes late, cause the traffic was heavy, I'd get the third degree. Now, if I'm not home before seven, who cares.

Or this:

> Last week, I'm sure my coworkers thought I'd gone crazy. I stopped in the middle of the hall looking for the source of a strange sound. Then I burst out laughing. I was the source of the sound. I was humming. Do you know how long it has been since I'd hummed anything?

When discussing solutions to the problem in general, the optimistic attitude remained consistent. Although they would always preface their offerings with "I'm not sure this will work, but ... " they always ended their discussions on a positive note. Almost to a woman, the last statement made was "Hey, if I can do it, anybody can do it!"

The women who participated while they were still in abusive relationships presented a still consistent but entirely different set of perspectives.[26] With each woman, one got the feeling that she did not really understand her own situation. Some denied they were being abused, at the same time describing the beatings they had received. Others would acknowledge the beatings but suggest that they were somehow responsible for them. They all knew something was wrong, abnormal, but they didn't know what to do about it.

The most overwhelming impression was one of betrayal— betrayal by their husbands, betrayal by their families, betrayal by the system and society at large. These women are adrift without anyone to trust (from their perspective). There is no one to talk to, nowhere to get help, no one to trust. They feel alone, confused and betrayed. "I once went to a lawyer for help. He sent a letter to my husband warning him to leave me alone. He beat me worse than ever" was how Joyce began her story. Tammy commented, "I'm just a housewife. He [her husband] is a well-respected retailer. Who is going to take my word over his?" Mary summed it up for all of them: "I'm alone. There is no one out there who can help me so I've got to look after myself. I'm just not sure I can."

There are a great many factors that appear to support or reinforce the right of a man to abuse "his" wife, while at the same time society pays lip service to the concepts of equality and individual freedom. The result is confusion. No one knows where to turn or what to do. The women are forced into inaction. Those who are committed to helping the abused women are overwhelmed or rendered ineffective by conflicting rules, policies, and norms. "What can we do?" is a question that is often asked but rarely answered.

Notes

1. There is not necessarily a connection between social maturity and chronological age. One can remain immature throughout life if the appropriate lessons are not learned. For example, profilers who are called upon to develop a psychological profile of a serial criminal frequently run into this kind of discrepancy. One profiler told the authors that several times he has hypothesized an age for the criminal that was far too low. It seems that if a person is incarcerated for any length of time, he is isolated from mainstream society and his socialization stops. His development is arrested, so to speak, as he learns the appropriate behaviors for a prison setting rather than for the outside world. The profiler is correct in suggesting the age of the criminal at the time he entered jail, not his age at release. In other words, if a criminal spends ten years in jail, is released, and then commits a series of crimes, the profiler will offer an age range of x to y but the reality would be x to y plus 10 years (the time he spent in jail). The profiler's estimate would indeed be too low in that it reflects the social maturity of the offender rather than his chronological age.

2. Note that situational insanity is also being used by mental health professionals to explain other aberrant behaviors such as suicide or attempted suicide. For example, many "Suicide Prevention" manuals point out that 95 percent of all potential suicides are mentally disturbed *at the time of the attempt*.

3. Not all men hold this view. Some want the equal partnership, just as some women want the "homemaker" role of their parents' generation.

4. This view was supported by the society as a whole to some degree. A prosecutor specializing in abuse and assault cases in Calgary complained to us that a man convicted of wife beating would get a small fine (under $500) or jail time of less than a month, while someone convicted of cruelty towards a pet dog would get a huge fine ($2000 or more) or jail for up to six months.

5. The individuals may or may not go through the roles at the same time. One may define the other as being in a role before or after the so-defined person defines himself or herself in that role. For example, a man may identify a woman as a girlfriend while she continues to define herself as just a friend. However, in the case of marriage they adopt the roles of husband and wife together, as there is a socially sanctioned ceremony marking the transition to those social identities.

6. Military wives face a higher risk of spousal abuse than do non-military wives, but the lack of community resources is only one factor. Others include socialization into a rigid hierarchy (the military rank system), which includes clear roles for the wives and an acceptance of violence as a means to an end.

7. This situation is more acute in "overseas" postings where the locals speak a language other than English and have customs that are very different from those of the military family. Indeed, in some locations the locals are actively hostile towards military personnel and their families.

8. The differential application of core values frequently operates along gender and age lines.

9. To be fair, similar advice was offered by Protestant ministers and Jewish rabbis in the first half of the twentieth century.

10. Indeed, the term "domestic dispute" implies that the problem is confined to the family unit and outsiders should therefore not interfere.

11. In 1977, a rapist was found not guilty in a California court for similar reasons. Since a lone woman was hitchhiking, she was advertising that (a) she was willing to enter any vehicle that stopped and (b) she was, therefore, less concerned about the consequences than an average female. As the court judgement read, it would not be unreasonable in that case for a man (the rapist) to believe that she would consent to sexual relations (Margolis 1982: 23).

12. "Shotgun" weddings have taken place so that a child conceived out of wedlock can "have a name" when it is born.

13. Of course, this was beneficial to capitalists as lower wages mean higher profits. They wanted women to be working, but at lower rates of pay than men.

14. To be fair, the RCMP tested all of its applicants, male and female, according to the same standards (unlike the Correctional Service, which used differential standards).

15. This is a myth that still surfaces from time to time today, despite a complete lack of empirical support for the idea of intellectual inferiority.

16. Fear of rejection may explain the burgeoning use of a "date-rape drug" in North American society. When a man drugs his date before raping her, he does not give her the opportunity to reject his advances and by so doing attack his masculinity. Interestingly, a man was recently convicted of raping his wife because he used a "date-rape drug" on her.

17. Since 1942, the United States has fought in World War II, the Korean War, the Vietnam War, the Gulf War, and numerous other smaller conflicts.

18. There are two interesting items worth mentioning in terms of appropriate dress. First, some members of society, usually the wealthy and the famous, are expected to violate norms. For example, the "Academy Awards" is supposed to be a formal black-tie affair but there are many people who watch the event on television just to see how far the movie stars will push the norm. Second, clothing norms are changing. In Ontario recently, a woman challenged an "indecent exposure" law on the grounds that it was discriminatory against women. She argued, successfully, that it is sexism when men are allowed to appear in public without a shirt on but women are not. The courts ruled that she was right and

struck down the law. Now it is legal in Ontario for both men and women to appear topless in public.

19. For example, it may be necessary to change the rules in the sport of hockey or outlaw marriage.

20. We do not advocate criminalization of these aspects of abuse; rather we are simply pointing out the inability of the authorities to deal with them. They are human rights issues, not criminal ones.

21. In Canada since 1984, wives can be compelled to testify and face potential perjury charges if they contradict their statements given to the police at the time the charges were laid (Kilgannon 1988: 2).

22. In 1984, the Canadian Law Reform Commission proposed that assaults committed against a spouse or any other family member be treated as aggravated assault, effectively making offenses between family members more serious than assaults outside the family (Kilgannon 1988: 2). To our knowledge, this recommendation has not been acted upon.

23. Here, this term is used to include anyone, professional or volunteer, who is involved in the spousal abuse problem, excluding the abused women.

24. This point of view, when contrasted with a front-line worker's view, would be similar to someone trying to deal with "world hunger" contrasted with another person trying to find supper for a specific homeless man.

25. In only one case was there a positive response. A western chief of police took the study, read it, and called us for advice on how best to approach the problem. Some suggestions were made, and to the best of our knowledge, he is in the process of implementing them.

26. The discussions tended to be confused and erratic. These were the most difficult interviews of all. They were certainly the most depressing.

Chapter 3

The Impact of Abuse

Domestic Violence

Everyone involved, from the abused woman to the police officer, lawyer, shelter worker, and psychologist, has one thing
in common: none of them understands why abuse happens. People seem surprised when it happens. One gentleman recently
commented, "I don't think there really is that much abuse going
on against women. After all, I look up and down my block and I
don't see any. Don't you think it's just a lot of talk?" It is highly
unlikely that any of that gentlemen's neighbors are going to ring
him up and say, "Oh, by the way, I was slapping my wife around
the other day. I do hope we weren't too noisy!" Generally, abused
women remain silent about their relationships; therefore, most
people have no idea how big the problem is and how much impact it has on society in general.

In 1993, a statistical study of violence against women came
up with some disturbing results. "One quarter of all women
have experienced violence at the hands of a current or past marital partner" (Statistics Canada 1993: 1). Further,

> This figure is even greater if we consider only those women who
> have ever been married or lived in a common-law relationship
> (29%). Fifteen percent of currently married women reported

violence by their current spouse; 48% of women with a previous marriage reported violence by a previous spouse. *These different rates may reflect the difficulty for many women living with a violent partner to disclose their experiences* to an interviewer, the increased risk of violence to many women during separation, or the great numbers of marriages that have ended because of abuse (Statistics Canada 1993: 4) [emphasis added].

There is no corresponding study available for the United States, but in general, the violent crime rate is much higher there. For example, according to the World Health Organization (1993), the annual homicide rate for the United States was approximately 4.5 times higher than in Canada's. For women, the homicide rate was lower but still over two and a half times greater in the U.S. than in Canada.[1] The differences in the frequency of other violent crimes are similar, and it can be suggested from this that the rates of wife abuse in the U.S. are at least comparable to those in Canada, if not significantly higher.

There has been considerable debate concerning a seemingly dramatic increase in violent crimes over the past few decades. The media give the public the impression that violence in the world increases every day and is rapidly reaching epidemic proportions. According to some researchers, the frequency of violence against women has apparently remained stable or even declined over the past thirty years, but what has changed is the women's willingness to report a physical or sexual assault (Silverman and Kennedy 1993: 204–7). Whether the increase is real or apparent, all researchers seem to agree that the "... risk of murder [or other violent assault] for women is still most likely related to being in a poor domestic situation" (Silverman and Kennedy 1993: 11–12; cf. Leyton 1997: xiv–xv).

In both countries, women who are currently being abused may downplay it or deny that abuse is occurring. As Margaret said:

My husband was angry about something that night. It didn't take much to set him off and he needed someone to direct all his anger at. He was trying to corner me but I managed to run from the house. I hid in an alley behind a fence. I crouched in the dark, fearing he would find me and hurt me. Later, I walked along in the

> alley trying to decide what to do. I heard a car coming and ducked out of sight. Now I was even more frightened, for the car was driven by my husband. I knew him well. I knew he was still mad and I knew I had to stay out of sight. By now, I was sobbing and praying and shaking. I had walked away from my home and didn't know who to turn to and *still did not want to involve anyone in a personal matter.* I would be ashamed and embarrassed. I was an adult. I was supposed to take care of myself and my children, yet here I was crying and sneaking down back alleys, trying to stay away from the roads and out of sight of all cars [emphasis added].

Margaret does not remember what happened the next morning when she finally returned to her home and her abusive husband, but she does remember it took several more years before she told anyone what she had gone through.

Domestic violence is common and comes in a wide variety of forms. There is "elder abuse," when adult children abuse their elderly parents. There is "sibling abuse," when children (usually teenagers) abuse younger siblings (and sometimes their parents as well).

> It is difficult to estimate the number of violent crimes committed by teenagers against family members, but research is starting to reveal the serious problem of violence by teenagers against their parents, brothers and sisters.
>
> Violence between brothers and sisters is widespread in North America (Focus 1992: 1).

That child abuse (both sexual and non-sexual) by parents is a serious problem cannot be denied. One need only read a newspaper or watch the news to realize that children are being hurt far too frequently by their primary caregivers. There have been a number of excellent reports in this area (for examples, see Bass and Davis 1988 and Blume 1990).

Personal Impact

A huge number of people are affected by spousal abuse. Some will be introduced here. Their names and some of their other characteristics have been modified to protect them (many of the abused spouses are still in hiding and live in constant fear of their former husbands).

The Statistics on Abuse

The women who were or are being abused are obviously the ones who are most affected. They are the receivers of the violence, and as such suffer physical damage ranging from minor bruises that heal in a matter of days to permanently debilitating damage and, in some cases, death. The following figures from the Statistics Canada (1993) Violence Against Women Survey present the cold, hard facts. Of all women who have ever been married, including those in common-law relationships, 29 percent were subject to some form of violent abuse. Some were only threatened (19 percent), while others were pushed, grabbed, or shoved (26 percent), slapped (15 percent), had something thrown at them (11 percent), were kicked, bitten, or hit with a closed fist (11 percent), or beaten up (9 percent). Some women were choked (7 percent), raped (8 percent), hit with some weapon (6 percent), or wounded with a gun or a knife (5 percent).

The frightening thing about these statistics is that they do not indicate how many times this abuse was received, nor do they include any indication of the severity of the abuse. For example, Linda was systematically abused for the twelve years she was married to Roger. Her statistic would have been listed above once under each of (1) being threatened, (2) being kicked, bitten, or hit with a closed fist, (3) being slapped, (4) being beaten, and (5) being wounded with a knife. This does not come near to expressing the horror she lived through for those twelve years. According to Linda, she was threatened frequently (she estimates at least once a day). She was slapped every time she did something that displeased her husband (roughly twice a week). He punched her several times every time he got drunk (usually on a Friday or Saturday night—sometimes both), and after a particularly serious bout of drinking, usually once a month, the violence escalated. He stabbed her three times in the last two years of her marriage. According to her minimum estimates, she was threatened no fewer than 4,380 times, slapped 1,248 times, kicked, bitten, or hit 624 times, severely beaten 144 times, and stabbed three times. In other words, she suffered 6,399 incidents of violence over a twelve-year period, resulting in uncountable bruises, black eyes, abrasions, nine broken bones, one miscarriage, and cuts that required a total of about forty stitches.

The Abused Women

From hundreds of abused women who participated in the study, three have been selected as typical. Here are their stories.

MARGARET

Margaret was born in the early 1940s in a small town where she was raised with eight brothers and sisters. Her parents were excellent role models and in general, she says, she had a wonderful, loving childhood. That ended abruptly when she became pregnant, at age 16, married the father of her child. She had two other children and remained married to her abusive husband until their youngest child was in his teens. At a time when she was seriously considering leaving him, he chose to leave her and begin living with his secretary. Whether she knew it or not, his leaving (as opposed to hers) was helpful in that she did not have to flee to a shelter or worry about him stalking her. Some time later he did make an attempt at reconciliation, which Margaret rejected.

She still runs into her ex-husband from time to time, usually at their children's homes, and he quickly falls back into the verbal abuse pattern he established during their marriage. Recently, she has made it clear to her children that she is not willing to visit them if he is going to be there as well. So far, this seems to have considerably reduced the tensions that had previously existed at her children's houses.

Margaret has remarried and is quite happy these days. Her husband is non-abusive, and even though the occasional memory of her abusive first marriage sneaks into the relationship, she seems content. She provided a brief autobiography:

> I can remember when I was five years old, and how independent I felt when I decided I should cross the railroad yard alone. There were only four or five sets of tracks, but to a five-year-old crossing over, eight to ten tracks seemed like an endless amount.

I was full of adventure and laughter. I loved people. I would organize little concerts, featuring my other brothers, sisters, and cousins. Today when I watch the old reruns of the *Little Rascals* I remember not only when I first saw them (that was when dad got the television set in the early fifties), but their antics bring back more of my own childhood memories. Ours was a busy neighborhood. We put on special productions in the neighborhood and charged a few cents for the admission. I remember setting up lemonade stands to earn cash. Those are great memories because years later when I became a mom, I'd remember all over again as I helped my own youngsters set up their lemonade stands.

Dad took us on a family holiday each year. I don't think I've ever known a more patient man, but then with nine children, he had ample opportunity to learn patience. He'd head out for our destination but it seemed he was always open to stop along the way whenever one of us spotted something that excited us. I look back on the kind of father he was and the great role model that he was, and then I look at the father that I gave my own children and I shudder. Family vacations after I was married were not taken with a patient man. The schedule was set and it was to be adhered to. If I had the map and made a mistake, everyone in the car suffered as they all had to listen to the verbal abuse.

Fortunately for me, I ended up with a dad who gave me a most wonderful and ideal childhood. Today, as I look back on the childhood I provided for my children, I feel shame that I stayed in the relationship as long as I did. I know that my three children loved their father, but they did not learn their patience from him. I guess if it came from anywhere, it was passed down from my parents to me to my children.

As a child I loved having large numbers of friends. I thought that everyone should be my friend. It made sense to me. One camping trip stands out in my mind. Dad drove into the camp and parked and I jumped out of the car. Mom and dad were taking things out of the car when I showed up with a new friend and introduced her to my parents. I can't remember when I didn't feel that we were all meant to be friends. I know I always felt badly when someone didn't care to be friends. I'd think about it for days, wondering what I'd done wrong.

I guess that my desire to be a friend to everyone was one of the first problems that showed up in my marriage. I recall the year I was a grade eight student. I was with a large group of friends at the provincial park. We ranged in age from 12 to 15 years old. I was one of the younger ones. A boy I liked was there and I was enjoying his company. I thought he was cute and he went to the same school as I did. We were in what would be known today as middle school. It wasn't an official date, but I think we probably felt it was. My brother's friends, an older group of boys, drove up and I ran over to say hello. They all spent a lot of time at our house. Mom and Dad made our friends feel welcome although it must have been a horrible strain on the grocery budget. Anyway, I went over to greet them in much the same way as I would my own brothers but when I returned to my own group of friends, the boy I liked was gone. Apparently he had become jealous with my actions and he stomped off in anger. Eventually I married that boy, and for more than twenty years that incident from our childhood was thrown in my face as if I was a fallen woman.

The love of theater and acting grew in me like a pumpkin seed. I went from singing and dancing for my family, the neighbors, and relatives to studying dance and theater. Mom started me off with folk dancing lessons, then ballet. Later, after my youngest child was born, I returned to study more dancing. This was when I discovered I was fickle. I studied adult ballet and then was introduced to jazz dancing. I soon decided that jazz captured the real me and I could move in the way I had as a child, with more freedom of movement and always able to experiment with new moves. I studied at the college for six years and was invited to teach there. I enjoyed teaching the children ballet, but my greater love was working in jazz.

During high school I continued to study dance, adding Latin American dance to my repertoire. I joined the drama club and excelled, taking the all round actor award.

I guess my love of the theater became the next big problem years later when I was married. I joined the local theater group and had bit parts for awhile. My husband complained a bit but appeared to be putting up with my hobby. He did until I landed the starring role in an Agatha Christie production. Suddenly he found fault with everything. He forbade me to be in the play when he discovered that the heroine received a hug from the hero at the end. I tried to leave the club but was talked into taking the role of a 60-year-old spinster. I guess, considering that I was not yet in my twenties, I should have viewed the new role as a challenge. I took the role but knew that if I wanted peace on the home front I must give up the theater.

Some twelve years later I was again bitten by the theater bug. I had been studying dance at the local college and noticed an advertisement for dancers and singers for a musical. We had a family consultation (that's where I would beg and he would make a decision) and it was agreed that as long as I went after a chorus-type part, that I would be allowed to audition. Well, I got the part but the whole thing was a disaster. I enjoyed everything too much and was told by my husband that I could choose between him and the theater. I was in the middle of an abusive marriage and too dumb to know that here finally was the opportunity to end it all, but I don't think that I was able yet to recognize that he was abusive. Instead, I felt that I must be doing things wrong and if I tried harder I could be a better wife and then he would have more patience. I blamed myself whenever he hit me, thinking I must try harder not to be so outgoing. Every time I heard him yell at me I would think, I have to try harder. Remember that I wanted to be a friend to everybody and I figured if I tried hard to be and to do what was expected of me, then I could make things work. I don't know if I could be referred to as a peacemaker, but I do know that it seems that I spent more than twenty years trying to keep the peace in a war zone. My home with my husband was that war zone.

The day that I was hit because my husband misplaced his wallet was about the time that I began to think that I desperately needed out of the situation I was in. It was also about the time that he told me that if I ever tried to leave him he would find me and he would kill me. I had seen how vindictive he could be to his enemies and I knew I was safer where I could see him than with him lurking behind every corner. I also wanted my children to have a live mother, not a dead one.

During my childhood I had many friends. One special one, from grade one to grade six, was my best friend. She was Oriental; I am not. She was treated like one of the family at my house and I was treated with equal respect at her home. We had sleepovers, played house and dolls, went sledding and did all the general things kids like to do. I can't remember if we played witch or not. I know I loved playing the old witch. I would be the witch and feed the kids water with green food coloring in it and buttered bread with sugar sprinkled on top. Of course we would pretend it was horrible witch food and I would cackle as I made my prisoners eat it.

Mom and Dad never gave us kids talks about all people being equal. They just lived that way. They had no racial prejudice. They loved all people and so I loved all people. I just thought that everybody did. It was awful listening to the list of hates that my husband had. This group of people were useless because of this and another group was worthless because of that. When I defended people I ended up in the dog house. If I remained quiet and said nothing then in my mind it was like I was agreeing with his prejudiced statements. It was stressful to be loyal to him in all ways and yet to hear the put downs.

Dad let us make tree houses and our next door neighbor let us play in his trees also, so it wasn't unusual to be climbing in the trees and swinging from ropes. For a while I had a very difficult time. There was a boy in grade seven who wanted to take me to a school dance and I couldn't decide if I would rather climb the trees and ride out to the old mine on my bike or actually take that step away from being a tomboy. I accepted the date but had to learn how to jive. I'd studied ballet and folk dancing to that point so I asked my sister to teach me to jive. She must have done a good job or maybe God just blessed me with a natural ability, because soon I had a regular dance partner and we started winning dance contests.

The dancing always seemed to be a part of my life. Eventually I studied country western dance, ethnic dance, more ballet, even break dancing. That last one really caused an uproar in my marriage. At the time I was on staff at a college and discovered a new dance was becoming popular. I thought it would valuable if I kept abreast of everything that was happening in the field and decided I should take a course. My husband, who generally looked at things from the half-empty instead of half-full perspective, jumped to the conclusion that soon I would go out to public dances and whirl around on the floor like a teenager. The discussion (which is another word for fight) caused quite an uproar at our home. It rankled him whenever I made an executive decision. He needed to be in control of his world, which meant everyone in his world. He was fine with me studying but didn't know how to give me credit for the brain I was blessed with.

I guess it follows that if I liked climbing trees as a youngster, I would enjoy other athletic type things. I did! During the first six years of school my best friend and I placed first in a ton of three legged races. I set a high jumping record in elementary grade that still wasn't broken years later when I had my family. It was great for me to have my son so involved in sports. He wasn't wild about the violence of hockey but he thrived on track and field, and in high school set some records himself.

I was blessed with three healthy, beautiful children. Sometime after the third one arrived, I ended up doing a talk show for television. Two people were also developing a fitness show about that time but threw in the towel when they discovered how much work was involved. I enjoyed dance, I was a teacher, and by then I was a fitness enthusiast, so I started thinking about producing the fitness show. Suddenly I was designing sets, arranging for crews, taping music, and writing scripts. I was also studying like mad, knowing that my physical education better be perfect. I even arranged to have a physiotherapist check all the moves that were to be done to be doubly certain that everything would be safe. About then I decided I'd also better beef up my education further, and I began studying anatomy and kinesiology.

I think that doing the two television shows was a type of replacement for the theater. I couldn't be on stage and I couldn't be an actor, but perhaps being the host of a two television shows could replace that.

My teaching position with the college was referred to as a hobby by my husband. He told me I could never survive in the real world and that I would never be able to make a living on my own. He put me down often enough that I always felt there was something that I had to prove. For years I thought I was trying to be great for my father, to show him that though I had married young I could still make something of myself. I wanted him to be proud of me. Finally I realized that my dad was always proud of me. It hit me one day that I was trying to prove to myself that I was wonderful, that I was worthwhile. I finally discovered after the breakdown of my marriage that the years of verbal putdowns had left me scarred. I had very little self-confidence. I was always trying to prove myself. Articles would appear in the paper and I would clip them out and think, Look, it's me, see what I accomplished. When I found that I wasn't mailing them to Dad, I began questioning myself about who I was trying to impress.

The television fitness show was taped for eight years. I saved the fan letters. I think I needed them. They made me feel worthwhile. It is too bad that the feeling could never last, but during those years there was always my husband there to let me know that I wasn't special and I wasn't wonderful. He not only tore me down but for a number of years he tried to undermine my faith in God. His ridicule was not reserved just for me. For some reason he decided to extend it to the children also, and he zoomed in a lot on our middle child. I cry when I think of the years of crap that he dished out and how I remained there and allowed my children to be damaged by his verbal abuse.

Being born to my mom and dad makes me feel that I have a Heavenly Father that loves me. I got such a neat start in life. My dad never yelled at me, ever. I never saw him spank any of his children, and with nine children that must have taken a load of patience. Well, I do recall Dad yelling once at some neighbor boys who climbed up on the roof of our garage. I can still see him in my mind, chasing those boys down the alley and yelling at them as he waved the broom at them. He didn't use any harsh words, though, unless you would consider cockeyed a foul word. My parents didn't use crude words. They displayed their respect for us at all times.

When I was fourteen years old I was working at a store part-time. My dad was the manager and he was back in the office with some other gentlemen. They didn't hear me as I approached the office, and I heard one of the men use the word shit. I don't like using it and I feel embarrassed writing it. I am sure it was my dad who used the word. I think it was his voice. Well, my dad went up on a pedestal after that. Imagine, he may have used rough words on occasion but he loved me so much he never spoke those words in my presence. Well, those parents of mine certainly gave me something to strive for as a parent.

My husband did not have the same kind of upbringing as I had and I do not know what kind of language his dad used; perhaps it was pristine. I wish that my children could have had a dad like mine who respected them and treated them as special. I know he loved them very much, but he didn't seem to express it well or often.

I don't remember my husband ever telling me that he liked my cooking, or telling me that I looked pretty. I look at old pictures of myself and I think I did look pretty, but I was never sure then. I think that it's sad to live with someone for over twenty years and to live in a limbo state where you don't know if you are really worthwhile, and you don't know if you really are pretty to look at. If you love someone, don't you want them to feel secure and happy? If you love someone, don't you want to tell them that you consider them special in every way? Otherwise, why did you marry?

I wanted to go to university and study nursing or physical education. I had no thoughts of raising a family, of getting married, of wedding bells, etc. My life was spread out before me. I was raised in a happy home with wonderful parents and equally wonderful siblings. One summer, when I was fifteen years old, I lost my virginity and became pregnant. I was scared. My parents were supportive. The boy (as he was not much more than that) at age sixteen returned to town and married me. I felt deeply ashamed for putting myself and my parents through that. One month after turning sixteen, there I was, a married woman. I was instantly responsible for another little human being. I wanted to be the best mom in the world and I had such good role models. How can you be the best mom in the world if you don't have a dad that wants to be the best dad? The best dad does not slap his wife around. The best dad does not tell his wife she is useless and stupid, especially when she truly is not!

One of Margaret's major regrets is that her middle child (Sandra) married a man just like her father and for about ten years lived in an abusive relationship as well.

SANDRA
After about ten years in an abusive relationship, Sandra ran for a shelter with her young daughter and a garbage bag full of her

belongings. Essentially they fled with nothing but the clothes on their backs. Today, she is rebuilding her life and going out with one man fairly steadily. When she left her husband, she swore to herself that she would never trust another man, but after four years her relationship appears to be working and the emotional scars have faded to some degree. Here, in her own words, is her biography.

I was born in a small town. I was afraid of the basement at my house. It was haunted. I had a nightmare about that basement. It was exactly the same every time (it continued into my adulthood, just less frequently): The stairs fold up into a slide once I'm halfway up and THEY are in the laundry room grasping and grabbing and pulling me down. Once in the laundry room, I'm laid on a concrete table like an operating table. It's dark. THEY are all around me. They tickle me until it hurts. I start to fall off the table. At that second, I wake up and catch myself as I'm about to fall out of bed. Every time, I have a weird tinny taste in my mouth for about two minutes. I could never figure out the taste but it always seemed linked to the concrete table. Maybe by the time I was twenty, the nightmare came only the night of the day I would tell someone about it. In my early twenties, it went away to be replaced by new fears.

My sister and I shared a bedroom all those years. It was great. Great for me. I was afraid of the dark. My Uncle Sam and Aunt June used to take me into Grandma and Grandpa's room. They would close the drapes and poke at me in the dark and scare me badly. Maybe that's why I was afraid of the dark.

During the early years, my mother was always there for us. I don't remember a lot of events with my dad. Seems like he worked and that's about it.

I went to kindergarten in that small town. I was five when we moved to a nearby city. My sister and I walked to school together. We would walk by the high school. I was scared. We would also ride our CCM bikes after the rain under street lights at night. We would find huge flying beetles and run over them. There were great trails and hills to ride on, too. Behind our apartment, it was open prairie.

Mom did most of the caretaker work at our apartment. She would give out jobs to all the kids in the building and we could win prizes like comics. Us kids would play soccer and dodge ball in the hallway. I kicked out once and hit a boy between the legs. I was in big trouble and didn't understand why. Mom explained it to me. We had access to the keys. Us kids would lock up the laundry room so we could have it to ourselves.

After less than a year, we moved to another, smaller city. I finished Grade I there. The principal of the new school scared me. He was gray-haired and never smiled. A teacher hit me in Grade I. She would use a ruler to hit kids across the palm of the hand if they were bad. One day I got up to help someone clean up a mess of paint. She hit me. I told my parents. My dad, I think, talked to the school. The next day I was late. As everyone was about to sit, I walked in. The teacher stood at the door glaring at me. "You little tattletale," she announced loudly. I was so scared, she even looked like a witch.

There were times my parents would go out and my sister was to baby-sit. After they left, she would leave. I had no problem caring for my baby brother but I hated being there in that haunted house. She would go across the street to Dairy Queen to be with friends. I'd sit at the picture window and just watch her. I'd cry and wait for her to come back. As long as I kept watching I wasn't really alone, so I was safe from the house. My sister and I didn't do lots together anymore. She was becoming "too cool" for a little sister.

We seemed to see Dad more often now. He was very strict. My mom was my best friend and both of us were scared of Dad. I called him "H & R Block" because like the commercial, when he spoke, you listened.

Over the next few years (Grades VII–IX), my parents separated. At first it was fun because Dad wasn't there, but then I began to feel like I was in the middle with everyone pulling me in every direction. I felt like a traitor to my dad, traitor to my mom. I just wanted out. Dad wanted to get back together but my Mom didn't want to. I tried to slash my wrists to get them to pay attention to me and to what they were doing. They did get back together and it didn't go well. My father slapped my face. My sister says, "you must have deserved it." At age sixteen, I quit school and moved out. I had to move back for a while but hated it. I finally moved out for good. Then I met Alan. I did everything I could to please him.

We moved a few months later. It was hard moving far away, but it was an adventure too. We were married and things slowly changed. It was a very slow progression. Things that were initially cute and caring (I thought) gradually became demanding and controlling. For instance, he might say, "you should wear a coat. It's kind of cold outside." It was a suggested request and I viewed that as, Oh, isn't that nice—he's being considerate and caring of my health. That became "Wear a coat!" and then "You have to wear a coat." I would respond with "Well, if I'm cold, I'll wear a coat." His remarks would be something like "You're too stupid. You don't have the sense to know if you're cold or not.

Wear a coat!" If I didn't wear a coat, there was hell to pay. In every way, in every thing that took place, there was a slow progression to reach that point where he had total control. I used to say, I think the truest statement in the world is "Love is blind." I excused him, minimized his actions and statements, because of love, because of love. That was my excuse. It was like he was the habit that I knew. I knew nothing else. I stuck with that. I loved him. I took his word for gospel. I did what I was told, all in the name of loving him, trying to help him through his hard times because he was always upset about work, or down about his children [by a previous wife whom he also had abused] or down about something. I thought that was my role, to try to make his life happier.

I definitely knew what my guidelines were, what I could and could not do. People say, Well, there must have been some happy moments and I'd say, Well, okay, so usually you think of happy moments as certain events on the calendar, like birthdays or Christmas, the birth of your child, and so I can think back to those events for years back, that yes they were fun but I wasn't totally me. I didn't have as much fun as I could have had because I always knew what my boundaries were. I always knew what line not to cross, or it was no longer going to be fun. It was going to be hell when I got home.

There was a commercial that used to be on television about a woman who forgot to mail a letter and all you would hear was her husband's voice calling her stupid, calling her down for not having accomplished remembering to mail this letter. Then a voice said that one of the worst forms of abuse is not the physical. It's the scars that are left by the mental abuse. And then in the ad the woman looked in a mirror, and although to look at her face she was fine, in her reflection she was actually covered in scars. The first few times I watched the commercial I was almost embarrassed to watch it in front of him because I thought maybe he would see on my face that I was relating to that commercial. It was like when you are in a room of men and a personal hygiene commercial comes on for women—you just want to leave the room. Well, when that commercial came on, I wanted to leave the room. I was afraid he was going to say, What? How come you are watching? Are you relating to that? I just wanted to leave. I guess that was one of the early things that started happening that stimulated me to think, Gee that voice of that man yelling at that woman, that sounds like the way he yells at me! Those are the words that I get called, and there is this commercial saying that it's wrong and look what it's doing to you.

In fact, I used to say to him, "You know, you call me stupid, you call me stupid, eventually I'm going to start believing I'm stupid. I'm fighting to believe that I'm not but if you tell a person enough times that they're stupid, they believe they're stupid." If you tell them enough times that they're bad, they start believing they're bad! And so that is what they become, but all my begging was in vain.

Margaret, Sandra's mother, offered the following comment on Sandra's upbringing and her marriage to Alan:

There definitely was abuse for Sandra's father when he was a child, and I've been able to trace that back to his birth and even discovered why there was abuse, more for him than for any of his other 15 brothers and sisters. The treatment he received at the hands of his parents showed an imbalance from the treatment of his siblings. His own parents apparently carried a self-inflicted guilt and passed it on to the child in the form of mean actions. As a child these would likely have been interpreted by the young boy as a lack of caring. He grew up feeling unloved and had a great difficulty in believing that he was lovable. His insecurities manifested themselves in a need to be in control. He was a jealous individual and in many ways Sandra's father and her husband were a lot alike.

I have a difficult time in assessing my own actions. I do not blame my childhood, nor can I, for my parents were loving and dependable. My siblings were loving and supportive. My childhood is filled with happy memories. It was not until I listened to my daughter describe the slow progression of events in her own marriage that I realized that I had reacted in much the same way. I wanted to create a fairy tale marriage where everyone was happy, and so I bent over backwards to be nice, to be pleasant, to give much more than I ever received. I soon realized I was no longer myself in his presence. I became afraid to laugh if there was another man around for fear it would set off his anger and jealous rages. By the time I realized I had become trapped in a situation I could not control, I had two daughters. I was ashamed to tell anyone that my husband occasionally slapped or hit me. At first I put it down to alcohol because his jealousy and unbelievable anger erupted when he had been drinking. (Later, he didn't even pretend to use alcohol. He'd just slap me when he was mad.) Like Sandra's husband, my husband—her father—also put me down. Early in our marriage he would laugh and lovingly call me a clown. I wanted so much to have people around me laugh and be happy that I was always clowning around, but gradually those remarks became, You're so stupid. Don't act so dumb! He put down most of what I did. I cannot remember him ever saying, You look lovely, nor ever hearing him praise my cooking, nor ever hearing him compliment my achievements. He held back his support and instead he undermined me as a person. I think eventually I became as insecure as he was, but in different ways.

The one thing that I regret and will always be eternally sorry about is what my fears and lack of backbone did to my children. I marvel that they love me, for I see that I let them down tremendously. Yes, I tried to be supportive of them, but in all honesty I became very afraid of their father and the repercussions of his anger. At one point he threatened me. He said if I ever left him, he would find me and he would kill me. I knew he meant it. I had seen how very vindictive he could be with others. It took me twenty years before I finally stood up and said, No more. How sad! How sad for all of us trapped in that horrible cycle of fear, abuse, and violence.

DEBORAH

Today, Deborah lives alone. Her sons are grown and live in a different city, as does her former husband. She teaches at an elementary school (having returned to university to acquire the necessary credentials) and engages in a number of hobbies and interests. She is currently involved with a man but is cautious in her optimism concerning where it will lead.[2]

Rather than write a biography, Deborah chose to write about her childhood memories of her father and how they affect her as an adult today:

DAD. I remember a life of growing up in a house where Dad was the boss. When Dad said you had to do something, you never questioned the reason why. He would often come into the girls' bedroom (which was located downstairs) and loudly state, "You girls get out of here and sweep this basement," or "Clean up your bedroom," or "Help shovel the snow," or "Mow the grass." Often, when I would hear him thundering down the basement steps, I would sit very quietly on my bed in hopes that he wouldn't come into my room. I never felt close to this man at all. He was a dictator, a despot and an autocratic parent. At mealtimes, Dad assumed the position and rights of the head of the table. He would walk through the door every night and ask, "What's for supper?" It was expected that my mother would have supper ready, or very close to it (if she knew what was good for her), because Dad would begin complaining until it was on the table. I believe that my mother unintentionally taught us to fear Dad, for she would hastily clean the house prior to his arrival and she would enlist the help of any child who happened to be within earshot. It was often a case of "quickly get that dusted or set the table before Dad gets home." All seven of his children were expected to be seated around the table when he sat down. If they came in late, he would have to move his chair to allow them in the kitchen and this always caused tension. In our house, Dad got to have quart milk (once in a while, as a treat, we children would be given a glass by Mom) and real butter, whereas we children were expected to drink either powdered milk or canned milk and margarine. At the table, manners were always impressed upon us (sit up straight, chew with your mouth closed, etc.). Seldom was there any conversation, aside from the typical question and answer stuff. Talk about pleasant things like holidays, birthdays or FEELINGS were never addressed, to my recollection.

I remember an incident where my older brother had been drinking at a party at the militia and fallen asleep in the washroom and got locked in over night. I remember the fear I felt [age approx. 14] when he and Dad got into a fist fight and Dad kicked him down the basement stairs. One of my biggest fears as a teenager was coming home pregnant and having my Dad kick me down the basement stairs. (My brother laughs today at this great form of birth control.) It was brought to my attention by a counselor that I use the metaphor of being kicked down or pushed down with respect to my father or/and men in general.

I remember running for the bus one evening and leaving the outside door open. Dad rounded the corner at that time and grabbed me by the hair and hauled me back to close the door. I remember crying all the way to the bus depot. I remember him pulling my hair twice over similar incidents [age approx. 12].

I remember my Dad saying, "You girls are good for nothing" many times and how much that hurt me as a child. (I believe one of the catalysts that kept me going when pursuing my degree was this belief. I set out to prove I was capable and smart enough.)

I remember one time when my Dad had borrowed my $20 that I had made baby-sitting and told Mom he was going to give me his mukluks (about four sizes too big) instead of returning the money. I remember Mom sending him downstairs to talk to me about it and I burst into tears because I was so terrified of him and I wanted my money back, and yet I was afraid I wouldn't get it [age approx. 13].

Christmas was always very chaotic at our place because there were seven children and two adults busily opening gifts. My memories of this time of year are good. We were always allowed to pick $10 worth of items out of the Sears catalogue and these were placed under the tree to be opened at Christmas.

SCHOOL. I was never a brain. I was teacher's pet in Grade XI and had a 81.5 average. Most other years, I slid by in the low

60s or high 50s. I quit school before the end of Grade XI as my dad was pressuring me to get a job and when I found one, I was overjoyed because this meant I could move out of the house.

I remember a time when I was living on my own and Dad found out that Richard [the man she eventually married] had spent the night at my place. Apparently he hollered at Mom and the family at supper time and slammed his fist on the plates. I didn't go home till Christmas that year and took my best friend with me as I knew he'd contain himself in front of her. He spent most of the time in his bedroom and only came out for a few minutes with his electric shaver in hand (going) and sat quietly at the corner of the living room. We never exchanged a word that Christmas.

Even today when I go home, my Dad tries to find something cruel to say to hurt me. I have stood up to him a few times but he still continues to be the "heavy." I often feel very uncomfortable around him but I do talk to him. He often wants a kiss good-bye or upon meeting and I often see it as a facade. He showed no affection to speak of as a child, so why now?

My Dad treats my Mom very disrespectfully and if I interject and come to her defense, he will attack me.

My Dad's influence affects my life in a negative way even today. I find I am intimidated by men (especially older, bigger men who I perceive as bullies or loud). I know I will try harder to please a male employer than a female and I am not relaxed around men who are in a position of authority over me.

I married a man who was very dominating and controlling, just like Dad (or, at least in my mind, he assumed that role).

I found I was attracted to men who distanced themselves or appeared aloof (in the beginning). I also dated a man for two years whose wife had been dominating and verbally abusive. I assumed the more dominant and controlling role in that relationship. I find that although I am attracted to that type of male, I am able to stay clear of them. I was in group counseling for over a year when my marriage broke up.

I do not have a very close relationship with my boys. While we talk easily, I do not feel comfortable talking feelings with my boys even though I have tried several times. My relationship with Donald (20) is more of a question and answer session. He has many of his father's qualities. When he lived with me, it was a constant power struggle. David (22) is planning to marry a woman whom I see as very much a subtle controller. The boys both have a relationship with their father but it is often an "on-off" kind of thing. My ex-husband still (ten years later) does not want to talk with me. I perceive him to be a very angry and bitter man.

Today I am in a relationship with a man who also had a similar upbringing and relationship with his father. (We'll see where this goes!)

MOM. My relationship with my mother has always been very close and warm. I now recognize that she has the same choices as I do and if she so desired, she could leave my Dad too. She chooses to stay, believing her religious beliefs "till death do we part." As a result of my relationship with her, I have many close female friends and seldom any problems with women. I can relate very well to most women and feel this is indicative of my upbringing.

Abused women are not stupid, nor are they handicapped in any other way. They are normal people with normal capabilities, needs, and desires. The types of women who are abused are not victims because they share a factor that marks them as potential receivers of abuse. On the contrary, they are ordinary women who happen to find themselves in an abusive situation. In fact, as far as we can determine, this is all that they have in common.

IMMIGRANT WOMEN AND ABUSE

Women who come to North America as immigrants face a particularly difficult challenge, especially if they are being abused by their husbands. For example, "Foreign-born women who have been sponsored by their Canadian- [or American-] born husbands [or, we believe, their foreign-born husbands who have obtained citizenship], may lose their immigration status if the marriage breaks down" (Focus 1993: 1), even if the reason for the breakdown is spousal abuse. They are not granted all of the rights that are given to North American-born women. (Under the United Nations guidelines, adhered to by both the United States and Canada, people seeking refugee status must show a well-founded fear of persecution based on race, religion, nationality, social group, or political opinion, *but not on gender*. Fear of persecution based on wife abuse is not a criterion for refugee status.)

"My husband beat me and I wanted to leave him," said Margarita, an immigrant from Guatemala[3] who was sponsored by her husband, also Guatemalan, who had come to North America several years earlier than Margarita and had obtained citizenship before her arrival. Margarita feared her husband but feared the situation in her home country even more.

I came here to escape the civil war, the death squads, the violence and the danger. There, we slept in the forest behind our house every night because we were afraid. Our neighbors had been murdered in their sleep so we slept hidden in the trees.

She approached some people at a governmental agency (she does not recall which one) about her husband abusing her. She was told to have him charged with assault. Only when she had done that could the agency help her. She talked it over with her female friends in the Guatemalan immigrant community. They told her not to do what the agency had asked. She was told a story, probably a myth, about another woman who had charged her husband with assault. As Margarita retold the story:

The woman called the police after a pretty bad beating—broken bones, missing teeth—and they came and took her husband away. He was convicted of assault [causing bodily harm] and received a sentence of one year in jail. The woman filed for divorce the same day he was convicted. Exactly four months later, two things happened: one, he was released from jail; and two, she was picked up by the immigration officials and deported.

Margarita followed her friend's advice because she did not want to be sent back to Guatemala. She chose instead to remain with her abusive husband until she became a citizen, which she eventually did.

Although the incident told to Margarita probably never happened (there is no such case in the court records), it is based somewhat in reality because "a woman can be deported if her husband is convicted of a criminal offense and sentenced to more than six months" (Lacroix 1989: 2)—a rather ironic twist.

An immigrant woman faces a series of other problems that are unique to her situation and make it difficult to get out of an abusive relationship. First, she is totally dependent economically on her husband. In all likelihood, she does not speak the language of her new country and so has no job prospects and no way to gain information on alternative sources of income. Second, as she is largely ignorant of the legal system and of her rights as an individual, she is also dependent on her spouse from a legal perspective. Both of these factors have been used by abusive husbands as control mechanisms. "The law says if you don't have a husband or a job, you have to leave the country and go home," "Our immigration papers say if you leave me, I get the children and you get nothing," and "Go! I'll call Immigration and you'll be sent home right away" are all threats that were by immigrant women. The women freely admit that since they couldn't read the documents or laws, did not know their rights, and had no one to turn to for advice other than their husbands, they had to believe their husbands. They had no choice.

Isolation resulting from the lack of friends or family close by and the language barrier was another in the series of problems faced by the immigrant women. They had nowhere to go if they left their husbands. Juanita, another Central American refugee, told of her visit to an emergency shelter.

> I was going to leave him. I couldn't take it any more so I went while he was at work. They were very nice. They let me sit, got me a coffee and found someone who spoke Spanish. They told me all about the shelter, showed me where I could sleep and told me who I should call to get money and clothes. Then they asked me if I had any questions. I said yes. I asked how my [immigration] status would change and whether I should go to the immigration authorities to get my own papers since all of ours were in my husband's name only. I had a lot of questions like that. They just stared at me. I saw them look at each other and shrug their shoulders. They had no idea what I was talking about or who to call. I left and went home. I cried while I made Enrique's supper.

There is little overlap between the social workers who work for the immigration departments and those who work in the shelters for abused women. Neither can answer all the questions as they are ignorant of each other's procedures, policies, and requirements. Inadvertently, this ignorance creates another wall to isolate the immigrant woman from the society at large and the help she needs. That is unfortunate, since many immigrant women who approach the authorities—either Social Services agencies or shelter workers—have already overcome a major cultural block just by making the approach. They must indeed be desperate in their abusive situation if they are willing to contact the authorities, given the backgrounds of many of the immigrant women. Many come from countries with oppressive political regimes wherein the authorities are to be avoided at all costs or approached only at great risk; these women have no information to suggest that the authorities in their adopted country are any different. A failure or rejection based on ignorance at this point is a serious setback from which it may take many years to recover—many years of continued abuse.

The Abuser

There are significant impacts upon the abuser at a number of levels and, logically, these impacts range in importance and severity: (1) in almost all cases the abusive relationship will end, which results in the abuser losing all forms of direct control he had had over his spouse; (2) because the relationship breaks up, the abuser may face economic difficulties when forced to give up some possessions to the departing spouse and, in some cases, pay support for the ex-wife and children (if any); (3) depending on the severity of the abuse and the degree of involvement with the legal community (the police and courts), the abusive spouse may suffer loss of prestige in his community and acquire a criminal record, as well as having to serve time in jail.

Generally, almost everyone felt that the abusers diverted the blame. "He blames me for all of his troubles." "He doesn't think he has a problem." "According to him, I am the one with the problem."[4] Few abusers acknowledge that they have a problem or even that they have done anything wrong. Naturally, this excludes them from taking advantage of any of the assistance programs that exist, even if ordered to do so by the courts.

In 1994, there were approximately 400 treatment programs for abusive men available across North America. Most impose qualifications for entry into their programs, including (but not exclusively) acceptance and recognition that they have a problem. As a result, many cases of spousal abuse are treated by the courts as assault punishable by incarceration without referral to treatment programs. John, for example, has recently married for the third time. Both previous marriages ended in divorce after he became abusive (each of the first two marriages lasted about ten years). In both of those marriages, he had been convicted of assaulting his wife and received either jail time or probation. A recent interview with his new and pregnant wife revealed that John was exhibiting abusive behaviors once again. The wife was already considering divorce action. Despite the minimum of twenty-one years of abusive behavior and a number of convictions for assault, John was never ordered by the courts to undergo treatment, and there have been no indications that he has considered that direction for himself.

Joel, a psychologist, was married to Lydia for almost a decade. Lydia felt that for the first few years, everything was great. Then he hit her during an argument. He instantly apologized and swore he would never do it again. That promise lasted two months until they had their next major argument. For the remainder of their marriage, Joel abused Lydia more and more frequently until Lydia fled to a shelter in fear of her life. Within a few months, Joel was dating another woman who said he began to abuse her while they were dating. She broke off the relationship after less than a year.

The information gathered about abusive spouses indicates that as is true for the abused women, there is little in common shared by even a majority of the abusers. Some have very little education; others are well educated. Many are unemployed or under-employed, but just as many are in high paying, prestigious jobs. Some were abused as children or witnessed others being abused, but others were never subjected to abusive behaviors. It is safe to suggest that the only thing these men have in common is the abusive behavior.

Whether their need is defined as a need to control their respective spouses or as a need to act out their violent tendencies with the spouse happening to be the most convenient scapegoat, the bottom line remains unchanged. These men are violent, clearly capable of seriously damaging another human being without remorse or regret. This latter assessment stems from the observation made by many abused wives that the level of violence escalates during the final breakup of the relationship. Instead of choosing to attempt to convince the wife to remain in the relationship, abusive husbands tend to attempt to beat their wives into giving up the idea.

The Families

The two people in an abusive relationship are not the only ones who are seriously affected by that relationship. Other members of the family are directly (and indirectly) affected as well.

When discussions focussed on the consequences of their abusive actions, consequences that ranged from loss of family to incarceration for protracted lengths of time, only rarely did the abusers indicate that they thought they had done anything wrong.

> We had a good thing going, Angie and I. We had a nice house. We went to a lot of parties and stuff. I looked after Angie, got her the best clothes, the best of everything. But one day she just ups and leaves, throws all that away.

Tim placed no emphasis on the fact that on the night Angie went to an emergency shelter, she needed fourteen stitches to close a cut he had given her over the eye, nor did he connect his abusive behavior with the breakup of his marriage.

> She left me. I didn't leave her. If it were up to me, we'd still be happily married. I'm sure if she'd sat down and talked to me, we could've worked everything out.

Like Tim, most of the abusers do not associate the marriage breakdown with the abuse. There is always some other reason and that reason always places the onus on the wife. It is her fault the marriage ended. Any consequences the abuser suffered as a result of his behavior also tended to be the wife's fault.

CHILDREN

Children learn all that they need to know about cultural values, norms, and behaviors from their parents and their peers (usually older siblings) and have those norms and values modified and fine-tuned during their years at school. If the family is dysfunctional, then the norms, values, and behaviors acquired by the children tend to be sociopathic, antisocial, or asocial (that is, they are not within the bounds of what society at large defines as acceptable). For example, a young man who was serving time in prison for rape resisted all of the correctional system's attempts at rehabilitation or resocialization. It was not that he was incorrigible. Simply put, he did not share the values that society at large held as appropriate. He had grown up in an abusive relationship followed by a series of foster homes (both parents were alcoholics; they lost custody of their son when he was nine years old). He had never learned the basic concepts of good and evil. Instead, he had a belief system that replaced "good and bad" with "good-for-me and bad-for-me." Everything he did was related to that dichotomy. Raping his date was good-for-me, and therefore good. Being convicted of rape and being sent to prison was bad-for-me, and therefore evil. The idea that good and bad involved the feelings of others never occurred to him (given his belief system) and so he did not understand that raping someone was bad or evil. He had, in his mind, done nothing wrong, and so did not deserve to be in prison. As the Correctional Service's rehabilitation/resocialization programs all presuppose that an inmate must first accept his guilt as an initial step, they were all doomed to failure in this case. This individual was released at the end of his sentence and re-offended almost immediately. He returned home (he was married with one child), beat his wife, then went to a bar, picked up a girl, and raped her in his car. He did another stretch in prison, during which his wife divorced him. Upon his second release, he went to his ex-wife's home and held her hostage, repeatedly raping and beating her in the presence of her child. Having done this, he visited his parole officer, arranged for a rent-controlled apartment, and went job hunting as if nothing had happened. He was arrested, charged, and is currently serving a life sentence in prison. He is frustrated by his present situation: "I was married to the bitch and she turned me in. For what! I was just doing what a man's gotta do. She wasn't no damn wife! She didn't want to give me what I needed so I took it. Then she turns me in like I committed a crime or something. Bitch!"

Children living with one parent who is abusive to the other quickly learn inappropriate behaviors. For example, a large percentage of men who grew up in abusive families are abusive to their spouses. They do not see anything wrong with the abuse. They have learned that this is the way one is supposed to act towards one's wife. Alan, Sandra's husband, watched his mother being beaten by his father. He grew up to physically and psychologically abuse all three of his wives.

Girls who see their mothers abused tend to seek out men who are "just like dear old Dad," entering abusive relationships more often than not. Sandra's mother was abused and Sandra ended up marrying Alan, who was remarkably similar to her father in attitude and behavior.

In neither case above is there conscious intent. The boys do not grow up intending to abuse their wives, nor do the girls grow up and deliberately seek out a man who will treat them the way Dad did Mom. Sandra repeatedly stated she did not recognize the similarities between Alan and her father until some time after her marriage had ended. They learn by observation and imitation (the keys to cultural training) without realizing that they are learning what society terms "deviant" behavior.

These tendencies to perpetuate the abuse are not the only problems that the children of an abusive marriage acquire. They tend to develop many of the problems that result from inappropriate cultural training. A brief list of those behavioral problems associated with the witnessing of the abuse of one parent by the other attests to the severity of the impact on the children of an abusive relationship (Alberta Solicitor General n.d.: 5–6). Children who observe violent behavior of a parent may:

- feel frightened, confused. and unhappy
- behave aggressively, become belligerent or withdrawn, and act fearful
- become depressed or even suicidal
- feel responsible for the violence
- exhibit self-destructive, accident-prone behavior
- have physical complaints such as headaches, stomachaches
- have nighttime difficulties such as insomnia, nightmares, bed-wetting
- seek punishment with behaviors such as lying or stealing (believing punishment means love)

- adopt rigid gender role identification, with girls acting withdrawn, passive, given to approval-seeking behavior, and boys becoming aggressive, acting out, bullying, and engaging in self-destructive behavior

Also, there is considerable anecdotal evidence that suggests that many children continue the cycle of violence when they become adults. Sons of abused women tend to become abusers, and daughters of abused women tend to marry a man "just like dear old Dad."

PARENTS AND SIBLINGS

Of the Abuser. Gaining access to the immediate families of abusers was difficult. This general reluctance to talk stems from two probable sources. First, an abusive son or brother could be a source of embarrassment: "a family should not air its dirty linen in public." Second, spousal abuse is illegal. It is a criminal act and families may not want to do or say anything that might incriminate the abuser. Families protect their own. For example, during Alan's assault trial (for choking Sandra after their separation), his sister was prepared to provide him with an alibi until she discovered that two other people were testifying to the fact that they saw Alan choke Sandra. (Alan's sister had already given a statement to the police saying that he had been with her at the time of the alleged crime. She recanted only after she became aware of the other testimony.) Since many of the families were unwilling to discuss the abuse for whatever reason, much of what is known of these relatives is secondhand and is quite likely biased.

Even those who spoke on the issue tended to avoid confronting the issue head-on. They were willing to talk about "marital problems" or "difficulties" but would not use the terms "abuse" or "wife beating." Several fathers and brothers (and one sister) insisted that the marriage in question was normal but added that their son or brother may, from time to time, be a "bit too strict." In one case, family members tried to minimize the actions of the males by explaining that "the boys get a bit rough but they don't mean anything by it."

The majority of the families already had a history of abuse. Margaret's husband, for example, used to tell her stories about being abused by his father, whom he characterized as a strict[5] disciplinarian. Two of Alan's brothers also grew up to abuse their spouses. Alan's father too was described as a disciplinarian who regularly "spanked" all of his children. Philip, an abusive husband who spent time in jail for assaults against his wife, described his home life:

> My parents were always yelling. My father would throw things around—usually my mother's stuff. They'd hit and kick each other. It was crazy. I used to go for long walks to get some quiet time.

Charles, involved with a therapy group for abusive men, presented a similar situation:

> My parents fought. Well, no. My dad fought. Mom just sat there and took it. Sometimes he'd beat her up, storm out of the house and go get drunk. Those nights were the worst cause after Dad left, she'd come to my room and beat on me. I can still hear her saying: "I'm staying with him because of you. This is all your fault."

Of course, in some cases abusive men came from functional, non-abusive homes. Those parents or siblings from the functional homes usually described the future abuser in terms of extensive histories of juvenile violence.

> We could never keep a pet around the house. They'd always go missing. My husband and I suspected John was doing something to them but we could never catch him at it.

That was what one mother best remembered of her son's childhood. A father spoke of the damage his son did:

> He was a holy terror, always on the edge. He had such a temper and any little thing would set him off. He'd put his fist through a wall or a window. I must've replaced fifty or sixty window panes that he broke.
>
> One time, he had this awful tantrum. It was, I guess, what you'd call a rampage. He went from room to room throwing things, stomping on things. He seemed totally out of control, but you

know, later when I was looking at the mess, no thing of his had been damaged, not one.

A stepmother of one abuser reflected on the actions of her stepson:

> I met Paul when he was eight years old. At the time, his parents were going through an amicable divorce, amicable, I think, for them but definitely not for the children. It must have been a confusing, horrific time for both children. Paul, the oldest, was introverted and academically brilliant. He was a likable boy but regularly led his younger sister on escapades that put them both in trouble and made it difficult to locate baby-sitters willing to take them on. I think even then Paul was acting out his anger and frustration with the adult world that turned his inside out.
>
> When Paul's dad began dating me and I was included in some family outings, Paul invariably wrecked them. Again, looking back on this, I think Paul was demonstrating his anger with a situation beyond his control.
>
> As Paul grew, he became fascinated with violence in movies. I recall when he was fifteen or sixteen, he actually made me nervous with his enthusiasm for movie violence. We even talked about this and, understanding my fears, he said, "Oh, but I'd never be violent against someone."
>
> Paul's mother took a job in a distant city and, in moving away, gave Paul's dad sole custody of the children. Paul never spoke about how this may have affected him but surely there may have been a feeling of abandonment.
>
> Our home was never a battleground. I think Paul's dad and I may have disagreed twice in front of Paul and his sister. Either my husband or I was at home when the children returned from school. We never drank or carried on in any violent manner. In fact, my stepson referred to me as "Goody Two Shoes."
>
> As Paul grew into a tall seventeen-year-old, he was lazy and lovable. His sense of humor was and is wonderful. He began dating and moved into his girlfriend's home town to be closer to her, and inevitably, she became pregnant. His wedding plans were disrupted when his girlfriend charged him with assault. I have spoken with the girl's mother and she told me that Paul had also been abusive to his girlfriend's younger sister. At that point I was not surprised, as shortly before Paul had met the young woman, he had disagreed with me strongly enough that he had threatened me.
>
> Today, the baby is calling somebody else "Daddy" and Paul has suffered, as he lost "the woman he loved" and his baby daughter. He moved away, sought help from a counselor for anger

management, and began a new job. Paul is sorry for his actions. I can't say that any one thing caused Paul to be abusive, although he may have finally been acting out all the anger he carried around. I do know that in an abusive situation, everyone loses. Paul did.

In one case, the husband's mother clearly blamed her son for his and his wife's marital problems, including the abuse. "He's no good. He's a bum. I don't know how she put up with him for so long." However, since those words were spoken in the presence of her former daughter-in-law,[6] there may have been a hidden agenda. It has been documented that in divorce situations where there are children involved and the wife gets custody, as was the case here, the husband's mother will side with the wife in order to maintain access to her grandchildren (Johnson 1993: 172; also see Johnson and Barer 1987).

This points out perhaps the biggest impact that the abuser's family members live with. When the marriage breaks down, the paternal grandparents (and aunts and uncles) of children born into the abusive marriage lose, or have seriously curtailed their contact with those children. To many, this is a serious problem. In order to prevent it from occurring, they will side with their daughter-in law, as in the case cited above, or pressure the daughter-in-law into staying with her husband despite the abuse. Several times women suggested that their mothers-in-law would use guilt, as in "The children need a father. Stay for the sake of the children," or promises, as in "We'll talk to him. We'll keep him in line," in order to prevent the marriage breakup and the subsequent loss of contact with their grandchildren.

Of the Abused Woman. The immediate families of the abused women can be divided into two camps based on whether that family had a history of domestic violence or not, because the reactions of the families to the abuse tended to parallel that division. Those families with a history of abuse tended to react much the same way the dysfunctional families of the abuser did (see previous section) while those that did not have a history of abuse reacted quite differently.[7]

The families with histories of abuse tended to discount or deny any wrongdoing and viewed the relationship as normal. In many instances, they applied pressure on the wife (their daughter or sister) to remain in the relationship. One father told his daughter that he would disown her if she left her husband. Another threatened to tell her husband if she didn't quit complaining about being beaten.

Families without abusive histories tended to be much more supportive. Both mothers and fathers of abused women encouraged their daughters to leave the marriage, as did a number of siblings. One brother gave an abused woman (his sister) a room in his home and found her a job in his company. Several others offered to go "knock some sense into" the abusive husband. In general, these family members did whatever they could to help.

Also, as the parents and siblings of an abused woman became aware of the abuse, they suffered emotionally. They could not understand why their daughter or sister would choose to remain with an abuser. Some even accepted some of the guilt: "He seemed like such a nice boy. I could kick myself for encouraging her to marry him." However, this guilt seems to be a natural reaction. The fact that their daughter is in an abusive relationship suggests, to them, that they failed to protect their daughter.

Despite the emotional and mental anguish the family of the abused daughter/sister suffers during the relationship, they rebound quickly once the relationship is ending or has ended. Their attitude becomes optimistic and hopeful. "She'll be back on her feet in no time. You'll see. Everything will be just fine" was a frequently offered perspective. Several parents did say they had one regret. They all wished their daughters had talked to them, told them about the abuse, sooner. "She should have told us. I'd had that bum tossed in jail years ago. But instead, it takes six years before she comes to us. God, what a waste." Brothers and sisters echoed that same sentiment.

OTHER RELATIVES

Research in this area was quite limited and certainly should be treated as tenuous at best. "Other relatives" were defined as anyone (other then the abused woman's or the abusive husband's parents and siblings) who considered themselves related, either by blood or by marriage, to either person in the abusive relationship. Their input was focused on (a) spousal abuse in general, and (b) the specific abusive relationship of the couple to whom they were related.

In the first case, they see spousal abuse much the same way as the general public does. Either they don't think about it much, or they are aware of the problem but have no specific knowledge about it. With regard to the specific abusive relationship, there is a strong tendency to minimize it. "They are having marital problems, but everyone does from time to time. I'm sure they'll work it out." Some deny it altogether. "He was brought up right. He'd never hit a woman." In only one instance was there a clear recognition that there was a serious problem in the relationship. However, even in that one case, the relative echoed a sentiment that they all seemed to hold: "It is their problem. If they want help they can ask, but until then we won't interfere."

These relatives tend to be only peripherally involved with the couple, seeing them more or less only at family functions and special occasions. As peripheral players, they exhibit no intense emotions when discussing the couple. In addition, their impact on the abusive relationship is minimal, as is the impact of the abusive relationship on them.

The Friends

There is a certain similarity between the friends' and families' reactions to abuse. The nature of the reaction seemed to center around the gender of the friend and the member of the abusive relationship whose friend they considered themselves to be. For example, male friends of the husband tended to minimize the abuse or offer justifications such as "he has been under a lot of pressure at work lately." A friend that does not sympathize quickly ceases to be a friend. Also, most male friends of the husband do not attach much importance to the societal problem of domestic violence.

Women, usually friends of the wife, are much more sympathetic to the wife's dilemma. As soon as the wife introduces the topic, the friends offer help, advice, or whatever the woman needs. They appear to be as ready to help as the wife's family and, in some cases, are able to contribute more and help more. One friend stated:

> Theresa first went to live with her parents but her husband kept going over there, hassling everyone. So I got her to move in with me. Then he couldn't find her. It was a lot safer for everybody.

When the abusive relationship ends, friends of the wife play a major role, largely as emotional supports, although they often contribute materially as well. Frequently they let the wife talk without judging her or her actions. Since friends are often of approximately the same age and background as the wife, they are most likely to empathize and understand, something the parents, being of a different generation, may not be able to do as well. Repeatedly, women who had left their abusive husbands and built new lives for themselves attributed their success to a network of friends (often only one or two close friends) who stuck by them.

Theresa spent several months in Barbara's apartment after leaving her husband. It was a difficult time for her.

> Some nights I'd wake up screaming. Barb'd be there to hold me. I'd get so depressed that I wanted to kill myself. She'd take me to a movie or distract me somehow. We went to a lot of movies. When I wanted to talk, she'd listen, sometimes for hours. If it weren't for Barb, I'd never have made it.

It appears that none of the emotions and reactions discussed above surfaced until the abusive relationship was at or near its end. Prior to that, most friends claimed to have no knowledge of the problem. "I knew they were having troubles but I had no idea he was beating her." Or, if they were suspicious, there was never any confirmation of the suspicions. Phrases like "we never talked about it" and "it never came up" were quite common indicating that a taboo exists against talking (even with close friends) about abuse.

In an earlier example ("Individualism and Independence," Chapter Two), a case was discussed wherein an abused wife was unable to talk to her female friend about the abuse. The friend gradually withdrew from the friendship rather than watch her friend suffer. This kind of thing turned out to be fairly common for both the wife and the abusive husband. Sam used to socialize with a co-worker until that co-worker began bragging about beating his wife.

> He seemed like a nice guy but once, after a few beers, he talked about his wife, what a bitch she was and how he had to "clean her clock" every now and again to keep her in line. It was upsetting. The guy was nuts. The next time he asked me if I wanted to go for a beer, I told him I'd quit drinking.

Sam explained that the topic was uncomfortable. "Who needs to hear about someone beating his wife? It's barbaric!"

On the other side of the friendship, when the abuser brings up the topic and the listener reacts badly, the abuser will usually terminate the friendship by dismissing the male listener as a "fag" or "wimp."[8] Apparently, some abusers feel the need to talk about the wife beating but do not want to be taken to task over it. They want a sympathetic ear.

The abused wife talks about the abuse to her friends only at or near the end of the relationship. She does not talk about it before that time. It is too embarrassing, too personal, too painful. Further, she is not prepared to discuss it even if the friend brings it up. Indeed, there were numerous examples of wives terminating friendships as soon as the friend broached the subject of their abuse: "It was none of her business. I didn't want her talking about my personal life all over town. I told her to leave me alone."

This kind of withdrawal seems to be a kind of defense mechanism. The abused wives have created an accommodation in their own minds. Some have convinced themselves that their relationship with their husband is normal, or that they still have some control over the situation. Others have developed a dependence on their abusive spouse. All are unprepared to face the fact that they had a serious problem. Rather than face that issue, they end the relationship with the friend who brought it up. In some cases, they become extremely angry and resentful at the friend's interference in their personal lives. As one friend put it:

I went from her closest friend to public enemy number one in a fraction of a second. To hear her talk, I was the worst person in the world and all I did was offer to help. She made it clear she never wanted to see me again. We never did get together after that. It was like she was a whole different person, not the person I knew.

Perhaps those friends who are reluctant to discuss the abuse are correct. If they want to maintain a friendship with the abused wife (and by doing so be in a position to help when asked), they need to "bite their tongues" and remain silent. But that too is not without risk—the risk that comes with waiting too long:

I still blame myself. Sheila was in trouble. Her husband was beating her and it was getting worse every day, or so it seemed. I used to stay up nights asking myself, "Should I call her. Should I go over there and get her?" One night, I couldn't stand it any longer. I called, but the police answered. She was in intensive care at the hospital. I found out later he'd beaten her with a bat. She died three days later. I cried for weeks.

In many cases, the abused woman becomes quite adept at hiding the bruises and keeps her suffering a secret. Her friends do not realize or even suspect that she is being abused. One of the authors recalled a discussion she had had with four other women, all close friends. The topic of spousal abuse came up, and three of the four admitted their ex-husbands had abused them. No one in this circle of friends had suspected that any of the others had been abused. That was one aspect of their lives that they had not shared. As Margaret put it:

I was in an abusive relationship for more than twenty-four years. During that time, I slowly distanced myself from my husband, but I knew that as long as I was with him, I had to protect him from public criticism. So I did. I don't think any of my friends really suspected what was happening behind closed doors.

Societal Impact

Wife abuse affects many people in addition to those who are directly and personally involved with it. The cumulative impact affects the general public and society at large. Many analysts express the impact in terms of dollars and cents. However, attaching an economic cost to it fails to describe the true nature of the problem. In fact, by placing such a value on human suffering trivializes it. As Chapman pointed out:

> The situation of the wife who is beaten with such regularity that she no longer thinks of herself as a person ... [is a tragedy that has] more than economic consequences (1978: 251–2).

If someone is beaten and so misses work for a day, one could argue that the cost of that beating in strict economic terms is equal to the lost wages. But if she is beaten on Saturday and is well enough to go to work on Monday as usual, does that mean that the beating carries no cost?

In newspapers and other media, the impact of a problem is often measured in economic terms and summed up in a single statement. Unemployment costs the government x billions of dollars every year. The "war on drugs" costs the tax payers y trillion dollars annually. Aside from being an artificial measure based on estimates and projections, this kind of impact statement is rendered meaningless to the average citizen simply because the numbers are too large to be comprehended. A billion dollars, or a billion anything, is a meaningless quantity because an ordinary person cannot conceive of it. This is illustrated easily by advertising techniques used to solicit contributions to fight famine (or another world problem). An advertisement that tells the viewer to send money because two million people are starving to death will not bring in as many donations as one that pictures a single emaciated child and says something like "Jorge is starving. Help us feed him."

The impact of spousal abuse is immense, but it is also insidious. Beyond filling hospitals with injured women and courts and jails with abusive men, it teaches children that violence is acceptable behavior and destroys the concept of the family as a "safe haven" protected from the violent world outside it. Indeed, given the increases that are being recorded in spousal and child abuse, the family is becoming more dangerous than the world outside. Also, the loss of potential that occurs must be considered. How can one measure what a child raised in an abusive family could have achieved, had he or she been raised in a normal, non-abusive household, against his or her real achievements? It is beyond calculation.

One group of people who are affected greatly by wife abuse consists of those who have some official or acknowledged connection to the spousal abuse problem. They can be divided into two broad categories. The first group intervenes to get between the abuser and his victim. The second group provides support for the victim, and sometimes for the abuser as well.

Intervention

There are basically two forms of intervention. There are people who intervene—that is, position themselves between the abuser and the victim—on behalf of the legal system. They are required by law to intervene on behalf of both or either party. The other set of people who intervene are not required to do so—and in most instances cannot do so—until they are asked by one or both parties involved.[9] Decisions made by the first group are legally binding on the parties (with some exceptions), whereas any decisions arrived at by the second group are not binding at all.

LEGAL INTERVENTION
The judicial system has an interest in keeping the peace and protecting its citizens from violations of their rights and physical well-being. The point at which the judicial system can intervene is codified into a set of laws that also stipulate the form the intervention must take and the steps that follow the intervention. There are three sections of the judicial system that intervene as part of their mandated duties. The police are the front-line troops. They intervene immediately. If the dispute must go beyond police involvement, lawyers get involved. On behalf of each party, they prepare to take that next step, which is to involve the courts so that there may be a legally recognized and sanctioned resolution with the full weight of the judicial system behind it. Naturally, some instances call for a different order and some even circumvent one of the levels, but the sequence described above is by far the most common. The complete process may involve a

number of interventions at any or all of the judicial levels, and may take many years to complete.

Police. The police are extensively involved in the problem of spousal abuse. For example, in 1992 it was noted that one in five (20 percent) of all aggravated assaults reported to police in the United States were aggravated assaults in the home (Senate Judiciary Committee 1992). Yet it has been suggested that the police are the worst people to be involved. Although things have changed and more women are becoming police officers, the police force is still a male bastion and many of its members have been socialized with the belief that in normal marriages, the husband is the boss and the wife is his subordinate. This results in a somewhat laid-back approach to spousal abuse (Martin 1978: 116). Many of the officers seem to think that, within certain limits, the husband has the right to "discipline" his wife. Some of the older officers passively resist the procedural changes that have been made in the past ten years or so because they find them ridiculous.

> They want us to charge every husband who messes up his wife's hair with assault. If we did that, we'd be in the station filling out paperwork all the time—leaving the streets free for all the real criminals.

Some of the new officers, including some of the women, are learning the "old boy" tricks and applying them, although we suspect they are using them for different reasons. A two-year rookie from Washington said:

> Weekends are bad. Drug dealers, rapists, murderers, prostitutes, muggers, they're all out there. I'd rather be hunting them down but, because I'm female and new to the force, I get a lot of the crud calls. Last Friday, I was given a dozen DDs [Domestic Disturbance calls]. I was tied up the whole shift while the other officers made a really great drug bust.

Some younger officers who feel they are missing all the action resent the domestic disturbance calls they get and use little tricks to speed them up. For example, they know that if they charge the abuser, it will take up to two hours to process him and file the reports, so they avoid laying a charge. One favorite method works if there are young children in the house. The officer lets the couple know that if one of them is to be charged, both are to be charged with disturbing the peace. At that point, the abused wife will back down rather than risk leaving her children alone in the house.

> You also take your time getting to the scene. That way you don't actually see any crime being committed. It becomes her word against his. She's less likely to press charges.
>
> My partner likes to arrive at the house with the siren going. That way, the people have a warning and a chance to settle down and clean things up before we get in the door.

Since many jurisdictions have implemented policies that state that the police must charge the aggressor in a domestic dispute automatically, the police tactics have changed a bit. More abusive husbands are being arrested but already some police officers have developed ways around the new policy. One officer from a southeastern state was quite candid:

> Most of our DDs are repeat customers. Every Friday night, we used to get a call from this woman. Her husband was beating on her. We'd go over there and the law says we have to arrest someone. So, this one time, we arrest her. She'd pushed him first. We took her downtown and gave her the full treatment. She still calls us, but not so often now—maybe once or twice a month instead of every week.

Although some police officers are sympathetic towards the husband or don't take the problem of spousal abuse very seriously, most officers are concerned and caring. They do not like men who beat up women. These officers welcomed the new policy concerning automatic arrests. An officer in Montana, a 15–year veteran, summed up the general perspective:

> We used to watch this guy get away with thrashing his wife time and time again. The wife was so terrified of him she wouldn't dare press charges. Man, you should have seen the relief in her eyes and the fear in his when we told him we had a new policy and hauled his butt off to jail. We've had a lot less trouble with him since then.

They like the new policy. They see it working but they still don't like domestic disturbance calls. Many officers think domestic disturbance calls are the most dangerous calls to get. They would rather be called to a murder scene or a hostage situation than a domestic disturbance, because with the former types of calls they at least have some idea of what they are getting into. Every officer has heard a story about an officer who was killed during a domestic disturbance by the person he was trying to protect. While he was trying to subdue a violent husband, the wife shot, stabbed, or bludgeoned the officer to death, depending on the version of the story. The story has assumed mythical proportions, and it colors the way the police handle domestic disturbance calls. "I never go in alone, no matter what. I always wait for backup." "Every time I get a DD, my gut flips over. I think, is this the one? Do I buy it on this one?"

The fear of domestic disturbances is real, and it is also understandable. The officers must enter a location, usually a residence, because someone has called them. Since the caller usually is not directly connected to the disturbance, the police officers have absolutely no information about the situation.[10] Police officers fear this unknown factor, since a domestic disturbance can be any crime being committed inside a residence. The legendary story of the officer killed by the wife, in our estimation, is a metaphor for that unknown factor. It warns the officers to be ready for anything but does not necessarily reflect reality in terms of spousal abuse calls. Abused wives do sometimes attack their "rescuers," but it happens only rarely.

That the police are not necessarily the best people to be involved in spousal abuse cases has already been suggested. The reasons given for that statement—that is, the cavalier way some officers approach those kinds of cases—are no longer true. The police in most, if not all, of the jurisdictions recognize the problem as serious and do their best to help victims of spousal abuse. However, we tend to agree that the police are not the ones who should be involved. Our reason, though, has more to do with the general mandates of police forces than the individual police officers.

The officers are there to "keep the peace." The simple existence of a policing body with the legitimate right to enforce the laws is sufficient deterrent to keep the majority of citizens in line. However, some people do break the law and the police try to "catch them in the act" or track them down after the fact and punish them for violating the "good order" of society. They perform a valuable service to the community. However, the fact that most crime is episodic is problematic. If one robs a bank or mugs someone, the crime occurs within a certain short period of time. A bank robber commits a crime only when he or she is inside the bank robbing it. The thief is technically a law-abiding citizen both before and after the criminal episode. Because most crimes are episodic in nature, the police perceive all crime—including spousal abuse—as "criminal acts." When they go to a domestic dispute, they rescue the victim, arrest the perpetrator, and "the peace has been restored." As far as the police are concerned, that is the end of it.

Spousal abuse, however, is not an episodic crime but a process that can last for many years or decades. The police are not equipped to deal with nonepisodic crimes. Anecdotal evidence suggests the police, in doing their job and dealing with the violent episode, contribute to the acceleration of the cycle of abuse and render the wife's situation more dangerous.

> You called the cops cause I tapped you a couple of times. I had to spend the night in jail with a bunch of drunks and perverts 'cause of you. I'm going to show you what a real beating is.

Thus did Ted forewarn his wife, Yvonne, before he beat her so severely she had to be hospitalized for a week. The police had arrested him for assaulting Yvonne around midnight. In the morning, a judge released him because (a) the jail was full, and (b) he had no criminal record. The police treatment of the abuse as episodic ended the initial beating but humiliated and angered Ted, who, as is typical of many abusers, did not believe he had done anything wrong. The judicial system then set him free to take his anger and frustration out on his wife. Police policy and perception have to take some of the blame for the second beating.

Some officers know that they sometimes make matters worse, and they are affected by that knowledge. One put it quite eloquently:

Yeah, it gets to me. The women look at me as if to say "What in hell are you doing?" They are absolutely terrified of their husbands.

Now, after we put the abuser in the car, I sit down with the wife and lay it on the line. I say "Look, lady, we're going to keep him for six, eight hours max. When we kick him loose, he's going to be really pissed at you. You need to get out of here. All we can give you is an eight-hour head start." Sometimes they take my advice. Sometimes they don't. That's all I can do.

As a final comment on this, perhaps the fear of retribution is one of the reasons that some women attack police officers who have come to rescue them from their abusive husbands. Perhaps they think that "if I defend him now, maybe he won't be so hard on me when he gets back home."

Another point to be made concerning the effectiveness of the police in spousal abuse cases relates to individual rights, which, in our opinion, hamstring the officers. They know that if they are going to help prevent further violence against the woman, they need to separate the husband and wife. Many officers say that they would love to do that. They would like to take the abuser "by the scruff of the neck and boot him out into the street" and tell him never to come back. However, the abuser has a legal right to live in his own home, and if he refuses to leave, there is nothing the police can legitimately do to force him out. In order to separate the couple, they must then convince the wife to leave. That is a difficult task, since the wife is being asked to give up everything—the house, furnishings, everything—to gain her own safety. It amounts to a punishment for getting beaten up.

Lawyers. The lawyers represent either the abusive husband or the abused wife whenever some step must be taken that involves the courts.[11] A lawyer is responsible for protecting the client's interest in the specific matters before the courts, and for guiding the client through the proper judicial channels. They are perhaps one of the few groups of people who do not act on their own feelings.

I represent a lot of abusive husbands because they, like all of us, should have their rights protected and have a fair hearing before the courts. I don't have to like them or what they've done, but I will defend them.

Interestingly, it seems that abusive husbands tend to use lawyers to defend themselves against legal actions initiated by others—specifically, criminal assault charges initiated by the police and prosecutors, and divorce proceedings filed by the wife—while the wife uses lawyers to start legal actions such as restraining orders and divorce petitions. This suggests that once lawyers become involved, there is a significant loss of the husband's control. He is no longer dominating his wife and initiating all actions, but instead must react to her initiatives to gain control over her life and the assets they once shared. However, the lawyers selected by the husband tend to be more experienced (and more expensive) than those selected by the wife, because when the wife seeks to end a typical abusive situation, she has left the household and he has retained control over most or all of the family assets.[12]

Abused women and their advocates tend to be somewhat resentful of lawyers for two reasons: (1) The lawyers represent their abusive husbands and so are seen as taking his side. The lawyer has become the enemy in that case (as is anyone who takes his side rather than hers); (2) Lawyers are among the few professionals who make money out of spousal abuse cases, money that comes directly from the pockets of the people involved. For the women, such an expense can be a serious hardship.

> I was getting $850 a month from Welfare for me and my child. Even living in subsidized housing, it's pretty well gone by the end of the month. The first lawyer I went to wanted $900 up front. I cried. I finally found one willing to wait until the divorce was settled to get paid, but I had to promise him a lot more than $900.

That is a fairly typical position for the abused woman, and she resents it. She realizes that her husband will be using their combined assets to hire a more expensive, and therefore presumably better, lawyer. And not only is his better lawyer going to get a settlement that is more favorable to him than to her, but there will be less money to divide because he is using it on the lawyer.

The women seem disappointed in a judicial system that forces them to pay to recover assets and personal objects that are already rightfully theirs. That disappointment manifests itself as resentment towards the people to whom they have to give the money—the lawyers.

In general, most lawyers are unaffected by spousal abuse. They concentrate on the legal aspects of getting what the client deserves (a fair trial, a reasonable divorce settlement) and do not concern themselves too much with the broader implications of the social problem.

> If I let all that stuff get to me, I'd be a mess myself. I want just enough information from my client to go after her husband, no more.

To be fair to the lawyers, it should be noted that the only time a lawyer deals with an abused woman is when the woman is seeking a divorce or a restraining order, which requires a divorce petition to activate. The lawyers are then focusing on the divorce and not the abuse, unless that abuse is being used to justify the divorce or divorce settlement. Those lawyers who do involve themselves with abuse or assault in the criminal courts are almost always working for the abuser, since a victim such as the abused woman rarely requires legal representation. Even then the lawyer is concentrating on the defense against the assault charge rather than the broader issue of spousal abuse. They intervene, but they are not personally or emotionally associated with the issue.

One lawyer did become personally involved in the issue. An active campaigner in the push to change the laws relating to spousal abuse, she admitted that when a woman comes to her for divorce papers and the marriage was an abusive one, her rates drop significantly.

> I charge as little as I can, and in some cases I do it pro bono because I know how tight money can be for them. I have to take a lot of other cases to be able to afford to represent these women.

Further discussions with her eventually revealed her motivation. She had been abused by her ex-husband. She has a personal interest in the issue.

The Courts. Two divisions of the courts are involved in spousal abuse, but like the lawyers, they never deal with it directly. The criminal court tries husbands who have been charged with various kinds of assault or murder with the wife as the victim. There is no charge of "spousal abuse" in any criminal code that was examined. Under some circumstances, the issue of abuse can be introduced during a trial, but usually only when and if the defendant had previous convictions for similar violent crimes against his wife. The civil court deals with divorce proceedings, but again it is one step removed from the issue. Indeed, since the lawyers generally work out a settlement before going to court, this section of the judicial system generally does not even see the divorcing couple. Only rarely do they appear before the court.

With regard to the criminal court, there has been considerable concern over the attitudes of prosecutors and judges have relating to spousal abuse. In 1991, on the same day but in two different courts in the same jurisdiction, one man was convicted of beating his dog and sentenced to sixty days in jail, while another man was convicted of beating his wife and received a sentence of thirty days to be served on weekends. The message that the courts valued a dog more than a woman was not well received and prompted a public outcry. As a result, the relevant government department began a review of all sentencing procedures. Seven years later, the review is still underway and no changes have yet been made in terms of assaults relating to spousal abuse.

It is likely that some court officials subscribe to the male superiority model and react to wife beating cases accordingly, but others are quite concerned. However, like the police, they are limited by law in what they can do about it.

GENERAL INTERVENTION
Many abused women, and some abusive men, have occasion to seek various kinds of help for themselves or their relationship that do not involve the criminal justice system. The assistance they need can range from medical care to advice.

Doctors and Other Medical Personnel. Abused women probably see medical personnel more than any other outsider. In a typical abusive relationship, the woman will be beaten so severely that she will require emergency medical treatment. When the relationship changes (that is, when she becomes pregnant or threatens to leave, or the abuser feels a need to escalate the abuse for some other reason), she will require medical treatment on a fairly regular basis. Interestingly, the beatings always seem to stop short of completely incapacitating the victim. She is always sufficiently ambulatory to get to the hospital. Generally, this appears to be a conscious intention of the abuser, who wants to avoid an ambulance call and the automatic investigation that goes with it.[13]

Although it is not yet legally mandated in most jurisdictions, there is tremendous pressure on the medical community to report any cases of suspected abuse. They are told, according to one informant, to look for patterns in the hospital visits (every other Friday, for example) and for patterns in the injuries. For example, if a woman shows up repeatedly with the same arm broken each time, that is supposed to trigger a report.[14]

Currently, the push is to have doctors or nurses report suspected abuse, which creates an awkward situation for everyone involved because these reports go to the police, who may or may not do anything about it. If they do, they may handle the situation improperly. Many of the doctors were quite willing to file the necessary reports but expressed doubts about police follow-ups. One provides spousal abuse information to the wife in her office and offers to contact a shelter for her, but refuses to inform the police of any suspected cases.

> No way! That's a sure way to get her killed. I reported one a few years ago. Turns out she was the wife of the cop who came to take the report. I ended up treating her again the next day. She was a mess.

Some are reluctant to get involved because of the general belief that what goes on inside a family is private.

> I have to ask, so I ask her if she is being abused. If she says yes, I call the police for her and they take over. If she says no, I believe her even if I know better. I am not getting into the middle of a domestic dispute.

Now that doctors and nurses are, by and large, asking questions relating to spousal abuse, there is a new trend developing among abused wives. They know that the medical personnel are going to be suspicious if anyone shows up in their emergency ward too often, so they are now performing their own triage. They determine the extent of their own injuries and generally will not seek medical help if they think they can handle it themselves. This, of course, increases the danger of untreated internal injuries. If they decide that medical treatment is unavoidable, they will go to different hospitals, sometimes many miles away. That way, no one hospital or clinic has a complete record of her injuries and no one will ask embarrassing questions.

> I kept a list of all the hospitals in a sixty-mile area. When he'd hurt me, I'd go to the next place on the list. That way, I'd only show up in one emergency room every three or four months, not often enough to set off any alarms in the doctors' heads. After a while, I started giving them phony names and addresses too. That way, there'd be three or four people with broken arms rather than one person breaking an arm three, four times.

That tactic worked for Phylis for six years until she ran into a doctor who remembered that she'd broken the same arm before. Although, according to Phylis, they joked about her being accident-prone without ever mentioning abuse, the conversation unnerved her.

> It really shook me up. I think it was while he was putting on the cast that I realized I couldn't take it anymore. I left the hospital and drove to my sister's place a hundred miles away. I never gave him another chance to hit me.

We talked to several emergency room staffers who believe that they deal with a huge number of abuse cases. One nurse suggested that whereas most people accidentally break bones or injure themselves during "active" times of the day, a lot of women show up alone needing medical treatment for "accidental" injuries during times the nurse felt were "inactive" times of the day.

> You expect those types of injuries between, say, 7:00 a.m. and 7:00 p.m. That's when most people are out and about. After that, people

settle down, pretty much. But these women show up at midnight saying they were on a ladder cleaning the walls and they fell, or they were picking up stuff and tripped on the stairs. Come on! People don't do that at that time of the night, especially if they are housewives and many of them are.

But you know the dead giveaway for me? They come in alone. At that time of the night, her husband should be at home. If he's home and his wife needs emergency treatment, he's going to drive her. If he doesn't and she's got to go alone, I'll bet you anything he's at home washing her blood off his hands.

The staff know it is a big problem but they don't know what to do about it. Do they report it or not? Do they confront the woman or not? It is very frustrating for them.

Marriage or Family Counselors. He was abusing me and I wanted him to stop, but I didn't want to break up our marriage. He was a really sweet man most of the time. I didn't know what I should do so I called a marriage counselor. Well, he insisted that if he was going to help, we'd both have to go and see him.

Professional counselors have learned that certain approaches work for different situations. Thus marriage counselors work as facilitators for conversations between a wife and a husband, family counselors bring the entire family as a unit into counseling, and individual counselors meet with the client one-on-one to help him or her work through his or her difficulties. Given this knowledge, if a marriage counselor is to help the couple work out their differences, he or she obviously needs to work with both of them at the same time. The counselor referred to in the above quote would have been glad to meet and talk to the woman about dealing with her own feelings, but she made it clear she wanted not to talk about her problems, but to save her marriage.

Several people in the counseling profession admitted that they have not had much success with spousal abuse cases. One said that the profession is not equipped to deal with an individual (the abuser) who as a rule is uncooperative.

I have watched about a dozen women bring their husbands in for a session. His body language is intense and it tells me he is at the session to please his wife, nothing more. He is not ready to talk, nor is he ready to take it seriously. In the twelve cases I've handled, they'll all come once or twice[15] and then he'll find an excuse to stomp out. They won't be back after that.

Abusers sometimes can be convinced by their wives to attend counseling, but only during the "honeymoon stage" of the abuse cycle. A typical abuser wants to show her that he is willing to work on the problems that "make him" abuse her. However, once he gets into the session, he quickly realizes that he cannot control the situation to his satisfaction. As Sam, one such abuser, noted: "She was going to tell him I beat her. That's the same as calling the cops. No way I could let her do that."

Jim took issue with something the counselor said, got angry, and walked out of the session. His wife followed just seconds behind him.

> I told her I thought the guy was a jerk and I wasn't going back to him. If she wanted me to go to more of these things, she'd have to find another one. Of course, I happened to be tied up the next time we had an appointment.

Marriage counseling can help improve married life for many people, but, according to the counselors, both the husband and the wife have to recognize that there are problems, make a sincere effort to resolve the issues, and work together to find mutually acceptable emotional compromises. The professionals readily admitted that abusive husbands are usually not ready to make any effort at all other than showing up at the session, perhaps because the husband does not recognize that there is a problem. These men by and large perceive their marriage to be "normal," and normal couples do not need a counselor. Further, they believe in a male dominance model and "real men" do not need help, especially from "touchy-feely types," "mama's boys," or "fags," labels given to counselors in general by those abusive "real men."

Marriage counselors are asked to intervene, to mediate between spouses, to help the couple work out the differences and "save the marriage." In abusive relationships, they, along with the clergy, are the only ones who will intervene in an attempt to save the marriage. (All others who intervene are committed to protecting the abused wife and urge her to leave the marriage.) Needless to say, regardless of their track record in helping save marriages that are non-abusive, their success rate with abusive marriages is zero.

Clergy. Most churches make strong arguments for the sanctity of marriage and emphasize the need to preserve it. It is a contract made "before God" and should not be broken. Because of this perspective, many churches empower their clergy to intervene on behalf of the church to help save a marriage at risk. Unfortunately, the church does not follow up this empowerment with any significant amounts of training. According to one retired Anglican minister, he was "winging it" his entire career.

> I took some university courses years ago but they were pretty general. The Church sent me on a two-week family counseling course once. The rest I learned by doing.

The clergy who act as counselors must be extremely careful to remain within the spiritual guidelines of their church when offering advice and counseling. A Catholic priest described his dilemma:

> I was talking to a woman I'd known for over ten years. She poured her heart out. Told me about how her husband was beating her. How she went to bed some nights wondering if she'd live till the morning but not really caring if she did. She pleaded with me, begged to be told what to do.
> Every fiber of my being screamed out, "Tell her to ditch the guy! Tell her to go to a shelter, leave him! Now!" but I couldn't. Church policy required us to preserve the marriage. Period. I told her to pray for guidance. Everything would be all right if she did. I have always regretted that!

Most churches, except the ultra-orthodox ones and some of the new "revivalist" or "fundamentalist" sects, are beginning to modify their stance with regard to abusive husbands and now tend to recognize them as special cases. The Catholic Church, for example, sponsors a number of shelters for abused women and offers professional counseling services in some cities. Other denominations are starting to train their clergy more extensively in the counseling area.

In past generations, the clergy were an important resource. They were the first ones turned to in times of family crisis. As one informant, a retired priest, noted, in many of the smaller communities the clergy were often the only resource available. However, church attendance appears to have been steadily declining all across North America, and increasingly, couples and individuals are choosing to go to secular professional counselors for help.[16] Despite the church's changing attitudes and increased training, the involvement of the clergy in marriage counseling is decreasing at a significant rate.

> Things are different now. I used to be really busy helping people who came to me. My appointment book was always full. Today, I am not so busy. Yesterday, my phone never rang. If I want to help people, I have to go looking for them. I volunteer now at a local interdenominational soup kitchen. In the old days, I'd never have been able to find the time.

Abused women who used their clergy offered opinions ranging from "he was a wonderful man and helped me a lot" to "he took my husband's side and as much as said grin and bear it." One woman called her minister a "life saver," while another claimed hers had "done more damage than good." However, despite this wide range of experiences, there was a consistent response to the question "Did your clergyman help you resolve your marital difficulties?" That response was a resounding "No."

Support Personnel

There are quite a few support services available to abused women, as well as some for abusive husbands. Most function at the community level. Others are governmental services administered through regional offices. The community support tends to be direct and personal, and sometimes specializing in serving battered women, while the governmental services tend to be bureaucratic, impersonal, and more general in nature. Both types of support services are useful and fill certain specific needs.

Community Support. Services found at the community level usually provide some form of immediate aid followed up by long-term support, although the emphasis of a particular service is normally one or the other. However, with the exception of emergency shelters, the support available at this level tends to be intangible.

Victims' Services. A relatively new service available in North America, "Victims' Services" are nominally attached to some police forces. In those areas that have such a program, its workers are the first people that abused wives are likely to see. Depending on the type of program, trained volunteers, or more rarely, paid professionals go as "ride-alongs" in designated police cars or operate out of a central office such as a room in the police station or city hall. When the police are called to a crime scene and there is clearly a traumatized victim, usually a woman, the officers will call for their "victims' services" team.

In order of frequency, victims' services personnel are called to assaults, sexual assaults (including but not limited to rape), burglaries (of residences of women who live alone or with children), child abuse, and murders (when the wife or some other significant female discovers the crime). Basically, they are called in whenever there is a victim who has been traumatized physically or emotionally. Their involvement permits the police officers to focus on the job they were trained to do while recognizing the needs of the victim by having a person there exclusively for that purpose. In cases of spousal abuse, it has become standard practice in some jurisdictions to call in the Victims' Services if the husband is arrested. If the husband is not arrested and remains in the home, the Victims' Services remain uninvolved.

This service is relatively new with less than 10 percent of major centers using it so far. Funding is shaky at best, and certainly less than generous. In at least one center, some funding comes from the government but most is provided by private charitable donations. One Victims' Services volunteer expressed concern:

> I don't get paid but there are all kinds of costs to cover. Simple things like telephone calls and gas for the car. How can I get to

the victim if the tank is empty? We lose a lot of volunteers because on top of having to work with traumatized victims, you can get all stressed out because there's no money for gas and we've had to put off training a new guy 'cause it isn't in the budget. It's always tense.

When these people work with abused wives, they are trained to make information on shelters available and offer to take the woman to one. They realize that immediately after a beating, few women, or few people for that matter, are capable of rational thought or coherent planning. Trauma tends to kick the brain into a kind of mental shock that insulates the person from the pain. It can take several hours for it to wear off but by then, in all likelihood, the husband will be back at home. The women who had had contact with the Victims' Services were generally appreciative and highly valued the "on-scene" service.

> He told me about the shelter and I knew I wanted to go there but it was like my tongue was numb. I couldn't talk. He then offered to drive me over. I nodded—and even that took a major effort—and off we went. He was wonderful. Without him, I would've just sat there and waited for my husband to come home the way I'd done dozens of times before.

Another said that the Victims' Services worker called her sister and sat with her until she arrived.

The Victims' Services program shows promise but it is too early to evaluate its overall effectiveness. The victims in general (not just the abused women) seem to be in favor of it, and the police officers generally welcome it and want to see more of it. The only problem is political resistance from a financial perspective. With budgets already strained at all governmental levels, politicians are reluctant to commit themselves to the expenditure.

Shelter Workers. If an abused wife decides to leave her husband and does not have access to family close by or to some financial resources, her only option is to go to a shelter. There she can obtain a safe place to live as well as food, clothing, and other necessities. The shelter provides her with time away from her husband so she can assess her relationship with him and her life in general in a secure environment. Frequently, the woman will arrive on the shelter's doorstep in need of all of these things. Sandra, for example, arrived with her daughter and one garbage bag filled mostly with her daughter's clothing.

The shelter staff, over and above providing the basic necessities, try to coordinate the overall "help package." They will set up appointments with counselors, guide a woman through the government bureaucracy, refer her to a reputable divorce lawyer, and the like. The shelter provides the foundation upon which the abused woman can build the rest of her life.

Despite all this, emergency housing and personal security are the shelter's primary concerns. Because of that, there is a great deal of suspicion of strangers. No one can find out who is living at a particular shelter at a particular time. All shelter records are confidential and available to no one except shelter staff and the woman herself, who has access to only her own file. Shelter workers are reluctant to talk to anyone about the shelter or about the clients, even in general terms. This caution is necessary, as there have been many instances when a husband has tried to locate his wife in order to "drag her home" or punish her for leaving him. It has already been noted that the time at which a woman is likely to seek the protection of a shelter, the first few weeks and months after the breakup of the relationship, is by far the most dangerous time for the woman.

Shelter workers, the majority of whom are women with perhaps as many as one-quarter having been abused themselves, are usually doing the job they love—helping women in distress— but rarely do they manage to sustain the professional detachment necessary to the job. Most are affected by the "horror stories" they hear and by the physical and emotional damage they witness in the course of their day. They must use some type of defense mechanism to protect themselves, and they do so with varying degrees of success. Some retreat into bureaucracy. Some retreat into themselves. Others quit their jobs; still others try to kill themselves. The helping professions, which include shelter workers as well as other social workers, doctors, nurses, and psychologists, among others, have a rate of suicide and attempted suicide significantly higher than the national average in either the United States or Canada.[17] Mary, a former shelter worker, discussed her suicide attempt:

> When I was married I was abused, but I eventually divorced him. I survived. I decided to help other women do the same and so I got my degree and got a job at the shelter. I'd listen to the women's stories and every one of them tore my heart out. It'd be lying there on the table bleeding, but I'd have to pick it up and put it back in because it was time to talk to another woman.
>
> Every night I'd go home exhausted. I'd fall asleep on the couch and dream. In those dreams, everything that had been done to the women was done to me by my ex-husband. I'd wake up screaming. I'd be afraid to go back to sleep. One night, I woke up. I was drenched in sweat. My heart was racing. I was so damn tired. I wanted to sleep. I had to, so I took all the sleeping pills I had, maybe a dozen. I lay down knowing I was going to have a long, long sleep.

She woke late the next morning, rested but unharmed. She had not taken enough pills to kill herself, but the pills gave her enough rest to enable her to think clearly. She left the shelter and started her own daycare center. She sleeps better now.

Psychologists/Psychiatrists. Most psychologists and psychiatrists are in private practice, but some are employed by agencies which sometimes deal with abused women. Only in the latter case would a battered woman come in contact with these professionals, as the women rarely have the funds to hire a private psychologist. Surprisingly, only one woman had had occasion to work with a psychologist, and that occurred because the psychologist was fresh out of graduate school and had taken a job at the Family Services Clinic temporarily. He was overqualified for the position and certainly did not plan to be with the clinic very long.

It is interesting that there is so little contact between this category of mental health professional and abused women who have been severely traumatized and are in great need of the services those professionals could offer. Perhaps there are parts of North America where battered women can avail themselves of psychological or psychiatric services, but there were apparently no such opportunities where the participants in the study lived.

Counselors. Most wife abuse counselors are not psychologists. Their training consists of either an undergraduate degree in psychology[18] or a two-year diploma in social work. They are not required to treat mental disorders but can deal with emotional problems in one-on-one or group therapy sessions. There seem to be a large number of counselors located in various private and government agencies, and some are available to abused wives at little or no cost. It seems, though, that they and other counselors are little used by the battered women.

Some of the counselors admitted to being unqualified to deal with battered women. One such counselor said:

> I was totally out of my depth there. I had two or three women who were telling me about all the terrible things their husbands had done to them, and they were telling me the reactions they were still having to that stuff even ten years after it stopped. Then they'd look to me for miracles. All I could think to say was "How do you feel about that?" and "Let's explore that a bit more." I felt totally useless and I'm sure I didn't do those women any good.

As one abused wife put it, she tried the counseling route but found it was better to sit down and talk to a good friend over coffee. "At least a friend won't be taking notes. She'll be listening to me." Another suggested that the other abused women living in the same shelter were good to talk to and certainly preferable to a counselor. "They have some idea what you've been through." Some counselors disagree:

> They need a compassionate but detached person to listen to them, not someone who lacks the training to understand. These women have complicated issues to resolve.

In response to that comment, a shelter worker said:

> Nonsense! All you need is some common sense and at least one ear that works. We had one woman who went to a counselor who told her she needed to get more physically active. He recommended a membership in a local health club. He said it'd only cost her about $100 a month and it would be well worth the cost. Ha! That was her entire food budget for the month and then some.

Several shelters are now organizing weekly self-help meetings for their current and former residents. They find them much more effective than the counselors available to them.

Maybe we'll start referring our residents to them again, but first they have a lot more to learn about what it is like to be a battered woman. Right now, they are a resource we are better off without.

Support Groups. Roughly one-third of the abused wives were in some form of self-help or support group. One woman had been attending the same Thursday night session for about ten years.

> When I first went there, I was like a little mouse in the corner. I just sat and listened. Everyone else there knew more than me. Now, I'm the "old lady" and never shut up. There isn't anyone but me left from the group I started with, but that's okay. I'm always meeting new people. I watch out for the first-timer, the little mouse. I sit beside her and smile a lot. I want her to know that I was the mouse but I survived. "I'm okay now but I was once like you." I think that is what a support group is all about.

Each support group has a nominal leader, usually an employee or volunteer attached to the agency or shelter that sponsors the group, who is responsible for booking the room and letting everyone know when and where the meeting is to be held. Originally, they had signed on as facilitators, but there seemed to be little need for a facilitator. The current leader of the Thursday night group laughed when that role was suggested for her.

> Facilitator? Half the time they aren't even aware I'm there. They all arrive and away they go. They are already deep into it before I even get into the room. If I started acting like a facilitator, they'd throw me out.

It was thought that those group leaders and facilitators would be negatively affected by the groups much as other "helpers" are, but that is not the case.

> It's actually uplifting. I'm always really up after one of these sessions. Sure, the stories are awful and it is hard to imagine human

beings doing some of those things, but you should see the love in that room. I watched one woman hug another after she told a particularly horrendous story. After a bit, they were both smiling. The hugs reduce the hurt.

I mean it. These sessions are truly amazing and effective. Every one of the happiest, most optimistic women in this group were, not so long ago, barely human, with self-esteem so low you couldn't find it with a dipstick.

GOVERNMENTAL SUPPORT

There are certain aspects of spousal abuse that require governmental involvement, but there is usually no governmental support specifically for battered women. Instead, their needs are addressed (theoretically) by a number of different departments that do not necessarily communicate with one another very well. Since this type of support tends to be bureaucratic and impersonal, the employees of these services are generally unaffected by the plight of these women. The women are no more than claims to process or applications to consider.

Welfare/Social Assistance. Almost invariably, a woman who leaves her abusive husband does so in a hurry, leaving everything else behind too. Chances are she will be unemployed and broke. She needs money to survive, so she must apply for emergency Social Assistance or Welfare. It would seem logical to assume that such claims would be speedily processed and automatically approved. Unfortunately, that is not the case. First of all, the applications must be filed during office hours and processed in order of receipt. One welfare office had so many applications for assistance (not all from battered women) that they could not guarantee a review of any application for at least three weeks. Second, in some jurisdictions, one must be a resident of the area serviced by a specific Social Assistance branch office for three to six months before they will accept an application for assistance. If, for example, a woman has fled to the home of her sister and she lives in a different district, the woman may be ineligible for help. Third, in some areas, if she has a home to go to (even if it is occupied by an abusive husband), she is automatically ineligible. Acquiring emergency money to live on is not an easy task.

Lack of Support

Despite all the individuals, groups, and agencies actively involved in the problem of wife abuse, the abused women believe, perhaps correctly, that there is only a limited amount of effective support available. As Tammy noted in an earlier chapter: "There is no one out there who can help me so I've got to look after myself." Ultimately, these women have so far had to absorb the huge emotional cost of the abuse all by themselves. While lawmakers and others pontificate and orate on the serious social problem facing our nations, the women are left to fend for themselves.

Notes

1. Violent crime rates in both the United States and Canada appear to have stabilized in 1995 (Leyton 1997: xx).
2. She readily admits that, for some reason probably related to her experience with her abusive husband, her relationships with men rarely last more than a few months.
3. Most of the immigrant women we interviewed were from Central America for a practical reason: one of the authors could speak their language (Spanish), so no translators were needed and the informants could communicate comfortably in their native tongue.
4. As an aside, the authors found that a large number of abused wives who had been out of the abusive situation for a number of years displayed little or no vindictiveness towards their former partners.
5. The use of the word "strict" was frequent. It suggests that what occurred (that is, the abuse) had some legitimacy in that the husband had the right to beat his wife but was a bit over-zealous. The difference between a disciplinarian and a strict disciplinarian is only one of degree rather than type.
6. A group interview was being conducted in the daughter-in law's home at the time.
7. Of course, there are always exceptions to the behavioral patterns. The overlap between history of abuse in the family and reaction to the abuse was not perfect. However, this may have had to do with how long a history of abuse there was in the family. For example, Deborah's family reacted as a typical abuser family would, siding with the abuser and pressuring the wife to remain in the relationship. Sandra's mother, who was also abused, behaved as a member of a family without a history of abuse would be expected to act.

Since Sandra's mother, Margaret, was the first in her family to be abused and Deborah's family has a history of spousal abuse going back at least three generations, the difference in reaction is not surprising.

8. There were no examples of an abuser talking to a female friend about his abusing his wife.

9. There is at least one other way to divide intervenors: on the basis of when they intervene. That is, one group intervenes when there is a person at risk or public disturbance; the second group intervenes at any other time. However, this type of division is not as clear, since the definition of a person at risk is arbitrary and situational. In addition, it would place the police in one group and all others in the second group. In our opinion, the division presented here is more useful.

10. It seems that for every wife who calls in a domestic disturbance, between ten and twenty neighbors call. Thus an estimated 80 to 90 percent of domestic disturbances are "blind calls."

11. Prosecuting attorneys are included in the next section on the courts. In this section, the discussion is limited to lawyers in private practice.

12. Usually the husband has a higher income to use as well. If the wife was not employed outside the home, she generally has little or no money for lawyers.

13. In many counties, a police officer is always dispatched to accompany an ambulance to provide additional assistance if needed, and to determine and report on the nature of the incident that resulted in the injuries.

14. There is anecdotal evidence to suggest that abusers even become habitual during the beatings, often hitting the victim in the same spots and in the same order every time. One informant had her right hand broken five times in two years, while another was punched in the kidneys consistently over a five-year period.

15. Most marriage counselors like to meet with their clients a minimum of eight or ten times. One or two sessions barely form an introduction to the issues.

16. In several major cities in the United States, members of the clergy have noted declining attendance at their church services as well as an "aging" of the attendees—that is, the average age of the people who regularly attend church has been rising. According to Catholic informants, there has been considerable discussion within the church hierarchy about the loss of young parishioners.

17. Suicide prevention specialists suggest that this is because those in the helping professions have no one to turn to for help except themselves.

18. An undergraduate degree (B.A. or B.Sc.) in psychology does not qualify one as a psychologist. At a minimum, one needs one postgraduate degree (M.A. or M.Sc.), although a doctorate (Ph.D.) is preferred. A psychiatrist must have an extensive education in psychology along with a medical degree (M.D.).

Chapter 4

Breaking Away

B ecause of the broad-spectrum impact that spousal abuse has, it should be considered a serious social problem. However, it is not merely an abstract social problem. For the millions of women who have been, are being, or will be abused by their husbands, it is a grave personal problem. They live with it every day and everything they do is affected by it. More to the point, it stays with them, and some of the psychological and emotional damage does not show up until long after the abuse itself has ended. For example, Margaret did not suffer her first anxiety attack until eighteen months after her divorce. "I didn't even realize it was connected to my abusive marriage until I talked to a counselor three years later. I have been away from him for seven years and I'm still trying to deal with all the garbage he planted in my mind." An outreach coordinator for a women's shelter said that "… some 67 percent of battered women suffer from panic attacks after they leave," and these attacks can occur over seemingly insignificant things. Margaret described one such panic:

> I'd be driving home from work and know that I was fifteen minutes late. I'd start sweating and literally shaking, knowing I was really in trouble. He is going to be angry. I'd turn the corner and see his car wasn't there. "Oh, thank God! He isn't home yet. I'm safe."

Then I'd remember that he was gone. He didn't live with me any-more. You can't believe how conditioned you can become to fear.

The abuse affects the women physically, emotionally and mentally. Sometimes the result is permanent damage. Often, the recovery from the experience takes many years. It is our opinion that society at large does not yet realize this. Many peo-ple think that abuse is an event or a series of events that ends when the marriage ends. It is not. It is a process that begins with the physical and/or psychological abuse but does not end until the abused woman has had sufficient time and resources to deal with the aftermath.

Breaking Up Is Hard to Do

The most frequent question asked by people with no connec-tions to the problem is the simple "Why do abused women re-main with their husbands?" Unfortunately, there is no simple answer to that question. Women do remain with abusive hus-bands for long periods of time. Margaret's marriage lasted about twenty-five years. Anita's husband died two weeks after their sixtieth wedding anniversary. She had "Free at Last" inscribed on his headstone and, over the few weeks following the funeral, proceeded to tell everyone that "that son of a bitch" had abused her since soon after their wedding night. That was the first any-one, family or friend, had heard of it. Why did she stick it out for sixty years and Margaret for a quarter-century?

Suffering Alone

An abused woman feels like she is the loneliest person in the world. She feels that no one else could possibly understand what she is going through, and they would probably lay a guilt trip on her if she left her husband. No one, so she believes, is able to help her except herself. There is some suggestion that in rare cases, this is true. Elizabeth was berated by her own mother, who called her "a slut" for "deserting her husband." Deborah was told by her mother that "God would make her suffer for leaving Richard."[1] Another woman's sister refused her phone calls and was pointedly rude when they met accidentally in a store. However, such incidents are few. Most people do indeed understand and are willing to help. Deborah's friends, for example, expressed relief when she finally left her husband. But despite the reality, the abused woman's perception is what counts, and many see themselves as alone and without emotional support. They will endure the marriage and the abuse rather than face their friends and family, who will, the abused wife believes, turn on her and blame her for the failure.

Low self-esteem is very common among women who have been abused. The longer a woman is in an abusive situation, the more likely it is that her self-confidence will be affected. Independent, capable women marry, and if the relationship is healthy, both partners can remain healthy. An abusive relationship is not healthy, and a woman can learn helplessness and hopelessness as a result of conditioning at the hands of her partner. The partner may use coercion and threats, intimidation, emotional abuse, isolation, or economic abuse. He may minimize what he is doing, deny that he is abusing, or simply shift the blame. He may use their children as pawns or weapons, or he may use the traditional male prerogative—"I am the master, I make all the decisions."

The learned helplessness syndrome that holds women in abusive relationships develops because of the pattern abuse generally takes: a slow tension-building phase escalates until an explosion or acute battering incident occurs, followed by a calm, loving respite. During the latter period of reconciliation, the husband's kindness and contrite, loving behavior make the battered woman's victimization complete. He does everything he can to convince her that he truly loves her and that he will change. She wants to believe him and becomes ambivalent about leaving him. If she stays, however, the cycle begins again. Eventually, as the cycle repeats and repeats, her responses become automatic and she readily accepts his excuses. She cannot break out: she has "learned helplessness." She has been conditioned to believe there is nothing that can be done to change the situation. She sees no escapes, no help, no alternatives.

Deborah was in an abusive marriage for fifteen years. She says, "my self-esteem took such a beating because of Richard [her husband]." He convinced Deborah that she could not possibly say or do anything intelligent. He verbally attacked her again and again. In front of their friends, Richard would interrupt Deborah as if to indicate that anything she said could not possibly matter. Seven years later, there are still times when she feels she's been hurled back in a time warp to Richard. Her self-esteem takes such a beating that she says, "I think to myself that I can't possibly say anything intelligent. I can't do anything intelligent. What the heck am I doing? I just want to sit down and cry."

Sandra says she feels much the same way. "I'm haunted by all those hurting words. I can't seem to forget the smallest things I've been told. They reverberate in my head." Alan told Sandra, "You've never accomplished anything and you never will."

The basis of socialization is that "the more often you hear or see something, the more likely you are to accept it as truth." Tell someone that he or she is stupid enough times and they will start believing it. Abusive husbands use socialization techniques[2] to get their wives to submit to them, and it works. Over the years, the wife will come to believe that she is stupid, incompetent, and useless. Self-esteem drops to incredibly low levels. This leads to an acceptance that she cannot get out of the relationship because she is not smart enough to survive outside the marriage. After all, her husband has been telling her for years that without him, she'd be nothing.

The low self-esteem also contributes to another reason that abused women remain in the relationship. Hand in hand with low self-esteem, many such women carry around a lot of guilt. Both are products of the manipulative abuse her husband has subjected her to. She thinks that he is an important, intelligent, wonderful person (so he constantly tells her) and she is a zero (so he tells her frequently); therefore, the abuse that "I am getting, I am getting because I deserve it. It must be my fault."

We also found that women who come from abusive homes do not see anything in the abusive marriage that is unusual or out of the ordinary. Being beaten by one's husband is "normal." Since they do not recognize that is it abnormal, it does not occur to the women that they should leave the relationship. For others, the abuse is so gradual and subtle at first that they do not notice. As Sandra said: "In every way, in everything that took place, there was a slow progression to reach that point where he had total control." Several informants admitted that it wasn't until after the divorce that they realized they had been abused. All they knew was that they were unhappy and uncomfortable in the relationship. They did not know why.

Fear is a prime motivator and holds many abused women in a relationship. Fear tends to paralyze people and render them incapable of making decisions or taking actions. Some abusive husbands know this, either cognitively or instinctively, and use it, but we feel that it is the fear of failure that keeps some women locked into a relationship. They are so beaten down that they cannot believe they can make it on their own. Some women, like Anita, hide the fear behind the adage "better the devil you know than the one you don't."

The women are afraid of what life will be like "on their own." For many, it is the fear of the unknown. They have never experienced life on their own. Margaret, for example, married young and went straight from her parents' home to a home with her new husband. Some women, in addition to never having lived alone, have never been employed outside the home. If a person has never lived alone and never had a job, having to face both at once can be a scary prospect, sometimes more terrifying than the beatings and other abuse.

Often women will remain in an unacceptable situation with an abuser because they are afraid of financial hardship. If they have children, the fear is still greater. Economic abuse is a common form of control in a battered woman's life, and statistics indicate that 95 percent of women who have left their partner live below the poverty line (Lindenburger, n.d.: 5). One woman said, "I'd rather scrub toilets every day than spend one more day with him."

Trish, Ann, and Sandra live in different cities and do not know one another, but they have a lot in common. All three sought sanctuary in a shelter for abused women within the past ten months and are on welfare today. Trish deeply appreciates the help from welfare. She does not yet have all the furniture she needs as a single mother with three children, but her friends are helping her create a new home. Ann is fiercely independent, and having to go on welfare is a tremendous blow to her pride. She is four months pregnant, just out of a shelter for abused women, and looking for work.

By leaving her husband and seeking aid in a shelter, Sandra eventually—but not voluntarily—gave up almost all of her possessions. She was able to keep what she could carry along with their baby daughter. When she left the shelter, she moved to an apartment with assistance from welfare. While she was in the shelter, her husband Alan also moved, taking with him what he wanted, including appliances that had been purchased on Sandra's charge cards. Alan told Sandra he needed the items because he was a working man and she was just a welfare bum. Sandra had quit her job to raise their daughter, and she felt devastated at having to accept social assistance (appreciative, but devastated). "It's just so embarrassing." Her shopping takes place now at the Salvation Army. She laughed as she found a cookie sheet at a bargain price: "... at least now I won't have to ask Alan's permission to bake cookies."

For many, the prospect of having to become a "ward of the state" and the associated social stigma are too high a cost to pay. They will remain with their husbands rather than face the outside world. At least they know what to expect.

If nothing else works to keep the woman in the abusive relationship, a relationship that clearly benefits the husband, he will use force or the threat of force. He will isolate her, maintain total control over finances, possibly disconnect the telephone. He will use whatever means necessary, including intimidation. Margaret's experiences reflect this attempt to maintain control:

> I can remember once when I had had enough and I really was going to leave him. My husband told me he would kill me if I left him. I believed him. He said "Wherever you go, I'll find you and I'll kill you." I believed him.

Holding the Family Together

In some cases, the partners realize that the relationship is troubled, but neither party is willing to give up on it just yet. They make various attempts to fix whatever they perceive is wrong with it. In most cases, the wife is the one to recognize that there is something out of place. Usually, the husband does not see it and therefore sees no reason to pursue solutions. However, both husband and wife will make attempts to stabilize what has become an unpredictable and unstable relationship. The wife is demanding change. She is becoming more vocal and resistive to the status quo. He is trying to cope with what he perceives as a sudden change in his wife's demeanor in order to re-establish the status quo. They are working at cross-purposes.

Margaret initially left her husband not because of the abuse, but because her husband was having an affair and flaunting it in front of her. "Even she was starting to be rude to me in public. I'd show up at the office to visit my husband and his secretary would give me that 'what the hell are you doing here' look. It was humiliating." A few months later, the affair was over and Margaret's husband wanted to come home. Everyone Margaret talked to about it urged her to give him a second chance.[3] She knew it wouldn't work even then, but she agreed to get back together anyway.

> I tried to get him to go to counseling. I tried just about everything to get him to change—when I was on my own, I realized he was the problem, not me—but within a few weeks [of them getting back together], he was back to his old abusive self.
>
> I stayed with him for a year—mostly, I think, to show my friends and family I honestly tried. My heart wasn't in it, though, and I got out. I should have done that a long time ago.

ATTEMPTS TO RECONCILE

Once it becomes apparent to one or both of the partners that the marriage is heading towards a breakup, the search for ways to prevent it begins in earnest. Ironically, the wife, who should be considering getting out of the relationship, is usually the one partner who makes a serious and concerted effort to address their problems and salvage what is left of the marriage. On the other hand, the husband, who is the one with the vested interest in maintaining the relationship, rarely even cooperates with the wife's attempts.

Some women will go to outside sources for help and advice concerning the relationship with the husband. They will talk with a member of the clergy or go to a counseling service. Initially, they will make the approach on their own, without informing the husband. In order to keep that initial contact a secret, the woman will make sure that the person she approaches is a complete stranger to both her and her husband. Susan would have liked to see her own minister but was afraid to.

> He plays golf with John almost every weekend. The thought of Reverend Martens [a pseudonym] talking to my husband on the golf course is just too embarrassing. Too dangerous as well. If John thought for a second that I was talking about us to anyone, I'd be in for it.

She sought out another minister from a nearby church and talked to him by herself. She was ambivalent about these meetings.

> Just having someone to talk to was really great, but I couldn't tell him everything. I wasn't sure how he'd react if I told him my husband beat me, so I didn't bring it up. I tried, but I just couldn't.

Susan was typical in that she was reluctant to initiate any discussion of the abuse. Had the minister himself brought it up, Susan feels she would have poured her heart out. Instead, they talked about everything else and she came away dissatisfied. She did take his advice, however, and approached her husband about marriage counseling for both of them.

Most counselors, including the clergy, will urge the wife to arrange for joint counseling. "You need both partners being proactive before relationship problems can be resolved," said one family counselor. "We can work on how the wife feels about the relationship by meeting with her alone, but to work on the relationship we need both husband and wife." Some women, like Susan, did try to persuade their husbands to get counseling. The majority of men simply waved it off as "psychological mumbo jumbo" and refused to go. Those who did go with their wives lasted between one and three sessions. They often found some excuse to terminate the session, like Terry's husband Peter:

> Peter just sat there for the hour. He didn't say a word, and no matter what the counselor did, he wouldn't open up. After we left, I asked him why. He said, "The guy's a fag. Probably never been married. What's he know about marriages?" No matter what I said after that, Peter wouldn't go back.

Terry's experience with Peter is not unusual. The husbands scuttle the marriage counseling. Some go further and demand that the wife stop any personal counseling she might be participating in. Peter's rationale for doing so was "I don't want my wife talking about our personal stuff to some stranger."

From a different perspective, the counselors are placed in an awkward spot professionally.

> The husband stomps out. His wife apologizes to me and rushes after him. It's the same every time and I think to myself, "There's another marriage down the toilet." But then I think, "Good! She should not be with him anyway. The guy's a jerk." I have to laugh at myself because I work with them to save a marriage that shouldn't be saved. I should have listened to my mother and gone to trade school.

Needless to say, any attempt at reconciliation through counseling usually ends in failure, and it is at this point that the abused woman comes close to giving up on the relationship completely.

SEEKING FORGIVENESS

With the possibility of counseling eliminated, the abused woman may threaten to leave, suggest a trial separation or simply leave her husband. In many cases this will evoke some strong emotions from the husband, as he is quite close to losing control or has already lost that control. Where once he was the dominator, controlling his wife like a puppet on a string, he has become irrelevant or is in danger of becoming so as far as his spouse is concerned. He is forced to react and he does not like it. As Bob stated:

> Everything was going well. We had a good marriage. Then out of the blue, she threatens to dump me. Man, I was floored. I had to do something, but what?

Apparently, the husband does not recognize or accept his responsibility for the impending breakup. He searches for other reasons. Bob blamed it on his wife's friends. "They never liked me. They finally poisoned her against me." Others lay the blame on society, television, or the woman's work outside the home.

> She's always hearing about divorce at work. The women in her office are all divorced. Probably always telling her the grass is greener over there. She's been brainwashed.

Because of this failure to accept responsibility for the marital problems—that is, not connecting the abuse to the wife's desire to leave—the attempts the husbands make have nothing whatever to do with the real problem. There seemed to be two non-violent approaches that husbands use to re-establish the relationship. Some husbands use either one or the other but most seem to use a combination of the two.

Initially, the husband will express deep hurt. He will cry and plead with her for forgiveness. "I am sorry, I will change" is a statement that was heard by many of the women.

> He would phone in the middle of the night, sobbing his heart out. He'd beg me to come home. He would promise me anything. He'd never hurt me again. He'd get help. He'd go to therapy. Whatever I wanted. He was so convincing.

Many of the women, like Deborah, found themselves weakening in their resolve. Many admitted that at this point they felt they were seeing the first real attempts by their husbands. Most considered reconciling, and many did.

> He wasn't his usual controlling self. That shell was cracking and I could see a real human being underneath. I wanted to get back with him and help him get out of that shell altogether.

He keeps the pressure up, displaying deep depression and crying whenever contact is made with his spouse. However, all of the wives, without exception, noted that as soon as the couple was back together, the crying and soul-searching stopped. Usually within a few weeks, the abuse was back, and frequently it was worse than ever before. One woman's husband started beating her before she even had her suitcase unpacked.

Other husbands will go the romantic route. Instead of crying and pleading, they will try wining and dining their wives, buying them flowers and balloons, and generally being on their best behavior.

> He suddenly became the man I married all over again. He was so gentle, so thoughtful. I had forgotten how wonderful he could be.

That was how Elizabeth described her husband shortly after she announced she was thinking of leaving him. They began sitting up all night just talking—something they hadn't done in years.

> He told me he had let everything get to him and he now realized that we had grown so far apart because of his behavior. To prove it, he took me on a holiday to the beach, a second honeymoon, he called it. He asked me to marry him again. It was so romantic I couldn't say no.

Elizabeth's new husband remained a romantic for a total of four weeks before reverting to his abusive behaviors. "He even took my next paycheck to pay for our holiday at the beach. I still can't believe I bought all of his 'I'll love you forever ' B.S. a second time. What an idiot I was." Elizabeth left for good five weeks after their "second honeymoon" and, in her words, "lived happily ever after."

THREATS OF VIOLENCE

There is a strong Jekyll and Hyde dichotomy in the husband's attempts to regain control and remain in the relationship. He will try romantic wooing and emotional appeals. If and when they cease to work, he will become malicious and vicious. He will use every means at his disposal to prevent his wife from leaving, to regain control of the situation. He blames his wife for all of the troubles and will force her, in any way he can, to remain with him and under his control.

Steven's wife Andrea made the error of telling him in advance that she was leaving him. He reacted by moving out first and taking their eighteen-month-old son with him. He then delivered an ultimatum: "If you don't come back to me, you will never see your child again." Andrea, in this case, did not capitulate but sought legal advice instead. The lawyer recommended that she file for divorce and sole custody. The police advised her that they could not help her as Steven was the baby's legal father and in the absence of court documents to the contrary, he had as much right to custody as Andrea did.

Steven, who is an impatient man, waited less than two weeks before returning the child to Andrea, but that did not end the threats.[4] He now says that if she files for divorce, he'll sue for sole custody of their son and Andrea will never see the baby again.

This was not the first time Steven had held a child as a way to control a wife who was beginning to break away. He had done the same to his previous wife. With her, he physically prevented her from breast-feeding the baby until she agreed to stay with him. She agreed, but fled shortly thereafter. During the divorce proceedings he tried to gain sole custody, but the effort was only half-hearted as he did not really want the baby. He wanted control of his wife. At one point, he mailed her a sympathy card, one that stated the sender was "sorry for the loss of your child." The implication of the message was crystal clear. Emotional blackmail can be a powerful tool.

In addition to using the children where possible, the abusive husband will threaten violence against anyone who means something to the wife. It is not unusual, for example, to threaten suicide. "I can't live without you. Leave and I'll kill myself." Both Margaret and Deborah heard those words repeatedly. Even after they had split up (the first time), Margaret would get late night calls from her husband. "If you don't come home right now, I'm going to kill myself." She spent more than one night talking him out of suicide. However, the suicide ploy, serious or not, only works a few times, after which a new tactic must be employed.

The most common way for abusive husbands to maintain control of the relationship is to elevate the abuse and back it up with death threats. Shauna, after declaring her intention to move back to her parents' place, was beaten every night for ten days. Between beatings, she was confined to her house.[5]

> As he hit me, he'd repeat that it was for my own good. He had to beat that notion out of me. He'd also say, "You leave and you'll get a lot worse than this. I'll kill your parents. Then I'll kill you." He'd emphasize each word with a punch. I was one big bruise by the end.

It took Shauna another five months to risk leaving him. This time, however, she gave him no warning. She waited until he went to work, then hitchhiked to the bus station and disappeared. She has had no contact with him since. She is too afraid to even file for divorce. "There's no way I want him to know where I am."

The threat of murder is used, and it is used frequently. Roughly two-thirds of the women in the study were threatened with death, and all believed their husbands capable of carrying out the threat. Although there are no statistics to back it up, we believe that a significant number of homicides reported every year in which the husband has killed his wife are motivated by the husband's belief that "she is going to leave me."

The Threads Unravel

Even after these attempts have failed and the marriage is on rocky ground, there will be attempts at reconciliation. However, most of the attempts are being made by the husband as the wife has, whether she is aware of it or not, already decided the marriage is over. Deborah, who kept a diary, wrote daily reminders to herself to resist any entreaties from her husband. The gist of her reminder went: "All men who abuse their wives love to welcome them back, but then they will turn on them and make them pay for leaving in the first place."

An abusive relationship rarely ends with a clean break. Sometimes it can take a year or more between the first tentative steps towards dissolving the relationship and the actual ending. It appears the abused wife is of two minds, for the steps she takes demonstrate her tentativeness or indecisiveness. One day she'll be determined to get out, but on the next she'll be telling herself that it wasn't all that bad. She may leave him but then come back a few days or weeks later. He may leave, or he may increase the abuse to reassert his control over her, or he may lay off her for a bit to see if that works. Whatever the case may be, overall the relationship becomes less and less satisfactory for one or both partners. It has to end.

There are a number of ways a "normal" (non-abusive) relationship can end: the split can be mutual with both the husband and the wife going their own separate ways, the husband can leave the wife, or the wife can leave the husband. However, for some abused women there are other ways that relationships can come to an end.

Suicide and murder, for example, become feasible options for some who see themselves locked into a hopeless situation with all "normal" escape routes blocked. They perceive their alternatives as: "Do I kill him or do I kill myself?" These desperate women have, through constant emotional and physical torture, been reduced to the level of the abusive husband. They consider resolving the problem with violence. A very few select the murder option, but most can not yet bring themselves to inflict violence on another person, no matter how despicable that person is. Instead, abused women prefer suicide. It seems that a majority of abused women seriously contemplate suicide at some point, while about a third of these go as far as attempting to kill themselves. There is no record of how many abused women have died at their own hands to escape their abusers.

Many abusive marriages end in yet another way that can be best described as "abandoning the relationship." One day, an abused wife will gather what she considers absolutely essential (in Sandra's case, it was her baby and some baby clothes) and flee to a safe haven, hoping never to see her husband again. Sometimes, she simply flees without any thought as to where she is going. She is simply going "away."

Escape to Anywhere

The women flee. They go "away." Some have been thinking about it and planning it for weeks, months, even years. Others simply do it without planning, almost without conscious thought. Elaine left the house one day as usual to get groceries. She went to the supermarket, bought what she needed and then drove home, or so she thought.

> I sort of "woke up" standing outside the front entrance of the emergency women's shelter with about six bags of groceries in my arms. I have no idea how I got there. To this day, I give my car the credit for saving me. It took me to the shelter all by itself.

Of course, not all abused women who leave their husbands go to a shelter—only those who believe they have nowhere else to go, no one to turn to. Nonetheless, it is a difficult and stressful time for the abused woman. Everything is in flux.

One woman who was abused for ten years but successfully removed herself from that relationship now coordinates an outreach program for battered women. She told us that

> The most dangerous time for a woman is when they start to take their power back ... once you start empowering yourself again and taking your power back, it terrifies the man. That's probably one of the most dangerous times. That's why separation, when they first leave, is a very very dangerous time, because he's lost his power and sometimes he'll do anything to get that back, including murder and suicide.

The statistical data support her comments:

> One-fifth (19%) of women who experienced violence by a previous partner reported that the violence occurred following or during separation and, in one-third of these cases, the violence *increased* in severity at the time of separation (Statistics Canada 1993: 4) [emphasis in the original].

However, the increased risk of violence is only one of many problems facing the women. They have to learn to live all over again in an entirely new and frightening context. For many, it will be the first time they have ever faced the world as adults without their husband. The cost in terms of security and comfort is enormous, and yet the women agree to pay the price. Talking to women who have just escaped, one can see that at that moment, they do not care about the massive changes they are about to experience and the gigantic hurdles they are about to face. Most are not even thinking about that yet. They are in survival mode, focusing in on "right now." They want to make it through the night and the day. They have escaped their husbands' tyranny and they are committed to staying free.

> As I drove to the shelter, I kept looking in the rear-view mirror. I thought he was going to catch me. A car jumped a stop sign in front of me and I instantly thought it was my husband trying to kill me. By the time I reached the shelter, I was a nervous wreck, literally shaking in my boots. I sat there for ten minutes, maybe more.

In response to questions about long-range plans, one wife who had been at the shelter less than twenty-four hours simply stared for a minute.

> What? I don't know. I plan to sit in my room for about a week and do deep-breathing exercises. Beyond that, who knows? I don't. I have about six dollars and one change of clothes, but I have everything I need—a safe place to sleep.

On Your Own

Some abused women are confident enough to strike out on their own. Margaret, who had been on her own for a few months before going back to her husband for a year and had a full-time job, was one of them. She packed up her and her son's belongings, located a low-rent apartment, and started over. She thought it was wonderful having her own place and not having to share it with anyone, but there were some problems.

> It was hard at first. It was quite an adjustment for my son, who had to go to a new school and leave all his friends behind. I overcompensated and tried to be both mother and father to him. In a way, that helped me get through the first few months. He was my lifeline.

She found the adjustment hard, and under it all was the conditioned fear she had lived with for years. She refused to admit it was there. By focusing all her energy on her son and her job, she managed to bury those fears even deeper, delaying their effects.

It seemed I just got busier and busier. I got a new job that required a lot of overtime. It was close to my son's school so he'd come over after school and hang out. I'd work and he'd do his homework. We'd grab a bite to eat somewhere and often we wouldn't make it home before ten.

I really didn't realize how busy I was until one night when I asked my son what he'd like for supper. He said, "Mom, how about homemade?"

Margaret is typical of many women who strike out on their own after leaving an abusive husband. Instead of confronting their own personal problems acquired over the years of abusive treatment, they take on the world and will not rest until they wrestle it to the ground. Not all women end up with what has been called the "superwoman syndrome" (we discuss this more later). Instead, they struggle independently with financial and emotional problems as best they can. Many have expressed a wish that they had had access to someone to talk to back in the first weeks, someone to help them sort out and explain what they are thinking and feeling.

I thought about counseling but that was too impersonal for me and a support group seemed somehow too public. My friends had their own lives and would get tired quickly of hearing about mine. So, I'd just sit in my apartment on a couch I got from Sally Ann for ten bucks and I'd cry. I'd cry but I didn't have the slightest idea why. For a while, I thought I was going crazy. Looking back, I suppose I was.

Living on their own permits many of the women to reintegrate themselves into society fairly quickly. That is positive, but it might also tend to delay the necessary emotional adjustment and recovery. Deborah, who also went out on her own right away, recognized this.

Me and my kids got set up pretty quickly. Financially we were okay but I'd spin out emotionally about every little thing. My boy would leave a plate or a knife in the sink and I'd blow up. I'd be reacting exactly how my husband used to react. I was an absolute bitch for about a year. In my mind, I was still living with him.

Family and Friends

Some women leave their spouses to "go home" to the house of their parents or grown siblings, or they may arrive on the doorstep of a friend's place. Each choice offers unique opportunities and unique difficulties.

PARENTS' HOME
Returning to the house a woman grew up in can be a tremendously uplifting experience, assuming that the family was functional and the woman's memories of that home were happy ones. There is an instant feeling of "safety" and "comfort."

> I walked in and my mom hugged me. She didn't say anything but she didn't have to. I was welcome and for the first time in years, my stomach didn't hurt.

Mary, who had suffered through a series of chronic stomach disorders including ulcers, all attributable to the stress of her abusive marriage, had phoned her parents the night before and asked if she could stay with them. They hadn't asked why. They had just told her to come on ahead. Her father offered to make the two-hour trip to come and get her and the offer was readily accepted—Mary had not yet figured out how she was going to get home. The next morning, shortly after Mary's husband left for work, her father arrived and took her home. They talked all through the trip and her father, previously unsuspecting of the abuse, was appalled but he said nothing. According to Mary, her father just drove and listened, never offering advice or criticism. He just heard her out.

> That first night at Mom and Dad's was wonderful. I ate like a horse at supper and went to bed early—around nine. I slept the whole night through. It was wonderful. I felt so safe.

Mary did not discover for some months that her husband had called while she was asleep. Her father told Mary's husband to stay away and never phone again. Mary's mother recalls:

> I can't repeat what Herb said on the phone. He used words I'd never heard him say before but I guess he got the point across.

He'd always been protective of Mary and he really laid it on that night. If Chuck even so much as called here again, Herb was going to use his shotgun on him. I could tell he meant every word.

Parents tend to be protective and nurturing. For several months, Mary remained under her parents' wing. She was able to talk about her abuse and gain emotional strength in that haven.

My mom could see I was nervous and jumpy even though Chuck lived about a hundred miles away. For the first few weeks, every time I had to go out—even just to the corner store—she'd come with me to protect me. It's funny now. I had had a sixty-year-old, five-foot nothing, hundred-pound bodyguard. But back then, she was my protector, my shield.

Of course, going home to one's parents is not always wonderful and idyllic, as Jodie found out. As in Mary's case, her parents offered unconditional support and love, but Jodie felt she was intruding none the less.

I was thirty-five with two small children. We invaded my parents' home and turned their quiet little place into a noisy chaos. I was always shushing the kids and picking up after them. My parents were very understanding. They said they didn't mind but I figured it had to get to them sometimes.

Jodie admitted that by coming home, she felt like she had stepped back into her teenage years. Although her parents treated her like an adult and an equal, Jodie felt obligated to adhere to the old rules, the ones she had grown up with, and that left her feeling emotionally stifled.

To be sure, it was all in my own head. They [her parents] were great, but I was confined. I made things tense for everyone. Finally, I moved into a small apartment a few blocks away. The kids and I still spend most of our time at Mom's but I'm much more relaxed about it all.

SIBLING'S HOME

Sandra, upon returning to her home province and thereby putting two thousand miles between her and her abusive ex-husband, stayed at her sister's house.

It was good for both of us in the beginning. I was on welfare and couldn't afford to live anywhere else. I could stay at Bonnie's and look after her kids and my little one during the day while she was at work. That way I could save her a bit of money on day care.

The arrangement worked well for a month, but there were clashes over "parenting styles" and other more, minor things like, who could watch what on television when. The relationship between the sisters deteriorated over the six months or so that Sandra lived with Bonnie. Finally, it reached a point where they were no longer speaking to each other. Sandra moved out and gradually relations improved until they approached normal. They speak to each other frequently and visit each other regularly, but both are still quite sensitive and often wonder what the other "meant" by some innocuous comment or remark.

None of the tension is really surprising, since the sharing of accommodation is a hardship, especially when there are familial obligations tacked on. Each sibling gives up a great deal of freedom and space to the other. About two-thirds of those who went to live with siblings (male or female) tended to develop difficulties similar to Sandra's. Interestingly, the problems they had getting along usually occurred only when the sibling was married and her or his spouse lived in the same residence, or when there were children involved. In cases where an abused woman moves in with an unmarried sister and neither have children, the experience tends to be more positive for both.

Friends' Homes

There were many cases of women fleeing to the home of a friend. It tended to be a very positive experience, especially if the friend was single and living alone. There were no familial obligations to hamper emotional recovery and no set rules.

I could tell her anything. I told her stuff I wouldn't dare tell my parents. We'd sit and drink hot chocolate and talk. I'd talk about what he had done to me. She'd listen and tell me what a jerk—or worse—he was. By the end, I think she hated him more than I did.

But, you know, the best times for me were when she'd talk about her happy times. I'd imagine them happening to me. She helped me see that the world wasn't all mean and nasty.

In every case that worked out positively, the abused woman lived with a woman she'd known for many years, usually since before the marriage began.[6] When husbands and/or children were involved, the experience was less positive than it could have been, but in every case, the experience was certainly not negative.

Several women who had family or friends to stay with chose instead to try it on their own or to go to a shelter. When asked why she chose a shelter when her long-time best friend had "thrown her front door wide open" for her, Marsha was blunt:

> I would have loved that, but my husband said he was coming after me. I did not want to let him anywhere near Cindy. He is too dangerous. I'd rather be uncomfortable and keep Cindy safe.

Another suggested that the friend or family member making the offer was making it pro forma, because they felt obligated to.

> I'm her only sister so she tells me to come and live with her for as long as I wanted. She was just saying that. Her husband would never go for it. He wouldn't want a sister-in-law hanging around all the time.

Into the Arms of Strangers

Some women have no friends or family available to help and lack the financial or emotional reserves to "strike out on their own." However, because of the duration and intensity of the abuse that is being heaped upon them, they must escape from their home. They are literally pushed into the arms of strangers: they head for the nearest emergency women's shelter. As testimony to the enormity of the problem, every town and city with a population greater than fifteen thousand has at least one such shelter.

The primary function of a women's emergency shelter is·to be a safe haven, a location where the husband's power and control ceases to exist. It is a temporary haven, designed to allow the women time to make more permanent arrangements without having to worry about immediate necessities. It is also a last resort. As one shelter worker put it:

> Most of the women we get here would end up on the street if we didn't exist. They have nothing, literally. One of our clients

showed up in the middle of winter wearing a light pair of slacks and a sweater. Everything she had to her name was in the pockets of her slacks—one small comb, six pennies, and a breath mint. That was it.

Shelters offer a range of services meant to streamline the transitions from abused wife to independent woman.

> We try to provide all we can. First, there are the basics—a bed, food, clothing. Then we provide counseling, daycare so mom can look for work or whatever. We hook her up with Social Services, lawyers, anything she needs.

The streamlining is necessary as the shelters have limits on how long a woman can stay, usually three to six weeks. The workers hope that by then the women will have found a place to live and have some source of income, either employment or welfare.

> Some women aren't ready to go after six weeks and we won't throw them out, but we do have to push them to get their act together. Usually, there are other women waiting for her bed.

The women who use the shelters come from a wide variety of backgrounds. Some were already on welfare or social assistance, whereas others came from middle- or upper-class homes. However, there are certain commonalities shared by all. Generally, as noted earlier, they have abandoned most or all of their assets along with their husbands. Most have never worked outside the home or have not been employed in some time. They were certainly unemployed at the time they fled to the shelter. In addition, their confidence and self-esteem are probably the lowest they have ever been. One woman described herself and the other women in the shelter as "the walking wounded."

> I'd wander around in a daze half the time. I was at a complete loss. What was I going to do? Where was I going to go? I didn't have a clue. The workers at the shelter would take me by the hand and walk me through the forms for social assistance. They'd remind me of appointments. Actually, they treated me like a brainless child which, of course, I was.

"Walking wounded," "shell-shocked," and "traumatized" were some of the terms used to describe the state of mind of most of the abused women when they arrived at the shelter. One woman couldn't remember her own name. They had to consult her driver's license to get it. Another was unable to speak. Many were in serious emotional turmoil. "I estimate that close to 80 percent of our clients are certifiably mentally disturbed when they show up here," commented one shelter administrator. "It can't be much worse in a refugee camp in Yugoslavia. These women have been victimized and we are lucky that there is anything left for us to deal with."

The women draw on some hidden reserve of strength to break the bonds and flee to a shelter like a marathon runner at the end of a big race. The women are totally spent, physically, mentally, and emotionally empty when they cross their own finish line, the front door of the shelter. Repeatedly, shelter workers remarked on this emptiness.

> The clients are exhausted, frightened little children. We offer them tea, a place to sit, and company and they are grateful for so little. That first day, we get them settled and into bed fairly early. They never argue. The next morning, you say hello and, you know, they have no idea who you are. As far as they know, they've never seen you before even though you spent two hours with them a little more than twelve hours ago.

Sandra's experience with the shelter was very positive. She felt that without the help she got there, she'd have been forced to go back to Alan. The shelter also helped her find the strength to face the world again. The shelter, then, provides a minimum of two essential services. The first, of course, is the safe haven. The second, equally important service is the programming and facilities to rebuild the woman's emotional infrastructure. The abusive husbands beat them down. The shelters build them back up again. Imagine having such low self-esteem that you apologize because you weren't abused as badly as some of the other women in the shelter. Such was the case with Mary Ann, who said that the way her husband squashed her hand (breaking four bones) was not as bad as Andrea's black eye and broken eardrum or the whip marks on Beth's back. This is the kind of challenge faced by the shelter workers.

As well as providing shelter for abused women who have left their husbands, these facilities sometimes offer services to women who are still living with their abusive husbands. These women come seeking information and advice. Patricia, an articulate former Women's Shelter worker, was quite negative about the success of shelters, particularly in terms of the first contacts that abused women had with them: "It aggravates the situation. She speaks to a counselor at the shelter and goes home armed with all kinds of information. She tells her spouse that he can't do this or isn't allowed to do that. She gets beat up even worse and it accelerates from there." Patricia questioned the competence of the shelter worker who offer women advice on how to handle the men who are abusing them.

> They get no training to speak of and because they have the title of counselor, they think they know it all. They tell the women to stand up for their rights, to be more assertive. They have no idea that all they are doing is setting up the abused woman for more pain. It never fails—within a couple of weeks, the woman is on the shelter's doorstep asking to be taken in. I may be cynical, but it is just possible that the shelter administrators are using the shelter advisors, mostly volunteers, as instruments to keep the shelters filled to capacity. If they gave them proper training, then the counselors would not give that kind of advice to the abused women, who would then be able to stay at home longer and have less need for the shelter. With empty beds, the shelter administration would not be able to argue for more funding.

Although the administrator's motivation was probably not as mercenary as Patricia suggested, there is certainly cause for concern. Initial contacts should be positive and certainly should not aggravate an already dangerous situation.

Whatever the shortcomings, emergency women's shelters serve an unfortunately necessary and vital function. They provide a safe haven for women whose homes have become battlegrounds. Every year, they save thousands of women whose husbands were slowly destroying their lives.

Legal Separation and Divorce

Even though the abused woman and her husband are no longer living together, they are still recognized by the legal system as a single entity—a married couple. In order to get on with her life, the woman must take the steps necessary to dissolve the entity and reclaim her own independent identity. In some states, a woman is ineligible for social assistance benefits as long as she is legally married to someone who is employed. It is the couple's income that is considered, not the individual's. Assets belonging to the married couple cannot be divided by the courts in many jurisdictions until a divorce petition is in place. Indeed, in many jurisdictions, an abused woman cannot obtain the legal protection of a restraining order before beginning divorce proceedings.

In most areas, divorce has become a relatively simple procedure. One party files a court petition for a divorce, with a copy being sent to the other spouse. Generally, the recipient will not contest the petition and it will proceed unhindered through the court system. If the other spouse contests the petition, it usually only results in a delay in the outcome. In years past, both parties had to agree to the divorce before it could be granted. That, needless to say, was used by some abusive husbands to control their wives even at a distance. The "no-fault" divorce circumvents that problem by permitting a divorce to be granted when either of the parties wants it, no longer requiring agreement of both.

Most divorce petitions in abuse cases are uncontested. However, the division of the couple's assets is usually a bone of contention. California and other "community property" states have simplified this aspect of the divorce considerably by automatically assuming that any assets earned or acquired during the marriage are community property to be divided equally between husband and wife. Most jurisdictions, however, lack that assumption, and it is left to the lawyers to negotiate a settlement.

Many of the women would have preferred to avoid the courts entirely, not because they wanted to remain married to an abusive man but because they did not want to risk having to see him again, even if just in court. Unfortunately, for various reasons, they needed the separation to be recognized by the legal system and so went ahead with the process.

> The bum I was married to had my credit cards and was using them. I couldn't cancel them—it's a long story—unless I could

show we were no longer together. Until I got the divorce started, I was still supporting him.

Many of the reasons are financial but some are career oriented.

It was like Catch-22. I'd charged my husband with assault so he had a criminal record. I wanted a job which happened to require that I be bonded. A person known to associate with criminals can't be bonded. I had to get a divorce before the bonding company would back me.

Perhaps the major reason for obtaining a divorce from an abusive husband has nothing to do with anyone other than the abused woman herself. She eventually obtains a divorce for herself, to provide a sense of closure for that chapter of her life.

There were two interesting patterns that showed up in the woman's approach to the divorce, especially if there were no children involved. First, roughly half of the women obtained restraining orders as part of the divorce package.[7] Second, almost all of the women put up very little fight concerning the division of the couple's assets.[8] The women traded their assets for freedom. Tammy explained the approach:

I knew that if my lawyer pushed for my fair share of our stuff, my husband would fight and stall. I had my lawyer tell his lawyer that if he agreed to not contest the divorce, he could keep everything. If, however, he did not agree, then I would push to get everything I could, including alimony. I knew the greedy s.o.b. would sign. It was over quickly.

Margaret stated her philosophy: "Material things can be replaced. Freedom can't be." Various versions of that idea came from many of the study's informants. The woman did not care that their abusive husbands were obviously gaining substantially from the arrangement. Tammy explained:

So? Materially, yes, the husband wins and I'm sure he brags to all his buddies how he took his ex to the cleaners in the divorce. But we see it as a necessary evil. I'd rather be broke and independent than rich and a prisoner of some sadistic creep.

Several shelter workers deplore the unfairness of it all and want to see the laws changed. At the same time, they see and appreciate the abused woman's point of view.

When children are involved, there are complications. In terms of custody, there are really only three options: (1) the wife gets sole custody, (2) the husband gets sole custody, or (3) husband and wife share joint custody. When abuse is involved, the wife can be expected to have to battle for custody of the children. Joint custody is not possible since it requires two conditions: (1) that the former partners live within a reasonable distance of each other, and (2) that there is a considerable amount of contact between the former partners. Neither of these conditions is desired by the abused woman, for obvious reasons.

The husband will almost always fight for custody, not because he wants the children (he usually does not) but because they can be used to exercise some control over his wife. However, this is one situation where a patriarchal society actually benefits the woman. She will be granted custody of her children unless it can be proven that she is an "unfit mother." Since our society values the mother-child bond, proving a woman unfit is a difficult, almost impossible, task. However, the husband will threaten to fight for custody on those grounds and unfortunately, many abused women have such low self-esteem they believe the courts will find them "unfit." There were a number of agonizing stories of women who literally became sick with worry as the court date approached. They thought they were going to have their children taken away from them. They needn't have worried, as in the vast majority of cases, the husband did not attempt to challenge her petition when the day of the court hearing finally arrived, and she was granted sole custody within minutes.

What tended to take the most time in court hearings was the determination of child support payments and visitation rights for the father. In at least some jurisdictions, these have become inextricably linked. Originally, they were combined to force "deadbeat" fathers to meet their financial obligations to their children. If a man wanted to see his children, he had to accept some financial responsibility for their care. Taken that way, it seems the right thing to do, but as with many things legal, it has been reinterpreted in a way that was not intended. Now, if an abused woman—or any woman, for that matter—wants the children's father to pay child support, the father must be granted visitation rights in return. In divorces that do not involve abuse this does not present a difficulty, but with abuse cases it poses a problem. If an abused woman wants or needs child support, she runs the risk of having to associate with the man who abused her, or at the very least, let the man who abused her use the children as a control device for years to come. It seems that in order to avoid that, many abused women do not seek any child support payments in the hopes that their ex-husbands will not insist on the visitation rights-support payment combination.

Some governments have developed a buffer program for women who wish to avoid direct contact with their former spouses but also receive child support payments from them. The husband pays the child support to the government, which then pays the wife. Despite complaints about slow payments in some cases, the program seems to be working. Sandra, who used the program, was relieved to be able to keep her location a secret from her ex-husband.

> I had to wait a few months for any money but, hey, Alan has no idea where I am.
> We did have to give him visitation rights but we got the courts to agree to supervised visits only. My mom and her husband agreed to be the go-betweens and supply Alan with their address. So far, thank God, Alan has shown no interest in seeing his daughter.

Long-Term Hiding

There are all kinds of abuse and all kinds of abusers, so it cannot be said that all women are abused in identical manners and to the same degree. They are subjected to varying degrees of physical and emotional torment. However, whatever the weapon—a word, a look, a fist, a foot, a bat, a knife or a gun—the women are beaten down and then beaten down again until they can't take any more, and it still doesn't stop. They have that in common.

When the marriage breaks up, the "fallout" varies as well. In a few cases, for example, the husband divorced the wife and never bothered her again. In the majority of cases, even when the wife left the abusive husband, an uneasy peace developed after a while. Both Margaret and Deborah speak to their ex-husbands on occasion, usually concerning their children. The women are uncomfortable when doing so, but both the husband and the wife are aware that his control over her is gone.

At the other end of the scale are those who escaped, rather than left, their husbands. Most people cannot begin to imagine what could force a woman to abandon everything and run, run from the one place that should be the safest of all—her home. The women tried to describe it but could not find the right words, perhaps because the necessary words do not exist. They tried phrases like "absolute terror," "abject fear," and "dread," but such words are meaningless if they have not been experienced. There is no frame of reference.

> I knew deep in my heart that if I stayed, I would not be alive by the end of the day. He hadn't said anything but when he looked at me across the breakfast table, I knew. "I'm dead."

To shelters, to the homes of friends or family these women flee, escaping from their husbands. For the lucky ones, that escape brings an end to the torment, but for some, the abuse continues. The husbands of these women refuse to accept that the marriage is over. They refuse to relinquish their control, their power.

There are those who like to simply test it every now and again. Garth, for example, was engaged to Yvonne for ten months, but she had enough sense not to go through with the marriage. He torments her just a little.

> I do believe I lived in hell for ten months. I thought I was going to lose my sanity. He never did take my self-esteem away but I did fear him for a long time. I haven't seen him in a year and a half, but when he comes back to town I can feel it. He always makes sure to let me know through my friends. It's like a black cloud.

Unfortunately for many women, their husbands vow to get their wives to come back or to punish her for leaving him. Regardless of the motive, the husband pursues his former spouse with a single-mindedness that is terrifying to the woman. She remembers only too well how bad the abuse was when they were married and knows it will be infinitely worse if he catches her. She lives in constant fear.

> I jump every time the phone rings. I sleep with all the lights on. When I go out, I check the street, doorways, passing cars. I can never relax.

Diane lives with terror daily. She is afraid of her husband and what he will do to her. She is in hiding about a thousand miles from her home. She uses an alias and has an unlisted phone number. She still finds it impossible to feel safe.

> He's out there searching for me. I know that one day he will find me. He'll watch my parents or steal my friend's mail, whatever it takes, but he will find me.

Some women have suggested a kind of Witness Protection Program for women like Diane. A shelter worker stated that "nothing short of a totally new identity and a complete severance of all ties to her past life will stop these men. They are obsessed."

Threats and Long-Distance Abuse

The abusive husbands discussed above are obsessed with settling the score and continue to torment their wives long after the marriage is over. Often, the abuse takes the form of threats by letter, by phone, or through friends, but it can be backed up with violence and the women take it very seriously.

Deborah's husband, Richard, purchased a gun shortly after his wife moved out. She never saw the gun, but she heard about it through her children. The young boys visited their father and were allowed to hold the gun and touch the bullets. Deborah knew that underlying threats were meant to bring her back to Richard's side, but she said, "I thought he was going to come after me, but to me, being dead was easier than going back to him. I would choose death rather than any more life with him."

Sandra was attacked by Alan after their separation. A judge had given Alan visitation rights to spend time with his nine-month-old daughter. Each time she met with Alan for the baby exchange, Sandra was harassed. She asked friends to accompany her, hoping to protect herself and baby Rebecca from Alan's screaming and ugly remarks. Alan attacked the friends with a barrage of insulting and demeaning comments. On one exchange, Sandra was alone. Alan assaulted her while she tried to back away, her arms full of baby and baggage. Alan was convicted of assault and sentenced to probation. Since then, Sandra has been living in fear. "I'm afraid someday I'll feel something cold and hard in my back."

The women complain to the authorities about these threats but generally do not receive much help. As Carol explains:

> The police officer was very nice and I could tell he wanted to do more, but he told me that unless Patrick [her husband] actually did something, the police could not do anything for me. He said, "We only have your word that he threatened you. That isn't enough."
>
> He did suggest that I complain to the phone company and try to get his phone disconnected. Fat lot of good that would do.

We got the impression that the authorities did not give much credence to the abused women's evaluation of the seriousness of the threats. Take the example of Igor, who was serving time in a federal prison for drug trafficking. While he was incarcerated, his wife Natalia divorced him. From prison, he repeatedly called her, threatening all kinds of horrific things, including murder. Natalia and her lawyer complained to the government department responsible for prisons, supplying documentary evidence that Igor had abused Natalia for years (he had been convicted three times for assaulting her) and a tape of one of the phone calls from him to her with the threats on it. Natalia insisted that the threats were genuine and that Igor should not be allowed to call her from prison. The government representative responded by saying that the prison could not prevent Igor from calling whomever he wished, and they could not monitor or record his calls without a court order. He suggested that Natalia just hang up on Igor when he called.

Apparently, the prison system did not take Natalia's concerns seriously enough for the calls continued. It appears that Igor also placed at least one call to his brother: about five months after Igor was incarcerated, his brother joined him, having been convicted of aggravated assault *on his brother's wife*, Natalia. She spent over ten days in the hospital as a result of that "unmotivated and apparently unprovoked" beating (according to the police report). Still the Correctional Service and the police did not act on Natalia's complaints of harassment and threats. Igor continued to call her two or three times a week until the day he was released from prison. (He was a "model prisoner" and was granted parole at his first hearing before the Parole Board.) Less than two weeks later, Natalia was dead. Igor had made good on his threats and beaten her to death with a bat.

A number of women were threatened and were sufficiently terrified that it affected their entire lives. For example, one woman moved to a new address every five or six months. Another had her unlisted phone number changed regularly four times a year. Several women refuse to have a telephone at all.

Although the telephone is still the weapon of choice for long distance violence, over the past few years there has been a growth in the use of the computer as a threatening device.

> I was so excited when I got an e-mail address on the Internet. I could keep in touch with a lot of my friends easily. Within a month, I started getting messages from him. The source was not identified, but it was him. At first, it was just typed messages, sometimes seven or eight a day, telling me what he planned to do to me. That was horrible enough.

Karen had to give up her Internet access and her e-mail address because even though she changed the address frequently, he managed to locate her every time.[9] She said that just as she started to get used to his threats, his approach changed.

> He started sending me photographs with the e-mail, photographs of mutilated, dismembered bodies in full color. It made me physically ill. God, it was horrible. He'd attach little notes like "This

will be you soon." I took them to the police, who dismissed the
photos as a cruel, sick joke. I had to quit the Internet.

Whether the long-distance abuse comes via computer,
phone, or mail, it has a profound affect on the women who
receive it. They are told that "it isn't over yet" and they must
protect themselves any way they can. They adapt, change their
lifestyles, try anything, but nothing they do alleviates the fear. It
is always there. Alicia, for example, escaped from her abusive
husband almost fifteen years ago. Since then, she has learned to
hate birthdays.

> Every year, every year, I get a card from him. Just getting it says
> "I know where you live." The card always says the same thing.
> "Enjoy this birthday because it may be your last." God, I hate my
> birthday and I hate him for doing this to me.

Attacks on Friends and Family

Immediately after the separation, the abusive husband typically
displays a considerable amount of anger directed at his estranged
wife and anyone associated with her. When his wife is not available to him, he seeks out other targets upon whom to vent his
rage. The anger seems to be uncontrolled, like a child's temper
tantrum, yet it must be calculated to some extent. Crystal who
hid from Larry at her grandmother's home described Larry's fury.

> He had an old address book of mine and one night about a month
> after I'd left, he started at the As and called everyone in that
> book. He'd call, ask for me, and if he was told I wasn't there, he'd
> launch into a tirade. He'd yell and swear, telling my friends that
> if they knew where I was and didn't tell him, he was going to
> blankety-blank it out of them. He also threatened them, warning
> them not to have anything to do with me or they would be dead
> just like I was going to be when he found me.

Crystal thought he was performing for her friends because the
same night he ranted and raved to all of her friends, he also
called a number of people who were more his friends than hers.
He didn't yell at them. One of those people told Crystal that
they'd had quite a pleasant conversation.

He'd call a friend of mine in a rage. Then he'd chat with a friend of his. He'd call another friend of mine and the rage was back. Maybe he was just trying to scare my friends into telling him where I was. Thankfully, no one did.

The abusive husband appears to have an objective—to "get to" his estranged wife—and he is resentful of any attempts to thwart him. Many friends or family members who got in the husband's way were attacked for intervening. Often the attack was verbal, but physical violence was not uncommon. More often than not, an attack, verbal or physical, works against him and solidifies the wife's friends and family into a defensive wall around her. For example, Cindy's parents initially wanted her to consider reconciliation. They had trouble connecting her stories of beatings with what they knew of their son-in-law.

Even as a child, Cindy had a flare for the dramatic. Everything was larger than life to her. She was upset with Jack and we thought she was stretching the truth a bit.

We changed our minds when Jack showed up here ... when Percy [Cindy's father] wouldn't let him in the house, he called Percy all kinds of names. He actually pushed him and threw him on the ground. If I hadn't yelled through the door that I was calling the police, I'm sure he would have tried to force his way in.

We had never seen Jack like that before. I guess he was showing us his true colors. Cindy was right to leave him.

The question arises as to why abusive husbands would persist in this kind of attack on friends and family when few succeed in their objective—to get to their estranged wives or to gain information that would lead them to them. There has to be another reason. The women offered a number of possibilities. One suggested that once the abuse is in the open (the husband could assume that his estranged wife will have told most of these people about his treatment of her) he no longer has to wear a mask of civility. He can behave however he wants without worrying about his "public image," since it has already been destroyed. Another woman thought that the abusive husband has a need to dominate and control, and if the person he usually dominates is not available he selects targets of opportunity. By exhibiting angry behaviors, he establishes control of any conversation and clearly dominates it by shouting down any attempts to inject reasonableness or logic into the discussion. If the other person resists, then he may resort to violence in order to achieve domination.

Stalking

Some abusive husbands who refuse to acknowledge their lack of control over their former spouses go beyond long-distance threats and harassment of friends and family to become stalkers. In blatant disregard for law and custom, they track their ex-wives with the intent of either getting them back under control or exacting revenge. This kind of behavior is far more serious and far more dangerous than the threatening behaviors discussed in the previous section.

There are two kinds of spousal stalkers. Each behaves differently and has a different goal in mind.

THE SILENT STALKER

The silent stalker is the husband who will, essentially without warning, kidnap or murder his estranged wife. Two cases are noted in Chapter One. More than half of the silent stalker cases end in a murder-suicide. Generally, the media will emphasize the spontaneous aspect of this type of murder-suicide. His neighbors and friends express shock and dismay: "He was such a quiet man. We never expected he'd do something this awful." However, the act is not at all spontaneous. When the police conduct psychological postmortems to determine the killer's state of mind leading up to the crime, it is usually discovered that the husband has been stalking his wife for weeks or months, searching for just the right time and place. He stalks her secretly, never letting her know what he is doing. His objective is not to torment her but to murder her.

It has been suggested that this type of stalker becomes fixated on the "if I can't have her, nobody can" idea, or somehow believes that she still loves him and they will be together always in the afterlife. They typically carry out the murder-suicide combination.

THE PSYCHOLOGICAL STALKER

The phenomenon referred to as psychological stalking is much more common. With this type of ex-husband, the motive for the stalking is to terrorize the ex-wife and make her life without him a "living hell." He is not invisible like the silent stalker. He lets his target know he is close by at every opportunity, and he lets her know what he plans to do to her when he gets the chance. He is continuing his psychological abuse and demonstrating to her that he still dominates and controls her, even from a distance. He will appear outside the supermarket just as she exits the building. He will go to the same movies and sit where she can see him. He will drive slowly past her place of employment. He will sit outside her residence.

The woman learns to know that he will go wherever she goes. To protect herself, she often will begin to spend more and more time at home thereby limiting her exposure to the stalker. She becomes a prisoner in her own home, and the ex-husband is the jailer. The stalker achieves his goal of continued domination and control.

Sandra's ex-husband would show up on the street outside her home at irregular and unexpected times. After five years, Sandra still barricades her door. She is also careful never to stand in front of her windows, as Alan is a former army officer and owns a rifle that he has threatened to use. His stalking ended when she fled the area a few months after their separation. However, Melanie's husband (and several others) kept up the "mind games" for years.

> Tim would hound me for weeks and then disappear. About the time I would be thinking he was gone for good, he'd pop up again. This went on forever. I'd move. He'd find me and follow me, then disappear and reappear again. He always smiled when we made eye contact but it was an evil smile.

The only solution to a psychological stalking is, according to those who have been through it, for the woman to escape once again to a place where he cannot find her. It means a second wrenching move, but there appears to be no other acceptable alternative.

Police Intervention and Court Orders

When the husband and wife are living together, the police can only respond to domestic disputes when there is a complaint, or when they themselves witness an altercation. Charges can be laid for assault, but little can be done about removing the offender or protecting the wife beyond that. Once a wife leaves her abusive husband, the situation changes somewhat, especially if a divorce petition has been filed. For example, most women who are concerned about further violence arrange to get a restraining order against their estranged husbands as part of the divorce package. Violation of the restraining order by the husband (that is, when he approaches within a specified distance of her) is a crime for which he can be arrested. The wife does not have to wait until he physically attacks her to involve the authorities. She can seek police intervention as soon as she sees him. In some cases, the order can be extended to forbid the husband from contacting his estranged wife by telephone or mail.

In addition, now that she has a residence separate from his, she can utilize a number of laws that are inapplicable in domestic disturbance cases. She can have him charged for trespassing if he enters her yard and ignores her demands that he remove himself. If he forces his way into her home against her wishes, the charge can be elevated to criminal trespass, or to breaking and entering or burglary. Further, if he attempts to harm her in any way, the resulting assault charges, which would not have the stigma of domestic disturbance attached to them, are usually treated far more seriously by the authorities.[10]

As is fairly obvious, the police and the courts offer significantly more protection for an abused woman once she has left her husband. That is ironic, because she needs it far more when she is still living with him. It is our opinion, and that of many of the formerly abused women, that the current laws and their enforcement do not address the concerns of an abused woman whether she still resides with her husband or not. When a man can choke his estranged wife, for example, and receive probation as a punishment, he is instantly free to hurt her again. When another can harass and threaten his wife from inside a prison or send her graphic messages on the Internet with impunity, one does not get the feeling that the abused woman's rights are being protected. Essentially all of the women called for drastic revision of the laws and more protection for women in general. They all felt the current laws favored the men at the expense of the women.

Rebuilding a Life

At some point in our lives, most of us experience change as a matter of course. We take on a new job and relocate to another town or city to be closer to it. We quit a job to stay home and raise a family. However, we rarely experience total change. Some aspects of our lives remain comfortably unaltered. When an abused woman flees from her husband and enters a shelter, the change is total. Everything that was familiar and comfortable remains under the control of the husband, including, in many cases, friends they shared and favorite public places. If, for example, they enjoyed a particular restaurant as a couple, the woman can hardly return to that restaurant and risk a confrontation. She experiences what can only be described as a "wrenching." She has literally ripped herself out of the fabric of her old life.

When most people experience change, it is usually to some extent planned and they have prepared for it. They applied for that new job, met some of the people they would be working with, checked out the local housing market and facilities, hired a moving company, and notified the post office of their impending change of address. All of this kind of thing tends to make the change easier, as they are already becoming familiar with their new location. It is not an unknown. The abused woman has no opportunity to plan her change beyond the "I have to get out of here" stage. She does not have time to prepare or to familiarize herself with the new location. Generally, she takes advantage of a "window of opportunity" to escape her marriage and flee to the shelter, which, up until that point, had existed only as an address on a piece of paper hidden in her shoe.

Further, in addition to the physical preparations, most people who are arranging a new situation undergo a kind of psychological or emotional preparation for the change. They perceive it as positive and look forward to it with confidence. The people who hired them think they can do the job, so they must be able to. They stress the advantages of the change and forge ahead. Once again, this is not how an abused woman will remember her change. For years, someone she once loved and respected has been telling her she is stupid and useless and would lose her head if it weren't attached. She lacks confidence. She approaches the move assuming she will fail. It is seen as negative and she looks upon it with dread.

An abused woman who escapes from her husband gives up everything that is familiar and comfortable on a moment's notice, without planning or preparation, and arrives at a shelter totally lacking in confidence and self-esteem, assuming the worst. That is not a good position from which to begin rebuilding her life.

A Brand-New Life

We found that most of the abused women who escape to shelters, in addition to not being prepared for flight to a shelter, are totally unprepared for what is to come after. They discover that they have to divest themselves of the remnants of their past life by filing for divorce, obtaining legal custody of the children, and, more importantly, getting to be recognized as an individual, independent of the "married couple." Many women have never considered themselves as individuals.

> I was married right after my high school graduation. I went from being Fred's daughter to being Derek's wife. I did not become Sharon, independent woman, until I was forty and living in a women's shelter. It was a revelation. It scared the s__ out of me.

Sharon and many others were terrified of being alone with sole responsibility for decisions.

> Dad made all the decisions when I lived at home. Derek, sometimes, early in the marriage, would ask my opinion on something, but he always made the decisions for us. I think the hardest decision I ever had to make during that time was which brand of toothpaste to buy. Now, I have to decide everything and I am sure I am going to screw it up.

Some women are overwhelmed by their new-found independence and the responsibilities that go along with it. They choose inappropriate responses. Some begin drinking. Others retreat into themselves. Some launch into all-out campaigns to find someone to take over the responsibilities. Michele was one of the latter.

> For two years, I dated everything in sight. I would throw myself at men hoping one of them would rescue me from the mess that was my life.

Her search was fruitless, a waste of time and energy. "All I did was postpone the inevitable." She laughs now at her behavior during those first two years. She jokes: "I didn't even have the sense to charge all the men I slept with. I could have made a decent living." However, at the time she could not see any alternatives. She certainly was not ready to handle her new life on her own.

The majority of the women in the study fumbled along, more or less on the right track, until they learned the skills they needed and gained the confidence to use them. Depending on how much had to be done to accomplish this, some women made giant leaps while others progressed in halting baby steps. For most, the process took years to complete, and for some, it never ends.

LACK OF SKILLS

Quite a few of the abused women lacked even the basic skills needed for survival. For example, one shelter worker observed that some of the women she dealt with did not know how to parent their children: "They have devoted so much of their time to trying to please their abusive husbands that they have neglected their children." In their former lives, their experience with the outside world was limited. A number went directly from their parents' homes to that of their husbands without ever having to learn how to live on their own. Jackie had never had to deal with money and budgeting.

> All my life, I got sort of an allowance. My husband would give me so much for groceries. He said, "When it's gone, it's gone." So I lived that way. I bought what I wanted and sometimes there would be money left over but most times, I'd run out the last

week of the month and we'd eat leftovers. If he didn't want that, he took us out to eat.

Until I left my husband, I'd never had a credit card or bank account of any kind. He looked after the bills and everything. Boy, it was a real eye-opener when I got out on my own.

About half of the women had not had a job or had been unemployed for a considerable length of time. As Jackie explained:

My husband didn't want me to work. He said it would affect his standing in the community. He'd say, "What'd the neighbors say if they thought you had to go to work? They'd say I was a poor provider." So when I went looking for a job after I'd left him, I'd always dread the "what experience have you had" question because then I'd have to say that the last job I had was working part-time in a corner store thirty years ago. That usually pretty much ended the interview right there.

The shelter workers found that these women had no idea how to put a resume together or how to go about looking for work. "We offer evening workshops to help them and sometimes, if we have the time, we'd go through the want ads in the paper with them." A shelter worker remembers a woman who burst into tears after spending an hour or so with the want ads.

I asked her what was wrong. She pointed to the paper and said, "I just looked through four pages of jobs, four pages, all kinds of jobs. I'm not qualified for a single one." It was heartbreaking to see a woman in her forties discovering she had no marketable skills.

Needless to say, these women have had to learn how to survive, how to find a job and how to keep it—all new experiences for some of them. Eventually some go back to school. Others start on the ground floor of a company and work their way up slowly, learning as they go. There are some, however, who find it impossible to enter the workforce. They end up on welfare.

Lack of Money

In today's modern society, women traditionally earn less than men do, even if they are in the same jobs and doing the same work. This, to some extent, accounts for why most single-income families with a woman as the "head of household" live below the poverty line (that artificial annual income level that divides the poor from the rest). It is much worse for abused women on their own for the first time with few or no marketable skills, because they find themselves in menial or unskilled labor categories getting paid a minimum wage.

Although the minimum hourly wage varies from state to state and province to province, it averages about $5.00. That works out to about $850 to $900 per month before deductions, based on a forty-hour week. Vickie sat in a coffee shop while she stared at her first paycheck ever from a fast food restaurant. For two weeks' work, the check was for around $350. She shook her head.

> You know, when I was living with him, we spent this much on groceries for two weeks. How am I going to pay for everything out of this? It is impossible. My rent alone is $300.

She eventually quit and applied for social assistance which, ironically, paid her more money and subsidized her rent. Janice, a mother with two small children, applied for social assistance immediately upon arriving at the shelter.

> I knew I'd never be able to make a go of it. The cheapest day care I could find wanted $190 a month per kid. At minimum wage, just getting someone to look after the kids so I could work would take half of everything I make. Why bother. Later, when the kids are old enough to go to school, then I'll look for a job.

Even those women who have some skills find it difficult to survive and get ahead. They cannot help but compare the material comfort of their old lives with their new ones. Paula is a receptionist for a dentist.

> Everything I own I bought at garage sales and even then, I had to wait a year before I could afford a couch. I still don't have a TV. I used to have everything. Now I have next to nothing.

We found that most abused women, particularly those who flee, are struggling to make ends meet. They live in subsidized low-rent housing or in the cheaper apartment buildings. Social assistance provided Janice with a tiny two-bedroom apartment in a downtown complex. It was all she could get, and she and her children have found there is a lot of adjusting to do.

> Try explaining to a five-year-old why we have to step over drunks in the hallway to get to our apartment. We have cockroaches in the kitchen and the whole place stinks like old gym socks or worse.
> We have a park next door but I couldn't let the kids play there. There are used needles and broken liquor bottles all over everything.

She came from a large, four-bedroom house in the suburbs, where the biggest problem was a neighbor who used his leaf blower too early on a Saturday morning. In her new home she has to carry a flashlight, because people keep stealing the bulbs out of the hall light fixtures, and a can of pepper spray, because offensive and belligerent drunks sleep in that same hall.

Perhaps the most serious impact this lack of finances has is that it significantly limits the future options available to the woman. She cannot hope to improve her education, gain worthwhile promotions, or get better jobs by upgrading her skills as these steps cost money, money she does not have.

LACK OF CONFIDENCE

There is another significant lack that affects their new lives perhaps more than any other: a lack of self-confidence. The abused women have been the subordinate partners in an abusive relationship long enough to have learned they are incapable of independent thought, which "is a good thing because if they ever did make independent decisions, they would certainly screw them up." They have been socialized to accept this as fact. Therefore they show up at the shelters with little or no self-esteem. "I am nothing. I am dirt. I am worse than dirt." This perspective will have an impact on everything that follows. They know they are going to fail, so many are afraid to even try. They make excuses and find reasons to stay in the shelter rather than face the new beginning.

Most of the shelters operate mandatory workshops and support groups in an attempt to bolster self-esteem and confidence, but it is an uphill battle. Even in the workshops filled with women just like her, a new arrival is reluctant to speak because she believes "no one wants to hear what I have to say." As long as the self-esteem is low, there will be little progress towards a better life for these women. For that reason, the shelters place their emphasis on building confidence. They begin to resocialize the women into believing that they are worthwhile as individuals and can make a positive contribution to society. Most of the women do not accept this for a very long time.

SUPERWOMAN SYNDROME

A few women, perhaps fewer than 10 percent, rebound from the years of oppression that they have experienced and regain their self-confidence rather too quickly and too well. These women, usually already employed at the time of their marriage breakup, tend to overcompensate for their years as a subordinate partner by developing an exaggerated estimation of their capabilities. They become "superwomen" capable of much more than mere mortals. Perhaps they are attempting to make up for the lost years spent with an abusive husband.

Margaret was a classic "superwoman" who, as a middle manager in a service industry business, became a workaholic putting in between eighty and a hundred hours a week at work (but getting paid for only 37.5 of those hours). Even at home, she would spend much of her time on the telephone making plans, setting schedules, or just making contacts. Her boss commented that she believed she could handle anything: "Any time I had a project that needed doing, she would be the first to volunteer no matter what else she currently had on her plate." Margaret said, "It was like I had something to prove. I was going to show everyone that I was the best manager ever. I believed I could run the whole place by myself."

This need to accomplish more spilled over into her home life. She was always on the go. Before she went to work in the morning, she would do a load of laundry, wash a floor, and phone a family member. After a ten- to twelve-hour day, she would stop on her way home to do some grocery shopping and/or some other errands. Once home, she would clean some more and make a series of phone calls. There was nothing she couldn't do. She was superwoman. Of course, she often forgot to eat or sleep. Margaret's typical response to the question "How was your day?" was "I only got half of what I wanted to get done done." Considering that she had planned to accomplish twice what was humanly possible, that was a fair response after a solid day's work.

We think that this "superwoman syndrome" masks a fundamental lack of confidence. The women are always busy because they are afraid that if people do not see them accomplishing seemingly impossible tasks, they will think the superwomen are slackers who aren't doing the job. They fear being found out as frauds. One "superwoman" told us:

> I was juggling so many projects in the air that I was sure they were all going to come crashing down around me any day. But all I could do was to keep juggling more and more, faster and faster. That way, if one got lost or messed up, no one would notice. They would all be too busy watching my hands.

Superwomen tend to burn out relatively quickly. Once they are forced to slow down or stop due to injury or fatigue or mental exhaustion, they are able to deal with their insecurities and lack of confidence and, with any luck, develop a more healthy balance.

Living with the Memory

It is likely that most abused women never fully escape the abuse. Its effects are felt for years, and some of them do not even appear until some years have passed. Louise said she didn't realize just how much she had been affected by William until she had been away from him for two or three years. She said she suddenly realized she had a warped view of a number of things. "I thought my new husband didn't love me because he wasn't jealous." Her abusive husband had been. She had been away from William for seven years when she said: "I still find times when the things he said will be back inside my head.... The memories I carry around."

The women leave the abusive relationship and take with them what they repeatedly called "excess baggage" but which is more properly termed the results of intense socialization. They have unconsciously learned to view the world the way their husbands taught them to. The women learn to behave in certain ways in response to certain circumstances or conditions. For example, Margaret became conditioned to having her children's toys picked up and put away by noon, when her husband would come home for lunch. Failure to have the house neat enough for him brought swift punishment. For years afterwards, long after the marriage had broken up, she would rush to clean up her own house, or panic if she hadn't yet cleaned and saw from a glance at the clock that it was past noon. These are conditioned and automatic responses that the woman has no control over.

Because they are conditioned responses resulting from socialization, they may not surface until the circumstances match those they were first applied to. Betty had been badly scalded the day her abusive husband dumped a bowl of pea soup on her. That was how Betty learned that her husband hated pea soup. Approximately ten years later, she sat down for a lunch her new husband had made for her. It was pea soup, something they had not yet had together.

> I freaked. I covered my face with my hands and ran into the bathroom. I couldn't stop shaking. It was like I had been transported back in time.

That residual training remained hidden until circumstances activated it.

One of the most tragic aspects of this kind of socialization is that in a normal functional relationship, seemingly innocuous events can trigger highly inappropriate responses which would have been "normal" behaviors in the abusive relationship. Those responses can be triggered anywhere and at any time. This can put an enormous strain on the individuals and the relationships they develop after the abusive marriage is over.

For example, Alice's husband George insisted that all of the food in the cupboards had to be alphabetized with the labels facing front. His mother, who also organized her cupboards that way, dropped in one day and at some time during the visit pointed out to George that one can was misaligned. After she had left,

George beat Alice for embarrassing him in front of his mother. From that day forward, he made spot checks on the cupboards, and if they were not up to his standards, a beating would follow. She learned to be very precise in the arrangement of cans. She also learned to sweat and shake when she heard a cupboard door being opened. Alice recalls how, many years later, that behavior returned when she was entertaining her fiancé and his parents in her home.

> I was in the living room and I heard a cupboard being opened. I raced into the kitchen and screamed: "Get the f__k out of my cupboard!" My fiancé's mother, who had been looking for sugar for her coffee and didn't want to bother me, just stood there with her mouth open. Although I apologized and tried to explain, the rest of the evening did not go well. We broke up soon after that.

The combination of kitchen cupboards and prospective mother-in-law triggered the panic and the inappropriate reaction. It was not something that was planned, nor was it expected.

The excess baggage of conditioned responses to specific sets of circumstances can never be completely eradicated. The women can go for years without even thinking about the abuse they were subjected to. However, when circumstances come together in just the right way, it is as if they never left that marriage. The years between then and now shrink to nanoseconds.

The people who have become parts of the abused woman's new social network have to deal with the baggage as well. It can put a severe strain on relationships and test the limits of friendship. The worst part is that there is nothing anyone can really do about it because it is unconscious and it is automatic, habitual. It is the everlasting residue of an abusive relationship. It is part of the subconscious memory, ready to surface when called for. Abused women must live with that memory for the rest of their lives.

In almost every case, the abused women recognized the toll abuse exacts from them and wanted to prevent other women from being abused. "No one should have to suffer like this" was the way one of them put it. Many have become activists, attending support groups, working crisis lines, lobbying politicians, volunteering in shelters, or helping out in some other way. Others were not ready or were not in a position to become active, but every woman the authors spoke to was willing to offer her ideas concerning what needs to be done. They were all committed to finding the solution.

Notes

1. Deborah's mother was an abused woman herself but because of her religious beliefs, she refused to even consider leaving her husband. She also felt that her daughter should suffer the abuse because that was the life "God has given her."
2. In political terms, this socialization process is called brainwashing.
3. No one in her family knew about the abuse. They thought it was just the "usual" marital troubles.
4. Likely, Alan did not realize how much energy, time and money was required to care for a toddler and work full time as well.
5. They lived in the country, and since it was winter when this incident occurred, he was able to effectively trap her in the house by taking all the car keys, telephones, and winter jackets.
6. There were no cases of an abused woman going to live with a male friend under similar circumstances.
7. Many lawyers are now automatically recommending restraining orders in cases of spousal abuse.
8. The only exceptions were when there were substantial assets in the form of bank accounts, securities, or property.
9. Tracking down individuals on the Internet is not difficult for someone familiar with the software and techniques. To test this, we arranged for an expert to find us after we changed our e-mail address. It took him less than an hour to complete the task, even though we had changed servers and our line access location as well as the address.
10. Not all of the laws are uniform across jurisdictions. For example, trespassing in some western Canadian provinces occurs when someone enters a building without permission. In many American states, one need only step onto the property without permission to be trespassing.

Chapter 5

What Can We Do?

During discussions with all the participants and stakeholders,[1] they presented a wide range of "ways to solve the problem' of wife abuse. The solutions proposed by the participants and stakeholders fell into two broad categories: (1) prevention, or preventative measures—solutions aimed at preventing spousal abuse from ever happening, and (2) termination, or protective measures—solutions designed to put an end to abusive situations that already exist. Interestingly, the former category was quite small with only a few suggestions in it, whereas the latter was a huge category featuring a wide range of potential solutions.

Preventative Measures

Potential Abusers

Most people approached the possibility of preventing spousal abuse with a somewhat fatalistic perspective. The general consensus was that an abuser may be compensating for a bad job or low self-esteem or having been mistreated by his parents, but the real reason he beats his wife is because he wants to, because it makes him feel good, because he can do it. Douglas and Olshaker (1997: 362–3), while discussing violent criminal behavior (a category that should include serial spouse abusers) from a criminal justice perspective, point out that intervention at an early age is the only way to prevent adult violence because "by the time it makes a blip on our radar [that is, a violent crime is committed], it's too late; the criminal personality is already well established." Some people were not prepared to give up on the adult abuser and offered ways to "get to" him. However, once the pattern is established—and this appears to occur at a fairly young age—it becomes almost impossible to break.

One abuser who was interviewed was in prison for aggravated assault against his wife. Michael did not perceive his assaultive behavior as bad. Rather, he was quite bitter that the police and the courts had put him in prison for doing what he thought was perfectly natural. He said: "Every now and again, kids get out of hand and you gotta beat them back into line. It's the same with women. They get uppity and start talking back, so you beat them back into line. What's wrong with that?" He made it perfectly clear that he had every intention of continuing to beat his wife when he was released from prison.

According to a number of psychologists, Michael is quite typical of abusers. One researcher suggested that trying to change his behavior now would be like approaching a heterosexual male and telling him that the laws now outlawed heterosexual sex, and the only acceptable and legal sex was between two males. Not only would the heterosexual find the new laws upsetting, he would in all likelihood defy them. Michael presumably feels the same way about beating his wife. Accordingly, most preventative measures were aimed at early childhood intervention.

CHILDHOOD

In order to prevent abuse from starting, a number of steps that could be taken were suggested. Many of them focused on the way a young boy is raised. These ideas tended to focus on the reduction of violence and aggression in the young boy's childhood and home.

1. *Socialization.* It was felt that boys' aggressiveness training was in need of modification. Aggressive or violent behavior must be avoided in the presence of the

children and the messages must be clear and unequivocal. For example, a mother cannot explain to a boy that it is wrong to hit his sibling and then punish him with a spanking.

2. *Non-destructive problem solving.* Many of those in the helping professions argued that at home, in preschool, and in kindergarten, children should be taught a variety of non-destructive problem-solving techniques. The idea is that all of the caregivers should promote cooperative endeavors and place a high value on cooperation rather than competition.

3. *Reducing availability of violent toys.* The counselors and psychologists were concerned about the availability of violent toys—guns, war-related toys and games, video games—and their effects on young boys. They felt that aggressiveness in young boys could be reduced by lowering the number of violent toys on the market. The proponents of this idea were not sure how or even if this could be done, but they saw it as important in the socialization process.

4. *Reducing media violence.* Similarly, the amount of violence the boy witnesses, on television in particular, is going to have an impact on his thought processes. If he sees repeatedly that "might makes right," it becomes his creed for life. Alternatively, if he sees cooperative and caring individuals on television, he will absorb their philosophy without being aware of it.

5. *Education.* Several social workers suggested that courses teaching the idea that "violence is bad" be introduced into schools at the Kindergarten or Grade I level. These courses should deal with anger management and life skills. The social workers felt that if young boys learned how to control their tempers and knew how to negotiate for what they wanted, they would learn that violent behavior such as temper tantrums and bullying is inappropriate.

6. *Breaking the cycle of abuse.* There were many proponents of the idea that the cycle of abuse must be broken

and that it should be done when the male is very young. The idea is to adopt "zero tolerance" for family violence. If a boy is in an abusive home, he is to be removed from that home and placed in a "normal" family environment.

7. *"Problem child" intervention: foster care.* Schoolteachers, lawyers, psychologists, and counselors all argued that childhood behavior, rather than childhood learning, could be associated with violent behavior in adults. They recommended that when a boy is identified as troubled, he should be placed in a foster home with "professional" parents who would provide a proper environment. The basic idea is to be able to monitor, recognize, and correct problem behavior when necessary. We feel that a comment was necessary here: We spoke to a number of child psychologists concerning this option, and all agreed that the idea, sound in theory, is utopian and unrealistic in practice. One suggested that it would send boys from "the frying pan into the fire" in that most often, foster care tends to have a more debilitating effect than does remaining in an abusive and dysfunctional family situation.

8. *"Problem child" intervention: psychological help.* The same people who suggested the foster care for "problem" boys also felt that as soon as they were identified, they should begin psychological treatment or counseling, either in their own homes or in foster care.

ADULT

Most people felt that by the time a male reaches adulthood, it is too late. He is an abuser who just hasn't started yet. Others felt that adult potential abusers may become abusive under certain circumstances, which, if they could be avoided, would not lead to abuse. Five ways were offered to diffuse the situation before the potential abuser becomes violent.

1. *Legalizing abuse.* Two abusive husbands and a brother of an abusive man suggested that the simplest way to eliminate the spousal abuse problem was to decriminalize it. "A man has the right to do what he wants in his own home. The government does not have the right to

interfere in a family's day-to-day life." These men wanted women to return to "traditional" values and recognize that a woman's place was by her husband's side, doing what he tells her to do and "getting smacked" if she doesn't. "We need to get rid of all that equal rights crap and get back to the way it used to be."

This solution is, without a doubt, absurd and totally lacking in merit. It does not propose a workable solution but rather speaks to the state of mind of the abusers themselves. It has been said a number of times that the abusers do not perceive their actions as wrong. The suggestion that wife beating be legalized reinforces that perception.

2. *Providing stress relief outlets.* "I wouldn't hit my wife nearly so often if I had some way to unwind," was how one man introduced this proposal. He argued that abuse is largely associated with, and caused by, pent-up stress and anxiety. "There should be sports to play or watch, entertainment, all that kind of stuff, to let a guy unwind after work." He wanted cheap season's tickets to the local professional sports games.

3. *Individual psychological counseling.* Many different people felt that as frustration builds, a man may lash out at his wife in an uncontrolled rage. They said that before the breaking point is reached, he should have the opportunity to talk about his frustrations and develop solutions without the need to become physically abusive.

4. *Support groups.* In addition to the one-on-one counseling, several professionals suggested that potential abusers should attend support groups with men who have already been down that road to learn how to deal with the pent-up frustrations that lead to abuse.

5. *Employment training.* The abusive husband, his family, and his friends all felt that abuse could be avoided or eliminated if potentially abusive men had opportunities for employment advancement. "There is nothing harder on a man than knowing he's going to spend the rest of his life in a dead-end job." They proposed a series of low- or

no-cost training programs for low wage earners that would permit the men to get ahead and thereby reduce frustration and abusive behavior.

Potential Victims

Members of the general public often make comments like "Why do they put up with it? If my husband slapped me just once, I'd be out of there so fast!" They do not realize the extent or the complexity of the abusive situation. When a woman in an abusive relationship is first married, her husband is not physically abusive. Rather, he is probably subtly controlling, and he is also possessive and jealous of her, wanting to spend every waking moment with her (a trait she finds endearing and romantic in the beginning). Soon the beatings begin and she is in pain, but she is able to rationalize his violent behavior—"He's working so hard, drinking too much, under a lot of stress." However, in the meantime, her self-esteem takes a nosedive. She thinks he beats her because she is doing something wrong. She tries to be a "better wife" but the beatings continue. Eventually, she simply gives up. "I am a really horrible person because no matter what I do, it is wrong and he punishes me. Let him beat me. I deserve it." From that point on, the beatings and abuse are normal, a part of their way of life. Informants offered a number of proposals designed to prevent this kind of scenario from developing and thereby prevent abuse.

CHILDHOOD

Much of what the woman perceives and how she acts as an adult depends on how she grew up and what kind of role models she had as a young child. If she is raised in a caring and nurturing environment, she will be strong enough to resist falling into the abuse trap. What follows are some ideas concerning what a woman must have during her childhood in order to help her avoid becoming a victim of abuse later in life.

1. *"Everyone is equally worthwhile."* Some abused women felt that the society was far too competitive. "The idea that in a race, or in any competition, you either come in

first or you lose affects us all" was how one friend put it. "You can run a marathon or climb a mountain, but if you aren't first, you are nothing." Young girls learn early that boys are faster and stronger, that boys win all the competitions and therefore boys are winners and girls are losers. Eventually, this winner/loser dichotomy is extended to all things, including marriages. The woman enters the relationship with the assumption that she is inferior to her husband. To the participants in this study, this idea was anathema. "It isn't true, but so many of us believe it." "We should be emphasizing that everyone's contribution is worthwhile and to be valued." Girls have to be taught that personal achievements and cooperation are important, and that even if they never win a race—the competing, the getting involved—is what counts. The informants suggested games and projects that promote cooperation rather than competition.

2. *Positive self-esteem.* Many of the participants were of the opinion that most of the problems plaguing society have roots in the low self-esteem of many of the people. Husbands get away with abuse because wives let them. They see themselves as unimportant, inconsequential. "I often thought of calling the police but I never did. I figured, who'd take my word over his? He's an important man in the community. I'm just a housewife." The solution to this problem is to use every means available to develop the positive self-esteem of people, particularly young girls. "Use the radio, the TV, the schools. Talk to them. Always tell them they are wonderful." Girls with positive self-esteem will be less likely to become victims later.

3. *Education.* Young girls need to be taught to recognize abuse for what it is—criminal violent behavior—especially if they are in abusive homes. Girls who grow up watching their fathers beating their mothers presume, because they do not know otherwise, that it is normal. As adults, they will expect to be beaten by their husbands. If they can learn in school that what their fathers

are doing is wrong and not normal, they will be much less accepting of violent behavior from their spouses.
4. *Breaking the cycle of abuse.* The "zero tolerance" policy for violence in the home applies for girls as well as boys. If a girl is in an abusive home, she should be removed immediately and placed in a non-violent, nurturing environment.

ADULT

Preparing a girl to prevent abuse later in life was considered critical, and so prevention proposals tended to center on the potential victim as a child. However, several people believed that there were two or three changes that could be made to prevent the beginning of an abusive relationship when the woman was already an adult.

1. *Trial marriages.* When two people marry each other, it is technically for life. It is a long-term commitment, and if a woman makes a mistake and marries an abuser, it can be difficult for her to extract herself from it, especially since family, community, society, and the courts are all assuming the life-time commitment. Some informants suggested that instead of the "till death do us part," long-term marriage, which can be ended only by going to court, there should be marriage contracts lasting for specific lengths of time, which one must go to court to renew. For example, one could get married for one or two years using a contract stipulating in advance precisely how assets will be divided at the end of the period, what the child custody and support arrangements will be, and so on. The contract would be legally binding on both parties and at the end of the contract's term, the marriage would be dissolved and assets divided unless both parties renew the contract for another set period of time.

Under this system, a woman who is being abused may choose not to renew the contract, and the relationship ends. She can then take advantage of the court-sanctioned structure to make sure she retains the portion of the assets specified in the contract as hers. This is a positive and built-in mechanism of escape from an abusive relationship, and since continuation of the relationship is based on mutual trust, the likelihood of a man becoming abusive in this type of relationship is diminished.

2. *Matrifocal family structure.* One of the more radical proposals, this requires a major change in the way the family is structured and how it operates. Several people suggested that society adopt a matrifocal, or "mother-focused," family as a basic unit by removing the adult male from the nuclear family unit. The suggestion was that the family should consist of a woman and her children acting together as an independent residential, economic, and social unit, while the husband lives elsewhere, and participates in the marriage and the family on a part-time basis. He may contribute to the family financially and emotionally, but he would not be an official part of the family.

The benefits of the shift to a matrifocal family unit are obvious in terms of preventing spousal abuse. It promotes a degree of independence in the woman, preventing the husband from completely dominating her and so making it difficult to begin an abusive relationship. Also, if the marriage breaks up, the wife need not relocate and give up all of her assets because she never surrendered them to her husband in the first place. There is also an element of security in this situation. If a man abuses his wife in a home they share, he cannot be forcibly ejected by the authorities, but if they maintain separate residences, he can be legally removed from her home, by force if necessary.

This solution was proposed by a number of abused women who were not aware that matrifocal families are common among African American segments of the population and are one of the fastest-growing family type among Euroamerican segments (cf. Haley 2000). The result would not be the empowered female head of household our participants perceived, as the matrifocal families that exist currently tend to fall well below the poverty line and their male children grow up without positive male role models. The freedom is illusionary, and unless much of the fabric of North American society can be altered, this solution is unfortunately naïve.

3. *Personal growth and awareness.* Adult women, because of the male dominance orientation of the society, suffer repeated attacks on their self-esteem and self-worth. In some jobs, they must be twice as good as their male counterparts in order to be accepted as equal. As the old joke goes, "men are aggressive, women are pushy." If a woman's self-esteem is diminished enough as a result of the societal perspective, she is a prime candidate for an abusive relationship that begins with the male dominating the female. Submissiveness caused by low self-esteem and insecurity has a tendency to encourage a dominating personality type to push harder, to be more dominant. Recognizing this, it was felt that all adult women who are not being abused should have access to various programs—educational, inspirational, motivational, and recreational—that contribute to personal growth and awareness. By taking advantage of these programs, a woman could bolster her self-image, gain strength, and thereby improve her self-esteem. It would then be difficult for someone to gain the kind of dominance over her that an abuser wants and needs. She would be too strong to permit it.

Both Groups

1. *New parent training.* Couples who have children are all amateurs when it comes to raising those children. Lacking experience of their own, they have only their own parents' experience to draw on. Their ignorance and their need to rely on their own parents' experiences often lead to mistakes. They learn as they go, and in the process, often learn poor child rearing practices. It

was suggested that at some point in his or her formal education, everyone be required to take at least one course on how to be a parent. The hope is that it will prepare them to be positive role models and have the necessary awareness of their responsibilities in the socialization process.

2. *Marriage training.* One counselor felt that people who are about to be married should take a marriage training course that teaches them how a nurturing relationship functions and what society's expectations are for the marriage and the couple.

3. *Not tolerating violence.* Several members of a support group felt that some kind of media "blitz" broadcasting the message that violence in any form should not be tolerated would be helpful. They suggested that potential abusers and potential victims would both benefit from the positive reinforcement of nonviolent behaviors. The support group did not confine its idea to the media: they wanted the community, the police, the courts—in short everyone—to carry the message everywhere.

4. *Education (recognizing spousal abuse).* In order to prevent abuse from starting, potential victims and abusers should be taught what abuse is and why it is wrong. The support group member who proposed this idea argued that "information is power," and that if a wife knew how to recognize abuse and saw the cycle beginning, she could act early to prevent it from taking hold. Simultaneously, if a potential abuser is fully aware of the unlawfulness of his urges, he may resist striking out.

Protective Measures

There was intense interest in developing a plan that would stop abuse after it had already begun. "Men are beating their wives and they must be stopped!" was the general attitude of the participants in the discussion groups. They all recognized, however, that there is no single solution that will end the problem instantly.

Instead, a variety of actions from a number of directions is needed. Their protective measures were divided into four major sections: (1) measures aimed at the abusive husband, (2) measures associated with the abused wife, (3) measures involving both partners, and (4) measures relating to the general public and to the community.

Abusers

TREATMENT

During discussions, terms like "sociopath," "psychopath," "crazy," "deviant," and just plain "nuts" were used frequently. Most people felt that an abuser was in some way abnormal and in need of treatment. However, even as the treatment options were being offered, they were couched in pessimistic terms. No one really felt they would work.

1. *Mandatory psychological treatment for offenders.* Many of the informants wanted the abuser placed in a mental institution under the supervision of a psychiatrist. They all believed that an abuser is mentally ill and needs to be treated with drugs or psychotherapy or whatever else might cure him. They stated that this treatment must be mandatory, as the abuser does not recognize that he is ill and sees no need for treatment. He will not go voluntarily.

2. *Anger management course.* Part of the psychological rehabilitation (or resocialization) of the abusive husband would be an intensive anger management program or course that emphasizes and teaches that violent behavior is not acceptable or appropriate.

3. *Life skills training and retraining.* Another educational/ treatment measure that should be available to the abuser is a course in life skills. These kinds of courses typically contain elements such as basic budgeting, job hunting techniques, and communication skills.

4. *Employment education.* A number of the abusers' relatives felt the way to solve the problem was to upgrade his education and thereby improve his job prospects. They suggested a variety of training courses sponsored

by the government, such as apprenticeship programs and university degrees. Educate him and get him into a job with a future, and stress will disappear. When the stress is gone, abuse should stop.

5. *Group therapy.* Group therapy was seen as another way to get the abuser to recognize that he has a behavioral problem. Interestingly, the strongest proponents of this idea were the abused women, who felt that the husband had to confront his behavioral problem (the abuse) and its psychological roots. The women also felt that since abusive men would never participate voluntarily, they should be compelled to do so by the courts.

6. *One-on-one therapy.* The abused women also wanted their husbands and others like them to be compelled to attend one-on-one counseling.

7. *Treatment for substance abuse.* A member of the clergy felt that the abuser would benefit from a substance abuse clinic or the like.

LEGAL RESPONSES

Since spousal abuse in its physical aspect is illegal, it is not surprising that the women demanded a number of legal responses to it to deter and punish the abuser.

1. *Tougher laws.* Many felt that the current laws governing assault are inadequate. In their opinion, one expects to be attacked by strangers and can take precautions, but no one expects to be physically attacked by a loved one and there certainly are no precautions one can take to guard against that. They want the laws rewritten to make assault on a family member a far more serious offense than an assault on a stranger.

> If I'm walking down a dark street late at night and I get mugged or beaten up, I'm partly to blame because I know better than to be in that kind of place at that time. But, if I'm at home, asleep, and my husband comes in and attacks me, he has to take full responsibility for the assault.

The women who suggested the tougher laws believed husbands must understand that they have no right to assault their wives, and that if they do, the consequences will be dire. The legal system should "stand behind the [abused] women."

2. *More serious legal penalties for offenders.* Associated with tougher laws are more serious penalties.

> My husband was charged with assault and got thirty days in jail. He referred to that time as a "vacation." He wasn't home eight hours before I was on my way to the hospital again.

The penalty for wife beating, one wife said, should be a minimum of two years in jail, with two more years added for each additional conviction.

3. *More police powers to arrest/charge abusers.* In many states, the victim must charge the abuser before he can be arrested. This puts her in a very difficult spot, since she is then directly responsible for having him thrown in jail. The women felt that in abuse cases, the police should have the power to charge the offender so they will "take the heat" instead of the wife.

4. *Ability of court to hold abuser without bail until wife is safe.* Under current laws, a person charged with a crime has the right to appear before a judge and request release on bail within a reasonable amount of time. In some jurisdictions, the bail hearing must occur within a certain specified time after the arrest. Some informants spoke of abusive husbands being back home in six or eight hours. One woman's husband spent three consecutive nights in jail for beating her each successive evening. Before he was released the third time, she fled to a shelter and he came home to an empty house.

> I would have left after the first beating, but he got home before I had time to pack. The second night I was too sore to do anything, but when he beat me up the third time, I was so angry I just had to leave. If I hadn't gone then, I think I would've sat in the living room with a shotgun waiting for him to walk through the door. Either way, I couldn't take another beating.

She and many others felt that once an abusive husband is arrested, he should be held without bail for a specific length of time. Forty-eight hours was suggested. That would give the wife time to clear out with a head start.

5. *Special courts for abuse cases.* A psychologist brought up the idea of a special court for cases of spousal abuse. He suggested a model similar to the family courts that now exist. "It should be responsible for all forms of family violence" and would, he continued, insure that cases of wife beating, now treated as assault, would get the attention they deserve.

6. *More vigorous enforcement of existing laws.* Many people, including police officers, agreed that the police and the courts need to treat spousal abuse with the seriousness it deserves. There are laws dealing with armed and unarmed assault that could be used to control abusive behavior, but in many areas, the police have been somewhat relaxed in their application of those laws to domestic disputes. It was felt that the authorities ought to enforce the laws already in place with vigor. Proponents of this measure feel that abusive husbands have been getting away with murder for too long.

7. *Corporal punishment.* In the spirit of "an eye for an eye," the victim's family and friends, as well as some of the front-line workers (from both the shelters and Victims' Services), wanted abusers to be subject to corporal punishment. One worker talked about caning as it is done in Indonesia, while another suggested using fists. The idea was to let the abuser know what it feels like to be beaten, and also to let him know that he will suffer each time he beats his wife.

8. *Public humiliation.* One victim's friends and a shelter worker argued that because abuse is such a secret, men get away with it too frequently. It was proposed that the abuser should be publicly humiliated in some way to shame him into mending his ways. A woman noted that a gas station in her neighborhood displayed a huge sign

covered with announcements such as "John Doe—pay your NSF checks." She proposed that public billboards reading "John Doe—stop beating your wife!" be put up. Announce the names of abusers publicly so everyone knows they are criminals.

One informant went a step farther and wanted a revival of the pillories used in the seventeenth and eighteenth centuries.

> Fix it so the abuser gets to sit with his head and hands in a yoke in the middle of a park or something. There, people could come to laugh at him, throw rotten fruit, and generally make fun of them. I don't think many men would want to go through that twice.

9. *Castration.* Two friends of an abused woman were convinced the only way abuse can be stopped is to establish a severe penalty, one that would serve as a strong deterrent. They suggested that once a man is convicted of spousal abuse more than once, the automatic penalty should be castration.

COMMUNITY RESPONSES

1. *Community action.* One shelter worker, who was also a formerly abused wife (twice), said that "We need more men confronting the abuser, telling him that his behavior is unacceptable and that the men in the community are not going to stand for it." She wanted everyone in the community, particularly the men, to impose social sanctions on the abuser in an attempt to get him to conform to acceptable standards of behavior. "They have to know that real men do not beat their wives."

Victims

Our informants realized that stopping wife abuse and protecting the victims from further abuse would require a concerted effort from all quarters. It was repeatedly emphasized that an abused woman cannot, as a rule, break away from the relationship without a great deal of assistance that continues after she is out of the relationship. The assistance and protective measures proposed for the victim came in three groups: treatment and education proposals, legal responses, and essential services.

TREATMENT AND EDUCATION

1. *Psychological counseling.* The abused women and the professionals involved in counseling (psychologists, counselors, the clergy) were convinced that an abused woman would benefit greatly from one-on-one psychological counseling on a regular and frequent basis. She has just emerged from a situation that has generated, for her, a great deal of confusion. Her perspective has become distorted, and in some cases, she has become totally reliant on her husband to tell her what to think and feel. She needs someone to talk to, someone to listen to her and to guide her towards a more balanced perspective.

2. *Support groups.* Equally essential are support groups, also referred to as therapy or self-help groups. In order to recover from her psychological and emotional trauma, an abused woman requires the opportunity to sit down with others who have had similar relationships. The sharing of experiences and freedom to talk without fear of judgment in a group of one's peers are therapeutic and healing.

3. *Employment readiness training programs.* Quite a few abused women suggested that the government sponsor a set of educational programs for abused women who have fled their marriages. They thought that many women who find themselves in that situation are unprepared to take almost any kind of job. Many have been housewives for "umpteen" years and have no idea how to look for a job, let alone do one. There should be a variety of courses ranging from basic resume writing to computer literacy, plus all kinds of other programs meant to prepare the woman to enter the workforce and get ahead.

4. *Self-esteem programs.* A woman in an abusive relationship is battered emotionally as well as physically. Her

self-esteem is so low she cannot identify herself as an individual. She is nothing more than an appendage to her husband, and is therefore incapable of independent decision-making. Having left her husband, she has to make it on her own, but if her self-esteem remains low, she will fail. Of course, failure will lower her self-esteem even further. These women need programs aimed specifically at raising self-esteem and self-worth. They have to learn to respect, love, and take pride in themselves again.

5. *Advertise services available to the abused.* A shelter worker doubted the effectiveness of the advertising currently being done in the area of services available for abused women.

> We print brochures and distribute them to wherever women gather, but I don't think it is enough. Actually, I'm not sure brochures are the way to go. More than one woman has been beaten for having one of our brochures in her possession.

This worker wanted shelter addresses to be featured on milk cartons, cereal boxes, and other common household products, as well as television ads, radio spots, and newspaper articles.

LEGAL RESPONSES

1. *More protection for abused women.* The police need to react more forcibly when it comes to spousal abuse. In addition to arresting and charging the husband, they must offer protection to the wife. If she chooses to remain in her home, there should be an officer there with her when her husband comes home. If she chooses to leave him, the police should take her to safety and if necessary post armed guards at her new location, wherever that may be. They must show the abusive husband that they take the wife's safety very seriously. Several people, including abused women, demanded more protection for the abused. "Right now, the police

are perpetrator-oriented. They deal with him and pretty much ignore the victim. That needs to change."

2. *"Instant divorce" and child custody for abused women.* If a man is convicted of assaulting his wife, the wife should be able to apply for and receive an instant divorce, along with sole custody of the children. If an abuser is faced with losing control of his wife and children, he may tend to be less abusive. More to the point, the woman would have a quick way out of an abusive relationship.

3. *Automatic court orders to keep abusers away.* A woman fleeing her abusive husband is often in danger, since a change in the relationship dynamics is often accompanied by increased violence. Case after case has been documented of an estranged husband stalking, harassing, injuring, and/or killing his estranged wife for leaving him. The women need protection. One way to accomplish this is through a system of automatic court orders. Once she has an automatic restraining order, the woman does not have to wait for the husband to do something (threaten or hit her, for example) before calling the police. His simply being near her becomes a crime. She sees him, calls the police, and they arrest him. Assuming effective enforcement of these automatic restraining orders, the women should be much safer.

4. *Easier access to lawyers.* Women with few assets of their own, and this includes many who flee their husbands, cannot afford "good" divorce lawyers because of the expense. Their husbands, on the other hand, can afford them. The women must make do with chronically overworked Legal Aid lawyers or endure enormous financial hardship to hire a lawyer. Some of the women felt that this was unfair. They need to have easier access to lawyers experienced in divorces, child custody cases, and the like. Most did not know how this could be accomplished. One woman thought there should be a government-backed loan program for women who have lost control of their own assets because they left the husband in control of those assets when they fled.

5. *Rapid settlement of finances.* Often when a woman leaves an abusive relationship, she also leaves behind everything she owns or has a financial interest in. Her husband retains possession of the house, car, bank accounts, and so on. She leaves with nothing. As she begins to rebuild her life, she files for a divorce that includes a financial settlement. In the current system, "possession is nine-tenths of the law" (even in community property states) and a woman faces a long uphill struggle to recover what is rightly hers. Her ex-husband can hire better lawyers since he has all the assets, hers as well as his, and he can drag his feet. It can take years and cost a great deal to get her possessions back. In reality, many of the women simply give up the fight and exchange all of their assets for their freedom, rather than put up with protracted and expensive legal wrangling.

Because of this, it was suggested that a "fast track" settlement process be instituted for abused women. They should be able to file an immediate petition and be granted a writ the same day. The bailiffs, or another court-appointed authority, could then seize from her husband a "reasonable" share of the couple's assets on behalf of the wife. The couple could then go back to court to "fine-tune" the settlement if they so desired. The obvious benefit of this kind of program is a significant reduction in the price paid by the abused wife for her freedom (and a corresponding reduction in the "reward" the husband currently receives for being abusive and driving his wife from their home).

SERVICES

1. *Rescue hotline.* A woman who is being abused can dial "911" and the police will arrive, but that is useful only during the actual beating or immediately afterward. "What about before or after?" asked a shelter worker. She continued, saying that in many cases, the women would have left their husbands a lot sooner than they

actually did if there had been someone, anyone, to give them some help and support. "Sometimes they need that little push to get past the inertia."

> We need a number a woman can call any time night or day. She calls and within a few minutes, some people show up at her place, help her pack a few things, and take her to a shelter, a hotel, her family's home, wherever she wants to go

2. *Resettlement program for the abused.* When people testify against dangerous and powerful criminals, they have the option of entering the Witness Protection Program. They are given new identities and are taken to a new place. They have the opportunity to start all over again. Several women wanted a similar resettlement program for abused wives. "My husband told me that if I leave him, he will track me down and kill me. I believed he could do it." This was not a rare sentiment. The abused women were seriously concerned for their own safety—and rightly so, in many cases. They need the chance to escape completely, to disappear. Some felt the way to do this is to get a new identity and move far away from him. Sandra, who now lives almost two thousand miles from her husband, still fears for her life. "If he finds me, I'm dead." She has changed her name, has an unlisted phone, number and even screens her telephone calls before answering, just in case. As another woman put it, "I can't use a credit card or have personal checks because my husband is in the credit industry. He has already found me twice. Both times I ended up in the hospital. There can't be a third time." There is strong support for an Abused Woman Protection Program.

3. *More and better shelters.* One shelter worker noted that although her shelter had twenty-two beds and a budget to house women in hotels on an emergency basis, there were nights when more women showed up than they could handle.

> One Friday, we had all of the beds full, ten people in the motel across the street, two women sleeping in the living room, another in the hall, and yet we had two more women and five children to find beds for. I ended up taking a woman and her three kids home with me for the night. It was unbelievable.

The shelter workers feel that there is a need for more (or larger) shelters to help deal with the spousal abuse crisis that many shelter workers and other professionals feel is upon us. The existing shelters are strained to the limits. In addition, some of the existing shelters are chronically under-funded and are forced to beg or borrow furniture and food. Some of these shelters cannot offer their clients decent beds because of a lack of funds. More money has to be invested in these emergency shelters to make the women feel more comfortable and more at home. They have just endured the shock of having to flee their own home.

> Can you imagine, a middle-class woman arriving at the shelter and being given a ragged towel, a torn dressing gown, and then being shown to a room she'll be sharing with two other women? Imagine her concern when her bed has a wobbly leg, only one blanket, and a sagging mattress. We have had some women actually think about going back to her husband rather than live like that. Something has to be done.

4. *Increased "Victims' Services" offered by police.* The front-line workers argued that there was a need for more Victims' Services personnel to offer counseling and other assistance to women who have just been battered by their husbands. They "need someone to hold their hand" and reassure them. They need someone there to help them get out if they want out. They need someone to offer them protection and security.
5. *Financial assistance.* A lot of the women stated that the main reason they stayed with their husbands rather than seek a shelter was financial. They knew they would have to go on welfare or social assistance, which for

them had a sort of social stigma attached. More importantly, they could not count on having much money to live on, if any at all. Many abused women wanted a special fund set aside that could provide short-term assistance to women in their particular circumstance. The money would be used to establish a new home and get the basics together, plus provide an allowance for job training or the like. This fund, enough to last up to six months, could be made readily available to any woman who had abandoned an abusive relationship. After that, if the woman still needed help, she could enter the regular welfare system.

6. *Easier access to counselors.* It is sometimes difficult to get an appointment with a counselor, especially in a large urban area. A government worker, who suggested that there be "emergency counselors" available without an appointment, explains:

> I had a woman in my office and she started having an anxiety attack. She was really stressed. I called her counselor for her. The earliest appointment we could get for her was a week from next Tuesday. Fat lot of good that'd do. I was so angry I could spit.

She has dealt with many abused women and has encountered this problem a number of times. She made it quite clear that she felt the system was "letting these women down hard."

Both Parties

1. *Marriage counseling.* A single minister put forward the idea that the couple would benefit from marriage counseling, which consists of the two partners sitting down and discussing their differences in the presence of a trained facilitator. He seemed to believe that even after the relationship has become an abusive one, the marriage is still worth trying to save.

General Public

1. *More reporting requirements for doctors who treat abused women.* It was felt that it is a doctor's duty to inform the police whenever they come across a suspected case of spousal abuse. No one really wanted this reporting to become a mandated requirement for medical personnel, but they did feel that the doctors and the nurses should take it upon themselves. The shelter workers in particular wanted the medical community to accept a greater degree of responsibility for sending women back into potentially dangerous situations.

2. *Penalize witnesses who do not report abuse.* Friends, family, or neighbors are often aware of spousal abuse but do nothing about it. This kind of selective inaction perpetuates the violence against women and, according to some lawyers and shelter workers, has got to stop. One of the lawyers wanted people who witness spousal abuse and fail to either report it to the authorities or attempt to stop the violence, to be treated as accessories to the crime and charged along with the abused husband.

3. *Greater public awareness of the problem.*

   The general public has its head in the sand most of the time. They donate money, time, energy feeding hungry children half way around the world, but they won't lift a finger to help a woman being tromped by her husband. Why? Because they don't really know what's going on.

   The counselor who made this comment wanted the public to be made aware of the situation and how bad it has become. "We have to tell them." There should be a "government-sponsored campaign to make the public aware."

4. *More public support for abused women.* Several groups of professionals and the abused women themselves thought that there was not enough of a show of public support for the abused woman, either while she is with her husband or after the relationship has ended.

> Once I was in a store parking lot with my husband. For some reason, he gave me a smack which sent the grocery bags flying. There were at least a dozen people nearby but not one of them came to help. They didn't have to pound the crap out of my husband, but they could have at least helped me pick up the groceries. No one would even make eye contact with me. It was so humiliating.

She went on to say that it would have made a world of difference if just one person had looked at her and acknowledged her. Other women concurred and discussed similar situations where people seemed to side with the husband, acknowledging him but ignoring her.

> If someone would say "stop that" or just "hey!" or even just look disapprovingly at the husband, things would be a lot better.

Other informants wanted more public support. They thought they would feel less alone if the public were more supportive of women in general and single mothers (many of whom are now single because they had had an abusive husband) in particular.

> It can be as simple as holding a door so me and my baby can get through, or saying good morning. Ideally, though, I'd like to see a parade downtown with thousands of people carrying signs saying "Abusers are Animals" or "Down With Wife Beating." I've never seen a rally for "Save the Wife!" "Save the Whale," "Save the Rainforest," yes. "Save the Wife," no.

5. *More media coverage of the problem.* Often, the media ignore spousal abuse.

> ... people just don't take it seriously because they never hear about it on TV. They call the police to complain about the noisy argument next door. They don't seem to care that a man is beating a woman there.

The media need to be responsible enough to broadcast the message so people can begin to understand.

> So many people don't think it's a crime because there
> are no crime shows about it. They figure if the talk
> shows don't talk about it, it doesn't exist. They are
> wrong.

The media needs to show them they are wrong.

Discussion

The authors examined the responses in terms of who made them
and who would likely gain[2] from them, other than the abused
woman, should the proposals be implemented. There was a kind
of desperation in the solutions the informants proposed. The
sheer volume and range of the suggestions indicated to the
authors that a "grasping at straws" attitude prevailed. No one
had a quick fix,[3] and most suggestions were made with dis-
claimers attached to them. Several informants went so far as to
lament that a solution to the problem was not possible.

In general, there were some interesting trends that exhibited themselves when looked at in terms of their sources, particularly if the participants were grouped according to their distance
from the problem.

The Couple

The two individuals most affected by the problem of wife abuse
are the abusive husband and the abused wife. [4]

THE ABUSED WIVES
Though the women did make some suggestions in terms of preventative measures, they were far more interested in protective
measures.[5] They thought that socialization of young boys was
important, as was reducing violence in the media and breaking
the cycle of abuse (that is, removing a boy from the abusive home).
However, they did not see any ways to deal with potential abusers
once they reach adulthood. As for potential victims (young girls),
they had several ideas; in fact, they introduced all four proposed
solutions in that area. They also suggested fundamental changes
in the structure of today's marriages as a way to avoid abuse. Trial
marriages and the matrifocal family were both proposed by them.

In the protective measures category, the wives offered a wide range of suggestions ranging from treatment for their husbands to a resettlement program for themselves and their children. In their opinion, in order for abuse to stop, these proposals would have to be introduced as a block. No single proposal would work alone. The women believed they needed all of them.

The women took the issue much more seriously than their husbands did, offering a total of twenty-seven potential solutions, nine times as many as the husbands thought of. However, none of these suggestions were to be implemented by the wives themselves, although they would certainly stand to gain by their implementation. This reflects a helplessness, a realization by the women that there is really very little, if anything, they can do by themselves to rectify the situation. Interestingly, no one else proposed solutions that required implementation by the abused wife, which perhaps indicates that everyone else agrees that there is little the abused woman could do.[6]

THE ABUSIVE HUSBAND

The men made only three suggestions. They all involved implementation by someone else but provided direct gains for the abusive husband. This suggests that the husbands do not accept any responsibility for the problem (if indeed they perceive that there is one). Because their suggestions contain an element of personal benefit for themselves, they might be interpreted as manipulative, and certainly as self-serving. The suggestions they made (legalize abuse, provide stress relief outlets, and provide employment training for abusers) reinforce that interpretation. It should be noted that other discussion participants made a total of fifteen suggestions that would benefit husbands, whereas the husbands made no suggestions that would benefit others. This indicates that the abused wives and some professionals were far more generous than the husbands were.

Family and Friends

HER FAMILY AND FRIENDS

When discussing preventative measures, the family and friends of abused wives placed an emphasis on the victim. They suggested the need to teach young girls that they are worthwhile and valued. They also said that all children (boys and girls) should be removed from abusive situations as soon as possible. When the potential victim is an adult, they said, she should have opportunities for personal growth. In addition, like the abused women, they supported fundamental changes in the structure of the family. Again, like the wives, they did not suggest any solutions that involved both potential abusers and potential victims, or any that dealt with the potential abuser as an adult. They saw that it was probably already too late.

Their approach to protective measures was not at all surprising, given that it is their family member or friend that is being abused. They offered no treatment options for the abuser but were willing to have him punished. Interestingly, they—unlike the abused women—wanted to see the abuser publicly humiliated or physically beaten. Those who offered these proposals were quite angry with the man who was beating "my sister" and "my friend." A brother suggested corporal punishment: "He should be beaten to within an inch of his life." Several friends of the women were prepared to go farther: "He should have his balls cut off."

HIS FAMILY AND FRIENDS

Abusers' friends and relatives presented a total of fifteen proposals, with six (40 percent) fitting into the Preventative Measure category. All of these six focused on the potential abuser *as an adult*, with half of them dealing with employment training. They offered no suggestions at all involving the potential abuser as a child, and did not even mention the potential victim.

Under the protective measures heading, their comments were similar. They wanted psychological counseling, anger management training, and employment training for the abuser, and, in general, made no acknowledgment that the victim had needs.[7]

BOTH SETS OF FAMILY AND FRIENDS

Most family members and friends on both sides offered a number of potentially useful ideas, although some of the husband's family and friends were reluctant to participate. More importantly, however, none of these proposals required implementation by either family of friends. Quite likely, they feel that their "hands are tied" and they can not do anything more than watch and worry. They did frequently comment on how useless they felt. This lack of confidence in their own ability to do something was not reflected in the suggestions made by others. Several other groups suggested that the family and close friends were responsible for breaking the cycle of abuse and teaching young boys that violence is not acceptable behavior. People felt that the family could and should be the most effective agent in controlling the amount of violence that young boys in the family are exposed to from all sources.

The Professionals

There are fourteen groups, sets of individuals, or agencies associated with spousal abuse. When asked about solutions to the problem, most people in these groups were quite enthusiastic and had strong opinions. The number of proposals coming from each group ranged from a low of seven, provided by representatives of the court and the clergy, to a high of thirty-four, offered by shelter workers. There are some interesting observations to be made about the suggestions as a whole.

The diversity of backgrounds and degrees of involvement with the problem generated a broad spectrum of potential solutions from the professionals. A total of 190 suggestions were received. They were almost evenly split between preventative (48.4 percent) and protective (51.6 percent) measures. Forty-two (45.7 percent) of their proposed preventative measures were within the "potential abuser as a child" sector. A further fifteen (16.3 percent) were within the "potential victim as a child" category. Of the ninety-eight protective measures proposals, legal responses (38.8 percent) outweighed the treatment proposals (23.5 percent). Their approach seemed to suggest that they recognized that the abuser needs treatment (15.3 percent), but in the meantime, the abused woman needs protection, support, and services (73.5 percent of responses).

Many of the suggestions offered by the several groups seemed to be self-serving. For example, of the six proposals made by shelter workers that were to be implemented by the shelters, three provided direct financial gain in the form of budget increases for the shelters. Add to those the proposals made by shelter workers that were to be implemented by others but also provided a gain to the shelters, and the number of proposals that provided gain to the shelters rises to five out of eight, or 62 percent. Other groups of professionals took the same kind of approach, offering solutions that provided some direct or indirect gain to themselves as well as to the abused women. Roughly 50 percent of the solutions offered by the police officers and the psychologists fell into the self-serving category.

The term "self-serving" in this context does not necessarily imply selfishness or moneygrubbing on the part of some professionals. Instead, it could be interpreted as a narrowly focused approach to the problem. The professionals are frustrated by chronic funding shortages in their areas. Shelters never have enough money to pay staff or to expand facilities. Counselors feel they are swamped and want more funding to hire more counselors. For example, one family counselor had a client list of about four hundred individuals or families. With that many clients, he is only able to see each one of them for half an hour every five and a half weeks, with no pay for working overtime. It seems that many of the professionals think first of solutions that both help abused women and resolve chronic deficiencies within their own spheres of influence first. These deficiencies would logically be near the top of any wish list. However, it must be noted with emphasis that once these issues had been addressed, the professionals usually went on to offer solutions that held no direct benefit for their own areas.

Many of the professionals placed the blame for the problem of wife abuse squarely on the government at all levels. Over half of all proposed solutions target governments as the ones who should implement the solutions. This is a message that says: "We are not responsible for the problem. That responsibility lies with the government." There are two interpretations of this perspective. First, the professionals truly believe that the government has failed the abused women by not providing for their safety and protection. Second, some of the professionals could be abdicating responsibility, deflecting it away from themselves by saying "It is not our responsibility," "We do not have the resources or the abilities to do anything more than we are already doing," or "There are others who need to be doing more." These feelings of hopelessness and helplessness pervade the professionals' proposed solutions.

General Trends

From all of the above, some general trends that bear repeating were discerned:

a. While the professionals paid equal attention to preventative and protective measures, abused women and their family and friends put the emphasis on protective measures.
b. The abusive husband and his family and friends offered far fewer solutions than did the abused woman and her family and friends, and they tended to focus on treatment rather than punishment. They also offered nothing that would change the situation in the future.
c. Everyone, except perhaps the husbands, seemed to agree that the only way to stop abuse once it has begun is to separate the husband and wife physically and emotionally. Only members of the clergy suggested marriage counseling as a viable option.

Despite the large number of solutions presented by the stakeholders, there was general agreement that one element was missing—a coherent, focused, and comprehensive strategy. Each solution was a Band-Aid, a temporary treatment of a symptom that left the disease itself untouched. In the next chapter, we will attempt to present one such strategy.

Notes

1. We define participants as including the wives, their husbands, families, and friends. We also define stakeholders as all those professionals who have a financial interest in the problem. These include counselors, shelter workers, lawyers, police officers, and others.
2. "Gain" is defined as some personal benefit, financial advantage, or increase in power.
3. One exception was the abusive husband who suggested that the whole problem would go away if a man were allowed to beat his wife just like in the "good old days."
4. The couple's children (who benefit from virtually any solution that reduces domestic violence) were excluded because suggestions were not collected from them.
5. Sixty-nine percent of all of their suggestions fell into the protective measures category.
6. They can decide to leave their husbands, a solution that does not appear on the list of solutions. The sense is that this possibility is a given, something the wife will do as soon as she feels there is sufficiently good reason and a support system in place with which she feels comfortable.
7. There was one exception. One mother of an abusive husband wanted tougher laws, more serious penalties, increased police powers, more vigorous enforcement of existing laws, and automatic court orders protecting the wife. This woman, whom we met at her ex-daughter-in-law's home, was attempting to maintain a good relationship with her former daughter-in-law (and through her, her grandchildren), so we expect that her sympathies would be with the victim rather than her son.

Chapter 6

The Future of Wife Abuse

A Backward Glance

The authors of this book have spent years working with women who have suffered greatly. What they have endured at the hands of "loved ones" can only be described as horrific—the stuff nightmares are made of. They would talk of fleeing for their lives, of being beaten, kicked, stabbed, and shot, of watching their worlds systematically destroyed, along with their own self-esteem. Women who have been free for ten years or more glance over their shoulders. expecting their ex-husbands to be lurking in the shadows. They jump when the phone rings or break into a sweat at the sound of a doorbell. Some women scuttle relationship after relationship out of fear, a fear generated not by their current partner but by a long-gone abusive former husband.

More importantly, despite all the women had been through, they seemed amazingly resilient. They were abused, in some cases for most of their lives, but in the middle of a conversation about that abuse they would stop and laugh, recalling some forgotten touching moment or amusing incident. Though the abuse did not strengthen them, it did not destroy them either. The women were stronger than the abuse and stronger than their abusive husbands. They survived and got on with their lives.

Many of the professionals we spoke to in the field of family relations in general and wife abuse in particular tried to instill in us a sense of urgency, or even of crisis. One could feel that urgency in the complex set of solutions they offered. They proposed preventative measures that dealt with long-term solutions but more time and energy were expended on expressing the urgent need for protective measures. This dichotomy, this division of solutions into preventative measures that lie somewhere in the future and have a sort of intangible quality, and protective measures that are urgent and immediate, consuming the caregivers' waking moments, makes sense on the surface. It certainly reflects the perspective of the caregivers. However, the dichotomy and the disproportionate focus on one of the two aspects reflect nothing more than current cultural norms and ideals, rather than a logical and justifiable approach to the problem.

For example, the social workers and others point to what appears to be a dramatic increase in the incidence of wife abuse and argue that this represents an epidemic. They feel that husbands are abusing their wives more and more. Close examination of the statistics and conversations with abused women could reveal a slightly different picture. In the Statistics Canada Violence Against Women study, the researchers state that

> Fifteen percent of currently married women reported violence by their current spouse; 48% of women with a previous marriage reported violence by a previous spouse. *These different rates may reflect the difficulty for many women living with a violent partner to disclose their experiences to an interviewer ...* (Statistics Canada 1993: 4) [emphasis added].

The suggestion that the rates for currently married women are considerably lower than those for previously married women may reflect the women's difficulty in disclosing current abuse to an interviewer is but an interpretation, an assumption with no data to support it. It is also possible that the difference between reported present and past rates of abuse reflects a reduction in the amount of wife abuse. This would be more in line with the stabilization of crime rates suggested by Silverman and Kennedy (1993: 204–7). The assumed reluctance of women to report current abuse suggested by the Statistics Canada survey does appear to contradict the observation that women seem to be more willing to report the physical or sexual assault (Silverman and Kennedy 1993: 204–7). If that alternative view is accepted, the urgency is reduced. Incidents of abuse seem to be increasing when in fact they are decreasing; however, that decrease is masked by an increase in women's willingness to report the abuse. Fewer women are willing to accept or tolerate abusive behavior from their husbands. That can be seen as positive and hopeful by all people working in the field.

Further, as was suggested above, the instinctive division of proposed solutions into preventative and protective measures is not as useful as it first seems, given that it may just be reflecting the current cultural values, values that members of the society use unconsciously.

Proposing protective measures reinforces the patriarchal notion that society is responsible for *protecting its women* rather than providing the tools necessary to enable women to protect themselves. It is an admission by both men and women that women are incapable of protecting themselves against men. This generates solutions that tend to assign the women passive roles, rather than proactive solutions with direct and active roles for the abused women. There are women's shelters rather than women's centers. The laws and regulations give the abusive husband all of the couple's resources and reduce the woman to poverty. There are seminars, courses, and self-help groups that help women cope with poverty, thereby recognizing that poverty is the inevitable result of her extraction from an abusive household.

Many of the proposals were merely extensions or elaborations of existing programs, programs that, by the participants' own admission, do not work as effectively as they could. Given that emergency shelters concentrate the abused women into identifiable enclaves (by advertising their locations to abused wives, they advertise to husbands as well) that exist in an atmosphere of fear and mistrust (all men tend to be suspect whenever they enter a shelter for any reason).[1] Most extant self-help and counseling groups contain only abused women and are often run by facilitators who were themselves abused. This creates a situation of mutual interdependence that suggests that women, being members of the weaker gender, need to band together to protect themselves from men.

The protective measures support the patriarchy, fostering an atmosphere of mistrust and perpetuating the idea that should a woman seek to leave an abusive relationship, she will have to sacrifice all that she has. The attitudes behind these measures may then be exacerbating the problem rather than ameliorating it. In order to deal with the situation and reduce the occurrence of wife abuse, another direction must be taken.

It can be posited that all individuals, including both abusers and those who are abused, are responsible for their own actions and the consequences of those actions. It has been our experience that the fact that many women will not leave an abusive husband is more often than not a conscious decision. Having weighed the pros and cons, she will not leave until she cannot stand the abuse one moment longer. One woman observed that she had reached the point where she had only two courses of action available to her: "Go to a shelter or kill him." The women do not leave until all other alternatives are exhausted. As a result, by the time the woman reaches the emergency shelter she is emotionally traumatized and unable to deal with even the most mundane matters. This condition, which is common among women who enter a shelter, reinforces the shelter workers' perspective that abused women are like children who need to be taken by the hand and guided through every step. Alternatively, women who leave their husbands (or whose husbands leave them) before the point of no return are not so badly traumatized and seem able to recover from the experience and re-establish their place in society much more quickly.

It is likely that the women stay with their husbands as long as possible because they recognize that to leave is to abandon everything they have earned and acquired in their lives up to that point, including assets, income, lifestyle, and, in many cases, friends and family as well. The cost of escape is obviously very high, and a great deal of abuse is heaped upon the women before they become willing to pay that price. Perhaps if that cost could be reduced, the women would leave the relationship before the abuse becomes permanently damaging (either emotionally or physically).

It should be the responsibility of the society and the community to foster an environment wherein the costs of leaving an abusive husband are significantly lowered. There would then be fewer traumas inflicted and subsequently reinforced. For example, when a woman goes to a shelter, she loses self-esteem in that she knows that other members of the society look down on women who flee to shelters as failures, people who were not able to make it on their own. Sandra identified this in her father's reaction to her moving to a shelter. Her father was upset at what her husband had done to Sandra, but Sandra thinks her father was more upset about her being in a shelter. He did not want her associating with "all of those losers" (the other women in the shelter). By going to that shelter, Sandra suffered first by having to swallow her pride and ask for help, and then had the loss of self-esteem reinforced by her father, who automatically labeled all women in shelters as losers.

From another perspective, most men will not become abusers whatever the circumstances, and some who might potentially become abusive do not because they are not afforded the opportunity. Other men will become abusers and will subject their wives to a wide variety of abuse because they can. They find that even if they recognize that what they are doing is wrong, the chances of getting caught—or if caught, punished—are minimal, and the benefits are great. For example, Peter was both verbally and physically abusive to his wife for several years. The police visited his home on several occasions, but each time he received no more than a warning. He was never charged, and yet, in his own words, "My wife treats me like a king. She waits on me hand and foot."

An abusive husband is not hindered by any significant costs for his behavior until his wife leaves him, or prepares to do so. At that point, he suffers a loss of control. His daily routine falters. His life is changing. It is at that time that abusive behaviors tend to escalate and the situation becomes more dangerous for the wife.

In this context, then, the problem of wife abuse can be reduced to one of finding a way to increase the costs of maintaining a set of abusive behaviors and reduce the opportunities potential abusers have to perpetuate that abuse.

Looking Forward

Although wife abuse may not be on the rise or be reaching crisis proportions, society cannot ignore it. Nor can society pretend that the many women who are currently being abused simply do not exist. Something must be done. Over the course of the research discussed herein, we have developed a set of approaches to the problem. They are not instant solutions, but rather directions that should be considered.

We have two logically compatible goals. First, given that there will always be potential abusers among the population who will abuse their wives if they have the opportunity, that opportunity must not be afforded them. Second, since women who currently find themselves in abusive situations quickly discover that the cost—both economic and emotional—are extremely high, the situation must be changed so that the costs of extraction from the relationship are borne not by the wives but by the abusers. Although these goals are somewhat divergent, there is a single underlying theme: "Society should not be protecting its women. Instead, it should provide the wherewithal for the women themselves to have the necessary tools to protect themselves and prevent the abuse from happening to them."

A Proposed Solution

Family and the Prenuptial Agreement

There is a cultural contradiction in North American society that has yet to be resolved. On the one hand, women are considered independent and equal to men in the workplace and elsewhere. On the other hand, that independence and equality have not yet been extended into their own homes. Once the workday is completed, a working wife is expected to look after her husband and children. In many cases, this is what she expects of herself. She sees herself as both a working woman and as a "traditional wife and mother." If she is not employed outside the home, she is not able to take advantage of the equality of the workplace. Being a "housewife" is perceived the same as being unemployed and has the same negative connotations. The role of wife and mother is chronically undervalued, and women suffer as a result.

This approach automatically gives the husband the superior position in the relationship, since, in general, a family is traditionally perceived as being "a man and *his* wife and children." This unconscious granting of the superordinate role to the husband may tend to facilitate abuse of that role. Before wife abuse can be brought under control, that perception must be changed. The wife and the husband must be granted equal status by society and *by each other*. The redefining process will meet with opposition and therefore can be expected to take a long time to complete. In the meantime, the change could be legislated. The new definition could be recognized in a legal sense relatively easily.

For example, it has become common practice for individuals with significant assets to ask their prospective spouses to sign prenuptial agreements. These agreements generally are a legal form of recognition that there are certain assets that belong solely to one partner and as such are exempt from any property settlement during a divorce, should that situation arise.

Using these prenuptial agreements as precedents, all jurisdictions, which already require the couple to acquire a marriage license before the wedding or at least register the marriage, could require the couple to prepare and to sign a general prenuptial agreement. That agreement would consist of two parts. The first would require both the husband and the wife to acknowledge their equality in the marriage. The second section would stipulate that should the marriage end in divorce, the assets acquired during that marriage would be divided equally.[2] Of course there should be some flexibility in the agreement to allow for unique or changed circumstances, but it is the simple signing of the document that is important.

By requiring a universal prenuptial agreement, the jurisdictions would require the partners to accept the equal status definition of marriage. In addition, each couple would have a clear understanding of the post-divorce division of assets before getting married. Understanding both that definition and the form the division of assets would take is important to the overall solution package being proposed here.

As a corollary to the redefinition of the marriage, society must also recognize the value of a single-parent family. Currently, many men and women look down upon a woman trying to raise her children on her own. It must be understood that a single-parent household may be a better, more stable environment than an abusive home situation with both parents present could ever be. Children need role models of both genders, but negative role models are of no value. "Staying together for the sake of the children" is no longer a valid concept.

Redefining the Crime

A crime against a family member and the resulting destruction of the "safe haven" that a person's home should be is different from a crime against a stranger. That difference, which is not currently recognized, should be acknowledged. There should be a separate set of charges laid against a perpetrator who is related to his (or her) victim. These new charges would allow the courts to treat the abusive husband differently from those who assault or threaten complete strangers.[3]

The arresting officers, rather than the injured parties, would lay any and all charges. (Currently in many jurisdictions, the victim is required to press charges before the authorities can proceed.) That would prevent the abuser from later applying pressure on his spouse to drop the charges, as she would not have the ability to do so. Also, there should be a "zero tolerance" policy for violence in the home. If a police officer is called to the scene of a domestic dispute and there is evidence of violent abuse, a charge should be laid. As will be demonstrated, under the new rules being proposed here this would all but eliminate the need for repeated visits to the same household—something police officers routinely complain about.

A New Court

In North America, there are already a variety of courts specializing in certain types of crimes and certain classes of criminals. There are family courts, juvenile courts, civil courts and criminal courts, which all operate under different sets of rules and procedures and have different outcomes. Just as society needs a new set of charges to recognize the uniqueness of abuse in the home, a new court to hear those charges is required.

In order for this new court to be effective, it must be granted a unique set of powers and procedures. For example, it should have evidentiary requirements similar to those in a civil court, so that a broader range of material would be admissible than is presently permitted in criminal court. At the same time, It should have the informality of a family court, to allow input from all parties without the restrictive limitations of other courts. Finally, it needs to have the ability to control the perpetrator, and, if necessary, to grant divorces and impose fair and equitable property settlements as well. The reasons for this arrangement of powers and procedures for the new court will become apparent shortly.

The New Procedure

If the proposed solution is implemented, the new procedure will permit the abused women to take control of their futures. Consider the following case.

A CRIME IS COMMITTED

A man is arrested for beating up his wife. Under the new system, he is charged with "familial assault." This new charge permits the authorities to place the abuser in custody immediately and hold him until his first appearance before a judge in the new familial court system. This first appearance would be similar but not identical to the "bail hearing" in the criminal justice system.

In the criminal justice system, once the accused has been granted bail and posted the bond, he is usually released to return home, as the posting of the bond guarantees only that the individual will appear in court as required. However, in the case of familial assault, that home is also the scene of the crime, a crime that will likely be repeated. In the familial courts, the first appearance before the judge results in several conditions being imposed on the accused in addition to the requirement to appear in court when called. The most important new condition is an immediate and all-encompassing restraining order forbidding him to return to his home or even make any attempt to contact his home (in person, by proxy, or by any other form of communication). He cannot go home, so his wife does not have to abandon her residence in order to avoid further abuse.

Restraining orders as they exist now are difficult to enforce, largely because the consequences of violating them tend to be minimal. Under the new laws, the accused abuser must post a substantial cash or security bond that will be forfeit if he violates the order. To add some weight to the order and to further increase the security of the victim, another condition can be placed upon the abuser: he can be required to reside in a designated supervised shelter created for just that purpose. He is free to go to work, but confined to the shelter when not otherwise gainfully engaged. In that way, the roles are reversed. The wife, the victim, gets to remain in her home and the abusive husband is placed in the shelter. All of the negative connotations of living in a shelter are transferred to the husband.

At this same court appearance, the judge has the power to do one other thing. He or she can place the couple's assets in trust, with the exception of sufficient funds for both parties to live on. This prevents the abuser from attempting to liquidate the assets, for example, by selling the house his estranged wife is currently living in. It also prevents the husband from denying his wife access to those funds for legal and lawyer fees and the like. As justification, the judge is able to use the prenuptial agreement that both husband and wife signed prior to their marriage. One additional benefit to this binding of assets is that if the abuser violates any of the conditions imposed upon him, the forfeited bond can then be taken directly from his portion of the assets and the wife is not penalized along with him.

Placing conditions on the accused with the associated threat of losing his own assets should he violate those conditions raises the stakes for the husband. The consequences of continued abuse have been made quite severe, quite personal and direct. The court has made it quite clear that the abuser is at fault. The court is clearly on the side of the victim and will not tolerate any further abusive behaviors. This provides some protection for the abused woman and validates her worth.

THE TRIAL

As demonstrated by the O.J. Simpson murder trial, the criminal justice system has evolved into a cumbersome and complex organization that clearly favors the accused and virtually ignores the victim. The new familial court would be different in two important aspects: it would be victim-oriented, and its mandate would be broader and less bound by restrictive rules of evidence. This would prevent the accused from hiding behind procedural and legalistic technicalities.

To continue the proceedings in the case described earlier: the actual trial is run by a judge, who questions the witnesses rather than permitting the lawyers to do so. The lawyer for the accused submits questions to be asked of the witnesses. This elimination of direct contact prevents any attempt to confuse, confound, or discredit the witnesses.

A wide variety of evidence, including statements from anyone who has been witness to abusive behavior of any kind (not just those behaviors related to the criminal charge), are permitted. The rules are similar to those allowed in a civil court. Since there is no jury involved, there is no concern that "ordinary citizens" will be tricked or prejudiced by the broader based evidence. The judge, a trained professional, is able to sort through it all in a fair and impartial manner.

Unlike the current family courts, where all cases are tried in camera, cases tried in the new familial court are open to the public and the news media. The court is clearly supportive of, and oriented towards, the wife. It is therefore likely that all who attend the trial will receive the message that the abusive husband is indeed the person who has caused the problem by committing a criminal offense, and that the victim, the abused wife, is acting appropriately by protecting herself through the court proceedings. The feelings of failure that the wife often feels now are removed and the social stigma is transferred from her (where it often resides now) to him. He is at fault. He is the failure. He is the one who should be looked down upon.

CRIMINAL DIVORCE

If the husband is convicted of the abuse, he is also guilty of violating the prenuptial agreement, specifically the section pertaining to the equality of the partners in the marriage. This permits the judge to rule on another aspect of the case. The conviction for abuse and the violation of the prenuptial agreement indicate a clear disregard for the sanctity of marriage. Thus in consultation with the wife, the judge is able to grant the woman an immediate divorce based on the husband's criminal behavior.[4] As part of the criminal divorce package, there is a property and asset settlement based on the prenuptial agreement, a custody order is proclaimed for any children involved, and child support and/or alimony payments are settled upon. In addition, one of the conditions of the divorce is a more or less permanent extension of the restraining order.

PUNISHMENT

Punishment of abusers is largely irrelevant in any solution package that is offered. Some people would argue that there needs to be some sort of deterrent in place. That is probably true, but most of the abusive husbands we spoke to would not or could not acknowledge that they had done anything wrong. They tended to interpret their imprisonment, the usual punishment for assault, as just another thing their wives did wrong. There is no deterrent value in incarceration in such cases.

What must be recognized is that the confinement of an abuser has no "rehabilitation" or "resocialization" value. The abusive behavior will be resumed as soon as the husband is released. Instead, the incarceration of an abuser satisfies two other needs. First, the physical aspects of the abusive behavior stop for the duration of the prison term.[5] Second, the jail sentence exacts some revenge for the abusive behavior.

Having said this, we recommend that a first conviction for wife abuse under the rules of the new court be reasonably lenient in terms of imprisonment, as the abuser has already been confined to a shelter for the period between the first hearing and the trial, has acquired a criminal record, has been handed an unwanted divorce with an imposed property settlement, and has had a potentially lifelong restraining order placed on him. Any additional punishment could be considered excessive. Perhaps a token jail sentence (thirty to ninety days) is sufficient for a first offense. However, any subsequent convictions will result in severe penalties, including a lengthy jail sentence (whether the victim of the subsequent abuse is the same as the first woman or not).

THE ORDEAL IS OVER

When the gavel falls to close that particular case, the abuser, as has been demonstrated, loses a great deal. He has lost his wife, and likely his children as well. He has had property settlements and child support/alimony payments imposed upon him. Permanent restrictions have been placed on his behavior in that he is forbidden any form of contact with his former spouse. He has lost the control he tried to acquire or maintain through abusive behaviors. He is now directly answerable for any and all future abusive behaviors. His reputation has been damaged in the community, for he is now a common criminal and abuser. Perhaps more importantly, he has been deprived of the opportunity to abuse a wife again, since any subsequent convictions will carry serious consequences. Any further abusive behavior would be very risky.

Alternatively, the abused wife gains from the court proceedings. She has gotten out of the abusive relationship and the costs have not been all that high. She was not forced out of her home. She had the choice of remaining there or going elsewhere. She also had the time to think through any decision she might make, rather than being forced to make a decision to flee to a shelter while sitting on a curb outside her home surrounded by police officers. She has assets available to enable her to afford any necessary changes. The abused woman did not have to hide from her husband. She did not have to avoid her friends and family to protect them from him. She did not give up her financial security, nor did she have to surrender her dignity.

Under the existing system, she would have had to be reactive, forced to respond to her husband's behaviors. With the new court system described here, she was able to be proactive, able to direct her own extraction from her abusive relationship. She worked with the judge to decide if she wanted a criminal divorce or not, and she worked with him or her in a relatively comfortable and safe environment to come to a fair and equitable financial settlement. By being proactive, she retained her self-esteem and emerged from the court with a positive self-image as well as a relatively quick settlement of all issues pertaining to her relationship with her ex-husband, ready and able to begin her new life.

A Step Back

We anticipate that this proposal will meet with considerable resistance. Some of the objections will be procedural. Some will be philosophical; others will be cultural or traditional. We do not intend, at his point, to address those objections. Instead, we choose to point out that the stated goals, which are (a) to eliminate as much as possible any opportunities husbands have to exhibit abusive behavior towards their wives, and (b) to reduce the costs the wife must shoulder for extricating herself from an abusive marriage, could be accomplished by the steps contained in this proposal. In addition, the proposal provides tools enabling women to protect themselves and prevent abuse from happening to them. Abuse would become a short term behavior because women would be able to leave their husbands much earlier than they do now and multiple convictions for criminal abuse would carry severe penalties.

Although the core of our solution package is the set of new laws, new courts, and new approaches to the problem, it should not be considered a "quick fix." Society cannot create this new system and then assume wife abuse will be immediately eradicated. The proposal amounts to a legislative solution, which will not immediately change peoples' attitudes, beliefs, and values. There is much work to be done in those areas. For example, individuals, as role models, need to send explicit and appropriate messages to children regarding the equality of the genders in the workplace and the home. Children need to see that controlling behaviors such as bullying are inappropriate and unacceptable. The message that violence in the home is wrong is crucial. In addition, it must be clearly demonstrated that abusive behaviors are the result of conscious choice (as there are alternative behavior choices), and those individuals choosing to exhibit abusive behaviors must accept the negative consequences of their actions. In short, we must examine all aspects of North American society (as discussed in Chapter Two) and make a conscious effort to modify them to reflect the ideal of equality.

A Final Statement

There is no doubt that wife abuse exists in North American society. There are many women who are forced to deal with abusive situations every day, but there are also a large number of people in many walks of life dedicated to helping those women. Many of the abused wives and their helpers have suggested ways to solve the problem. However, no matter how valid or workable those solutions, they are imperfect. Everyone is focused on his or her own small part of the problem. Also, each individual usually deals with immediate problems on a case by case basis. An abused woman wants to get out of her situation. She is not interested in the problem of spousal abuse in general. Shelter administrators are concerned with obtaining the necessary funds to serve their clients properly now. They cannot be concerned with the situation twenty years from now.

Because these solutions (which do work in an immediate sense) are short term, they tend to be more pragmatic than they should be. The solutions tend to have one thing in common. The woman who was in the inferior position in an abusive marriage is removed from that relationship, but not from the inferior position. She tends to be treated as a child by the police, shelter workers, counselors, and others who, because of the nature of the immediate solutions, seem to take on the role of parents guiding her through the necessary procedure. She is not given control over her own life.

If changes are to be made and effective long-term solutions to wife abuse are to be generated, the broader picture must be examined. We have proposed a set of solutions, but that was not the intent of this work. Instead, we have tried to present that broader picture for all to see. We did not set out to solve the problem but to provide the information necessary to stimulate thought and discussion. In our opinion, that goal was accomplished.

Notes

1. One shelter in the southern United States has banned all men. Any police officers, maintenance workers, or legal representatives entering the premises must be female. One of the authors asked the administrator of the shelter what would happen if there was a fire and no female firefighters were available. She shrugged and responded: "I guess the place burns down."
2. Some people would argue that this is the same thing as saying that the marriage is bound to fail. However, since the majority of marriages already end in divorce (see Haley 2000), this prenuptial agreement is nothing more than an acknowledgment of reality.
3. We do not wish to imply that one crime is more serious than the other. They are, however, quite different from one another, and that difference should be recognized.
4. If the wife chooses not to seek a divorce at this time, she is at least making an informed decision under conditions she herself controls.
5. There are numerous cases of incarcerated husbands phoning their wives and being verbally abusive and threatening. On occasion, an abusive husband would arrange for a friend to act as his proxy and physically attack the wife on behalf of the husband, but these cases are rare.

References Cited

Alberta Social Services. n.d. *Wife Abuse: What is it? What to do about it*. Alberta Social Services. Edmonton.

Alberta Solicitor General. n.d. *Victims of Family Violence: Information and Rights*. Alberta Solicitor General. Edmonton.

Anderson, C. A. 1997. Effects of violent movies and trait hostility on hostile feelings and aggressive thoughts. *Aggressive Behavior* 23: 161–78.

Anderson, C. A., and Dill, K. E. 2000. Video games and aggressive thoughts, feelings, and behavior in the laboratory and in life. *Journal of Personality and Social Psychology* 78(4): 772–90.

Armstrong, S. 1994. Hope In Hell, Heroes in Bosnia. *Homemakers Magazine* 29(4): 18–31.

Ayto, John. 1990. *Dictionary of Word Origins*. Arcade Publishing. New York.

Bachman, R., and Linda E. Saltzman. 1995. *Violence Against Women: Estimates from the Redesigned Survey*. Bureau of Justice Statistics, Washington, D.C.

Bard, Morton, and Joseph Zacker. 1974. Assaultiveness and alcohol use in family disputes. *Criminology* 12(3): 283–92.

Barker, Joan C. 1993. Shades of blue: female and male perspectives on policing. In *The Other Fifty Percent: Multicultural Perspectives on Gender Relations*, edited by Mari Womack and Judith Marti. Pp. 349–60. Waveland Press. Prospect Heights.

Bass, Ellen, and Laura Davis. 1988. *The Courage to Heal*. Harper & Row. New York.

Bellah, Robert, Richard Madsen, William Sullivan, Ann Swidler, and Steven Tipton. 1984. *Habits of the Heart*. University of California Press. Berkeley.

Bernard, Jessie. 1972. *The Future of Marriage*. Bantam Books. New York.

Blackstone, W. 1765. *Commentaries*. London.

Blume, E. Sue. 1990. *Secret Survivors*. John Wiley and Sons. New York.

Bohannan, P. 1971. *Divorce and After*. Anchor Books. New York.

Bryson, B. 1994. *Made in America: An Informal History of the English Language in the United States*. William Morrow and Company, Inc. New York.

Bureau of Justice Statistics. 1995. Women Usually Victimized by Offenders They Know. U.S. Department of Justice Press Release (August 16, 1995).

Campbell, Joseph. 1949. *The Hero With a Thousand Faces*. MJF Books. New York.

C.A.W.E.S. 1993. *C.A.W.E.S. Acknowledges Its 10th Anniversary*. Central Alberta Women's Emergency Shelter. Red Deer.

Chapman, Jane Roberts. 1978. The economics of women's victimization. In *The Victimization of Women*, edited by Jane Roberts Chapman and Margaret Gates. Pp. 251–68. Sage Publications. Beverly Hills.

Dill, K. E., and Dill, J. C. 1998. Video game violence: A review of the empirical literature. *Aggression and Violent Behavior* 3:407–28.

Douglas, John, and Mark Olshaker. 1997. *Journey into Darkness*. Scribner. New York.

Durkheim, Émile. 1938. *The Rules of Sociological Method, Eighth Edition*. Edited by George E. Catlin. Translated by Sarah A. Soloway and John H. Mueller. Free Press. New York. [Originally published in 1895.]

Edmonton Women's Shelter Ltd. 1995. *Violence Against Women*. Edmonton.

Ember, Carol R., and Melvin Ember. 1996. *Cultural Anthropology. Eighth Edition*. Prentice Hall. Upper Saddle River.

———. 1994. War, socialization, and interpersonal violence. *Journal of Conflict Resolution* 38: 620–46.

Focus. 1987. Understanding abusive men. *Focus: Family Violence Prevention* 2(2): 1–2.

———. 1992. When teens abuse parents and siblings. *Focus* 6(3): 1–2.

———. 1993. Immigrant women: overcoming abuse in a new country. *Focus* 7(2): 1–2.

Franssen, M., Q. Tingley, and B. Franssen. 1994. *In The Name of Love Stop Violence Against Women*. The Body Shop. Toronto.

Gelles, Richard. 1972. *The Violent Home*. Sage. Beverly Hills.

Gleick, Elizabeth. 1996. No Way Out. *Time Magazine* 148(26): 12–15.

Gregorash, Lesley. 1994. Husband Abuse. Paper presented at the 1994 Conference on Men's Health Issues. Edmonton.

Haley, Shawn. 2000. The future of the family in North America. In *Essays on Culture Beyond the Millenium,* edited by V.M. Razak. FUTURES 32(8): 777–82.

Harris, Marvin. 1993. *Culture, People, Nature: An Introduction to General Anthropology, Sixth Edition*. HarperCollins. New York.
———. 1981. *America Now: The Anthropology of a Changing Culture*. Simon & Schuster. New York.
Health Canada. 1994a. *The Effects of Media Violence on Children*. Health Canada. Ottawa.
———. 1994b. *Canada's Treatment Programs for Men Who Abuse Their Partners*. Health Canada. Ottawa.
Hiatt, Les R. 1975. *Australian Aboriginal Mythology*. Australian Institute of Aboriginal Studies. Canberra.
Howard, Michael C. 1996. *Contemporary Cultural Anthropology, Fifth Edition*. HarperCollins. New York.
Johnson, Colleen Leahy. 1993. In-law relationships in the American kinship system: the impact of divorce and remarriage. In *The Other Fifty Percent: Multicultural Perspectives on Gender Relations*, edited by Mari Womack and Judith Marti. Pp. 163–73. Waveland Press. Prospect Heights.
Johnson, C. and B. Barer. 1987. Marital instability and changing kinship networks of grandparents. *The Gerontologist* 27: 330–35.
Kilgannon, Gerry. 1988. Wife abuse in Canada — new attitudes, new laws. *Focus: Family Violence Prevention* 3(1): 1–2.
Lacroix, Suzanne. 1989. Double isolation: the case of the abused immigrant woman. *Focus* 4(2): 1–2.
Lederer, Wolfgang. 1968. *The Fear of Women*. Harcourt Brace Jovanovich. New York.
Leyton, Elliott. 1997. *Men of Blood: Murder in Everyday Life*. McClelland & Stewart Inc. Toronto
Lindenburger, S. n.d. *Make a Difference*. The London Coordinating Committee to End Woman Abuse. London.
Linton, Ralph. 1959. The natural history of the family. In *The Family: Its Function and Destiny*, edited by R. Anshen. Pp. 30–52. Harper and Row. New York.
Maggio, Rosalie. 1991. *The Dictionary of Bias-Free Usage: A Guide to Nondiscriminatory Language*. Oryx Press. Phoenix.
Margolis, Maxine. 1982. Blaming the victim: ideology and sexual discrimination in the contemporary United States. In *Researching American Culture*, edited by Conrad Kottak. Pp. 212–27. University of Michigan Press. Ann Arbor.
Martin, Del. 1983. *Battered Wives*. Simon & Schuster. New York.
———. 1978. Battered women: society's problem. In *The Victimization of Women*, edited by Jane Roberts Chapman and Margaret Gates. Pp. 111–42. Sage Publications. Beverly Hills.
Murdock, George P. 1949. *Social Structure*. Macmillan. New York.

Newman, R. 1986. Symbolic dialects and generation of women: variations in the meaning of post-divorce downward mobility. *American Ethnologist* 13: 230–52.

Otten, Alan. 1991. Drop in early marriages may have lasting impact. *Wall Street Journal* November 26: B1.

Rheingold, J. C. 1964. *The Fear of Being a Woman*. Grune and Stratton. New York.

Robbins, Richard H. 1997. *Cultural Anthropology: A Problem Based Approach*. *Second Edition*. Peacock Publishers. Itasca.

Sanday, Peggy Reeves. 1990. *Fraternity Gang Rape: Sex, Brotherhood, and Privilege on Campus*. New York University Press. New York.

Senate Judiciary Committee. 1992. *Violence Against Women: A Week in the Life of America*. Senate Judiciary Committee, U.S. Congress. Washington, D.C.

Silverman, Robert, and Leslie Kennedy. 1993. *Deadly Deeds: Murder in Canada*. Nelson. Toronto.

Statistics Canada. 1993. *The Violence Against Women Survey*. The Daily 1–10. Statistics Canada, Ottawa.

Storr, Anthony. 1970. *Human Aggression*. Bantam Books. New York.

Troll, L. 1971. The family of later life: a decade review. In *Decade Review of Family Research and Action*, edited by C. Broderick. National Council of Family Relations. Minneapolis.

Wallace, Anthony F. 1970. *Culture and Personality*. Random House. New York.

Ward, Martha C. 1996. *A World Full of Women*. Allyn & Bacon. Boston.

Weitzman, Lenore. 1974. Legal regulation of marriage: tradition and change. *California Law Review* 62(4).

World Health Organization. 1993. *World Health Statistics Annual*. WHO. Geneva.

Yanigasako, S. 1977. Women-centered kinship networks in urban bilateral kinship. *American Ethnologist* 4: 207–26.

Index

abuse
- acceleration of, 19–21
- criminalization of, 227, 228–30
- cycle of, 17–19, 190–91
- denial of, 81–82
- involving third party, 16, 171
- legal definitions, 68–71
- legalizing, 191–92
- long distance, 169–72
- of child, 82
- of elder, 82
- of husband, 4, 21n. 6
- of sibling, 82
- political reaction to, 72–73
- rates of, 1–2, 68, 80–84, 221–22
- redefining, 227
- types of, 8–16
- willingness to report, 81, 125–27, 211–13, 221–22

abused women
- betrayal of, 76
- empowering, 222–24
- protection for, 205–7

abuser, 101–2, 214

abusive relationship
- cost of ending, 140–45, 153–87, 222–24, 225

alcohol, 30–32, 83

anger management, 190

army wives, 41, 77n. 6

assault
- familial, 228
- physical, 1, 2, 8, 14–17, 75–76, 81, 83–84, 123, 189
- sexual, 1, 14, 61–62, 81

attitude, 28–29
- about family and marriage, 32–33, 42–43, 46–49, 53–54, 225–27
- divergence in, 33–34
- toward abuser, 230
- toward competition, 193–94
- toward sex, 61–62
- toward spousal abuse, 23–25, 211–13
- toward violence, 62–66, 198
- toward women, 23–24, 32–33, 34, 224
- wife's, 20–21, 225–27
- with a weapon, 16–17, 83–84

authoritarianism, 10–11

behavior
- abusive, 7
- criminal, 189–90
- learned, 7–8, 24–26, 66–67
- manipulative, 146–50
- suicidal, 151, 153, 174

blaming, 101, 103, 104, 148, 150

Capitalism, 53–56
children, 10, 20, 48–49, 101,
    103–6, 118, 151, 166–67,
    206
clergy, 129–30, 147
community
    aggregate, 43
    factors, 40–43
control of wife, by husband,
    9–14, 16, 102, 145, 168
core values, 44–45, 68, 78n. 8
counseling, 36, 127–28, 192
    easier access to, 210
    family, 127–29
    marriage, 127–29, 135–36,
      147–49, 211
court orders, 176–77, 206, 228–29
courts, 68–69, 123–24, 201–2,
    227–31
    new, 227–28
crime, episodic, 120
crime rates, stabilization of,
    221–22
criminal
    code, 68, 70–71, 124
    record, 231
cultural
    aggregate, 66–68
    factors and mechanisms,
      43–68
culture change, 44–45

date-rape, 78n. 16
defense mechanisms
    withdrawal, 113–14
destruction of property, 15–16
divorce, 36, 48–49, 112–13,
    163–67, 206, 225–27
    criminal, 231
    settlement, 122–23, 164–66,
      226–27
doctors, 6, 27, 124–27
domestic disturbances, 117–21
dominate, need to, 34, 197

education, 46, 190, 198
    concerning spousal abuse,
      198
    formal, 27
    of abused woman, 204–5
    of women, 59–60, 194–96
effects, long term, 140–45,
    184–86
English language, 45–46
ethnic background, 5, 98–101

family, 6, 46–49, 157–59
    attacks on, 172–74
    factors, 32–40
    impact on, 103–11
    matrifocal, 196–97
    nuclear, 46–47
    psychological distance
      from, 50
    redefining, 225–27
    structure, 48–49
    traditional, 44–45, 46–49,
      53–54, 58, 226–27
fear, 144–45, 155–56, 168–69,
    220, 222
feminism, 60–61
financial hardship, 144, 155–56,
    209–10
forgiveness, 148–50
friends, 6
    attacks on, 170, 172–74
    help of, 52–53
    home of, 159–60
    impact on, 111–14
front line workers, 71–75

gender
    bias, elimination of, 44–45
    differences, 56–58
    equality, 59–60
    relations, 56–61
    rigid identification of roles,
      106
    roles, 37–39, 47–49
government policy, 68–71

harassment, 13–14
hiding, 167–69
homes, abusive, 26, 115–16
homicide. See murder
humiliation, public, 9–10, 11,
    173, 202–3

ignorance of policies, 100–101
independence, 50–53
individual
    aggregate, 29–32
    factors, 24–32
    impact on, 82–114
individualism, 50–53
intervention, 116, 124–130
    foster care, 191
    legal, 116–24, 176–77
    problem child, 191
    psychological help, 191
intimidation, 10, 15, 145, 150–52,
    169–72
isolation, 9, 13, 41–42, 49, 51, 145

knowledge, 24, 26–28

laws, tougher, 200–201
lawyers, 6, 22, 27, 121–23
    access to, 206–7
learned helplessness syndrome,
    142

marriage
    redefining, 225–27
    sanctity of, 47–48
    trial, 195–96
media, 63–64, 115, 212–13
    violence on, 190
mental illness, 32, 77n. 2
methodology, 4–8
minimizing, 13
monogamy, 49
    serial, 49
murder, 3, 17, 18, 81, 152, 153, 174
mythology, 51–52

neolocal residence, 49–50

outside influences, 20

panic attacks, 140
parents, 6, 25–26
    home of, 144, 157–58
    impact on, 106–10
    nonsupportive, 109–10,
        141–42
    of the abused, 109–10
    of the abuser, 106–9
    supportive, 109–10, 157–58
parents and siblings
    of the abuser, 106–9
    of the abused woman,
        109–11
patriarchy, 53–46
personality, 29–31
police, 6, 22–23, 57–58, 68–70,
    117–21, 227
    greater powers for, 200–202
poverty, 145, 180–82
pregnancy, 20
prenuptial agreement, 225–27
problem solving, non-destruc-
    tive, 190
psychiatrists, 134–36
psychologists, 6, 27, 134–36
public awareness, 211–12

rape. See assault (sexual)
rebuilding life, 177–84
reconciliation, 146–48, 173
rehabilitation. See resocialization
relatives, impact on, 110–11
Rescue Hotline, 207–8
resocialization, 104, 231
resources. See support
role models, 66

schools, 65–66
self-esteem, 30, 53, 61, 142–44,
    162, 182–83, 193–94,
    204–5, 220–24

separation, legal, 163–67
shelter
    for abuser, 229
    policy, 73–74
    women's, 2, 140, 154–55,
        160–63, 168, 208–9,
        221–24
    workers, 6, 22–23, 132–34
siblings, 6. See also parents and
    siblings
    attacks on, 106–10, 158–59
skills, lack of, 179–80
Social Assistance. See Welfare
social maturity, 77n. 1
social status, 27, 161
socialization, 25–28, 46, 103–6,
    189–91
society, impact on, 114–16
solutions
    preventative, 188–98, 218,
        221–22
    proposed by abused wives,
        196–97, 213–14
    proposed by abusive hus-
        bands, 214
    proposed by authors, 220–24
    proposed by family, 214–16
    proposed by friends, 214–16
    proposed by the clergy, 210
    proposed by the profession-
        als, 198, 209, 216–18
    protective, 198–213, 218,
        221–23
    self-serving, 216–18
sports, 8, 65
spousal
    roles, 37–39, 47–49, 225–27
    rights, 33–34
stalking, 174–75
status of women, 7
strangers, 43–44
stress
    ability to cope with, 35
    relief, 192
Superwoman syndrome, 156,
    183–84

support
    available, 35–37, 41–42,
        207–10
    community, 131
    governmental, 137
    groups, 136–37, 192, 204
    lack of, 138
    personnel, 130–37
    network, 41–42

temperament, individual, 24–25
therapists, 6
therapy. See also treatment
    group, 74, 200
    one-on-one, 135, 200, 204
threats. See intimidation
toys, 64–65, 190
training
    centers, for abusers, 101
    employment, 192–93,
        199–200, 204–5
    marriage, 198
    of new parents, 197–98
    for abuser, 107
    for substance abuse, 200
    lack of, 102
    of abused woman, 204–5
    of abuser, 199–200
trust, abusing, 11–12

urbanization, 40

Victims' Services, 131–32, 209
violence
    domestic, 4, 22–23, 80–82,
        111
    physical. See assault
        (physical)
    psychological, 2

welfare, 137, 145, 161
withholding, 9, 10, 12
Witness Protection Program,
    169, 208
women in the workforce, 56–59